Berlin '45 AIRBORNE DIVISION

8. AUGUST 1945

★

The General and His Daughter

Photo of Major General James M. Gavin for the cover of the *Sunday News*, February 24, 1946, taken at the time of the Victory Parade. (Photo courtesy of Barbara Gavin Fauntleroy)

★

The General and His Daughter

The Wartime Letters of
GENERAL JAMES M. GAVIN
to His Daughter BARBARA

Barbara Gavin Fauntleroy
Commentary and Notes by Starlyn Jorgensen
Edited by Gayle Wurst

FORDHAM UNIVERSITY PRESS

New York : 2007

Library of Congress Cataloging-in-Publication Data
Gavin, James M. (James Maurice), 1907–1990
The general and his daughter : the wartime letters of General James M. Gavin to his daughter Barbara / edited by Gayle Wurst. — 1st ed.
p. cm. — (World War II, the global, human, and ethical dimension)
Includes bibliographical references and index.
ISBN-13: 978-0-8232-2687-0 (cloth : alk. paper)
ISBN-10: 0-8232-2687-5 (cloth : alk. paper)
1. Gavin, James M. (James Maurice), 1907 — Correspondence.   2. Generals — United States — Biography.   3. United States. Army — Biography.   4. United States. Army — Airborne troops — History.   5. World War, 1939–1945 — Aerial operations, American.   I. Wurst, Gayle.   II. Fauntleroy, Barbara Gavin.   III. Jorgensen, Starlyn.   IV. Title.
U53.G38G38   2007
940.54'1273092 — dc22
[B]
2007000873

Printed in the United States of America
09 08 07   5 4 3 2 1
First edition

To the World War II paratroopers of the 82nd Airborne
and to those gallant young men who were lost along the way.

"Most soldiers like to write letters; it is a form of self-expression otherwise denied them. They can talk shop, etc. all day long but they can talk to no one as they can their own kin. Letters mean a great deal to them."
—from letter of June 25, 1943 from James M. Gavin to Barbara Gavin

Every soldier needs to know that someone at home is thinking of him and praying for him, that someone cares whether he lives or dies.
—Barbara Gavin's annotation to her father's letter

★ CONTENTS ★

★ ACKNOWLEDGMENTS ★

This book would never have been written without the war stories, kind words, and encouragement of the World War II veterans of the 82nd Airborne, my dad's "boys." It began as "You ought to put those letters in a book" and progressed to "When is your book coming out?" Here it is, my brothers.

I am particularly indebted to Gayle Wurst and Starlyn Jorgensen. Gayle, the niece of a 505th Parachute Infantry Regiment veteran who served under my father, has been our agent and gentle editor. She sent the letters manuscript to Fordham University Press, where the director, Bob Oppedisano, and his team recognized its value and used their many talents to turn the manuscript into this handsome volume. Starlyn is another daughter of the 82nd Airborne, whose father fought with the 456th Parachute Field Artillery Battalion. A most knowledgeable historian of the Division, she has transcribed the letters and expertly described the battles and the context of the war into which my Dad's letters fit.

Gerard M. Devlin, paratrooper veteran of the Korean and Vietnam wars, author and friend of my father, has contributed immeasurably with his introduction, as has Dr. Rufus Broadaway, who was my father's junior aide-de-camp as they jumped into Holland and is now a physician of great renown. I also want to thank Colonel Edwin Sayre, General Richard Seitz, General James Johnson, General Ed Thomas, General James Lindsay, General Wayne Downing, Phil Nordyke, Ed Ruggero, and James Megellas for generously endorsing this book.

Finally I would like to thank my husband, Clancy Fauntleroy, for his patience as I labored to find the right words to describe my memories and for his skill as our photographic producer.

— Barbara Gavin Fauntleroy

Gayle Wurst

The General and His Daughter presents for the first time the complete and unabridged wartime correspondence between General James M. Gavin and his daughter Barbara. The 209 letters, which begin when General Gavin was thirty-six years old and Barbara was nine, constitute the majority of his private correspondence during World War II. Written between the eventful times of early spring 1943 and December 5, 1945, they start at Fort Bragg as (then) Colonel Gavin, commander of the 505th Parachute Infantry Regiment, prepares to move to New York Harbor, where he will embark for North Africa and the European Theater of Operations to lead the first American mass regimental combat jump in Sicily. The correspondence closes upon his return to the United States as the commander of the 82nd Airborne Division, which he led in the Victory Parade up 5th Avenue in New York on January 12, 1946.

The letters Barbara received came in many varieties—V-mail, handwritten notes, "captured" German letterhead, Division stationery, and numerous other forms—and were written from shipboard, foxholes, field tents, cellars, palaces, and busy offices. They were often composed in haste and under duress, and several convey her father's intimate thoughts just before or after a combat jump. Yet despite these difficult circumstances, Gavin writes with remarkable clarity, speaking intelligently, directly, and honestly to his young daughter. The letters, infused with love, concern for her welfare, and the desire to help her understand his absence and his many responsibilities, sparkle with humor, playfulness, and attentiveness to the everyday affairs of a precocious little girl. He also sent many curious, colorful, and fascinating mementos—shoulder patches, foreign coins, stamps, insignia, silk maps, pennants, and a cartoon drawn especially for her by her favorite childhood author, Munro Leaf. Barbara even received her father's medals and decorations in the mail, sent to her for safekeeping.

The letters have all been carefully transcribed by Starlyn Jorgensen with a view to faithfulness to the author's originals. They have, however, been formatted into paragraphs to make for easier reading; many were written on wartime V-mail, with minimal space, so that the use of paragraphs was precluded. General Gavin's grammar has been preserved, including the (very few) errors, which are presented without editorial comment. In many instances, Gavin was writing on "captured" typewriters with a foreign arrangement of keys; we have thus corrected most typographical and spelling errors, which were nevertheless far and few between, and rectified capitalization and punctuation where necessary. Omissions were also rare, and we have silently supplied a missing pronoun or two.

With very few exceptions, General Gavin dated his letters, and they are here presented in chronological order, arranged into chapters that chronicle the six campaigns of the 82nd Airborne Division in World War II and the Allied Occupation of Berlin. Textual apparatus has been kept to a minimum, in order to preserve the flow of the letters as General Gavin's personal chronicle of the war. Starlyn Jorgensen has framed the letters within brief italicized overviews of the 82nd's operations, concisely and unobtrusively supplying essential biographical and historical information. Within the text of the letters, her short textual notes, contained within square brackets, identify places, people, and other significant references at their first mention. Longer personal notes within the text, bracketed, italicized and identified with the initials *BGF*, are provided by Barbara Gavin Fauntleroy, creating a subtle father-daughter "dialogue" between the lines.

Several contributions by people who knew General Gavin well and were close to him in different ways supplement the letters. The volume opens with a foreword by Dr. Rufus Broadaway, an aide-de-camp to Gavin, which testifies to life in the field with the General and to the admiration and loyalty he inspired in his "boys." Gerard M. Devlin, noted airborne historian, the author of a forthcoming biography of Gavin, and the general's friend in later life, has graciously supplied the introduction. Framing the letters themselves are essays by Barbara Gavin Fauntleroy, which look back to the years of her childhood. They chronicle her feelings, impressions, and experience as "the General's daughter," and discuss the circumstances that led her father to select her as his representative on the home front and special private correspondent. Factual notes and additional commentary by Starlyn Jorgensen appear at the end of the letters. A bibliography of cited sources and selected works for further reading and an index of proper names complete the volume.

★ FOREWORD ★

Rufus Broadaway

Major General James Gavin told me that he wrote letters to his daughter Barbara. Indeed, he wrote to her more than two hundred times while he commanded the 505th Parachute Infantry Regiment and later the 82nd Airborne Division during World War II. When her father left for war in April 1943, Barbara was nine years old. With the publication of *The General and His Daughter,* she now generously shares many intimate thoughts of a famous father to his loving daughter during exciting and perilous times.

General Gavin was my personal hero. I had parachuted into Normandy on D-Day. Shortly after returning to England, I was given the great privilege of serving as his junior aide-de-camp during the airborne invasion of Holland, the Battle of the Bulge, and much of the remainder of the war in Europe. I was with him for most of our waking hours and came to know him well. As the junior officer, it fell to me to receive an almost incoherent telephone call on December 17, 1944. This was the first alert of the 82nd Airborne Division to the German breakthrough that began the Battle of the Bulge.

In addition to being a great commanding officer, General Gavin was a fine human being, in every respect. He was basically gentle and soft-spoken. He was kind and considerate. I do not recall his acting harshly under any circumstance. He was not given to profanity or to dirty jokes. He called me "son."

Almost any afternoon while we were in reserve, the General would say, "Son, let's go for a run." It was an opportunity that I cherished. Although he had a dozen years on me, his long legs seemed to carry him with less effort than my shorter ones. I have run most of the rest of my life, including many marathons. Many times I have recalled the inspiration from my general.

War, however, is necessarily cruel. The objective is to kill the enemy and to do so as efficiently and effectively as possible. Many of Gavin's men have recalled seeing the tall officer with stars on his helmet in the thick of battle as he shared the dangers of combat.

On one occasion in Holland, the enemy had penetrated the southern end of our defensive line. General Gavin immediately went down to see for himself. Soon he was prone (as was I) on a railway embankment and he was furiously firing his M-1 rifle like the infantryman that he was. In another instance, while battling in the snow of the Ardennes during the Battle of the Bulge, we came upon a soldier who was attempting to put on his boots. The General asked him where his socks were. He replied that they were lost. When we returned to headquarters, General Gavin gave me a pair of his own socks and had me personally take them to the barefoot soldier.

Gavin recognized the importance of his leadership role, but he never demanded privilege. When General Dempsey sent up a caravan trailer for Gavin's personal use in Holland, Gavin instead used it for Division Headquarters and slept in a foxhole like any other soldier. When I suggested that I might sleep in the caravan, he gave me a quizzical look and said that he did not think that was a very good idea! Soon after, the caravan was hit by artillery.

James Gavin, the major general, was also a man of great personal integrity. At one point there occurred a serious misunderstanding with General Ridgway. Gavin thought that the honorable course was to request reassignment, an action that would cost him command of the 82nd Airborne and probably a grade in rank. Fortunately, Ridgway regretted his behavior and accepted Gavin's explanation, ignoring Gavin's request to be relieved of command. Gavin observed that he himself had learned a lesson in restraint.

These and many of the General's other sterling qualities are amply expressed in this volume. But perhaps above all else, his letters to Barbara demonstrate a loving and enduring bond between father and daughter. Rarely does he address her as "Barbara." More likely it is as "Butch" or "Babe" or simply "Beautiful."

More than a simple account of his activities, these letters in which he shares with his daughter his experiences at war provide considerable insight into his personality. Gavin also here reveals his personal and private feelings, perhaps nowhere else recorded, at moments of exceptional historic importance. He wonders, for example, that Providence has spared him through numerous combat jumps and through the campaigns in Sicily, Italy, Normandy, Holland, and the Battle of the Bulge. Throughout, he frequently speaks of his high regard for his officers and troops. He believes them capable of anything, and his troops respond to his strong and fearless leadership.

Another side of General Gavin is displayed in his considerable correspondence to Barbara during the occupation of Berlin, when the European campaign was finished. Gavin related immediately and closely to the Russian officers. Vodka helped! Acting essentially as the mayor of Berlin, he involved himself directly in getting food and firewood to the German people.

General Gavin states that he kept a diary, but his letters to his daughter, at the time his only child, seem intended to provide a further view. It is as if the General, a man of both war and deep humanity, needed to confide in this dear child his thoughts, his sly humor, a view of his inner strengths and fears, and to express his love for her.

The letters in *The General and His Daughter* have never before been published in whole. Those few that have been made public have been cited by authors of books on the 82nd Airborne or in *The Panther*, the newsletter of the 505th Regimental Combat Team Association. Now, for the first time, Barbara generously offers the larger reading public the entirety of her father's letters in a most personal way. Here they are to read over and over, for historians and novices, for soldiers and peacemakers, for fathers and families everywhere.

Gerard M. Devlin

History has shown us that there are very few men who become a legend in their own time, and even fewer who have come to be known as a Renaissance man. But during his truly extraordinary and productive life, James M. Gavin easily qualified for both of these lofty titles.

I first met him in 1972 upon joining the General Gavin Chapter of the 82nd Airborne Division Association in Lexington, Massachusetts. In those days our chapter was almost entirely comprised of grizzled battle-scarred World War II paratrooper veterans who still were tough as nails and great admirers of their courageous wartime leader. Our monthly meetings were held in a private function room at the U.S. Air Force Noncommissioned Officers Club located at nearby Hanscom Field, and consisted of the usual happy hour which was followed by a formal dinner and short business meeting.

Much to the delight of all chapter members, our greatly revered general would occasionally attend one of those meetings. Prior to his arrival, a lookout would be posted at the large window overlooking the club's parking lot. On sighting his approaching car, the lookout would alert us by saying, "Hey, quiet down. The General is here" — at which point every man in the room (including me) would rush to the window to observe our chapter chairman meet and guide the General into the club. Entering the room one step ahead of the General, the chairman would ever so formally announce, "Gentlemen, our commanding general." As is the military custom, we would snap to attention, facing the door to see the good-natured General briskly entering with a big smile on his Irish face and also to hear him say in a booming voice, "Thank you, gentlemen; please carry on. And most importantly, let's all have a drink!" Glass in hand, he would circulate among us, warmly shaking hands and just being one of the guys.

During the following years, when I began my career as an airborne historian and writer, the General was most helpful and generous with his time, explaining to me in great detail the World War II combat operations of his 82nd Airborne Division. So I therefore am grateful to have been asked to write the following words concerning this great American patriot.

James Maurice Gavin was born March 22, 1907, in Brooklyn, New York, to a young immigrant woman newly arrived from Ireland. Only a few months after his birth, dire personal circumstances forced his mother to place him in the Angel Guard Home, an orphanage administered by the Roman Catholic Diocese of Brooklyn. There he remained until shortly after his second birthday, when he was adopted by the Gavin family of Mount Carmel in Pennsylvania's anthracite coal-mining region.

Though he consistently achieved extremely high marks in school and demonstrated a great thirst for knowledge, his adoptive parents abruptly terminated his education when he completed the eighth grade. The only reason he was given for this discouraging turn of events was that the time had come for him to start helping support the family, which had fallen on hard times because of recent work stoppages in the coal mines. For the next few years he held several low-paying jobs and dutifully contributed all that he earned to the family. Throughout this long and stressful period, he spent most evenings at the town library studying the same subjects his former classmates were being taught in school and also pursuing his new-found interest in American military history.

On his seventeenth birthday, still facing a bleak outlook for any opportunities to achieve some measure of success in life and with tension mounting within the family, he ran away from home and joined the army. His first duty assignment was in Panama, where, even though his pay as a new enlistee was only twenty-one dollars per month, he faithfully sent half of it home each payday. Because of his earlier success in self-education, plus his natural good soldierly qualities, he quickly mastered all basic military skills and rose to the rank of corporal before reaching the midpoint of his three-year enlistment. Shortly thereafter, he achieved even greater success by winning an appointment to the U.S. Military Academy at West Point, New York, through competitive examination.

Upon graduating in June 1929, he placed in the top third of his class and was commissioned a second lieutenant. Three months later he married Irma M. Baulsir of Washington, D.C., to whom he had become engaged during his senior year at the academy. There then followed a series of routine infantry assignments in the United States during which he was promoted to first lieutenant in 1934. It was while the Gavins were stationed at Fort Sill, Oklahoma, in November 1933 that they announced the birth of their daughter Barbara, who would prove to be the only child of their marriage.

Several months prior to Barbara's birth, Irma had briefly returned to her parents' home in Washington so that the blessed event would occur in the thoroughly modern Walter Reed Army Hospital located there. Accompanied by his wife and young daughter, Gavin left Fort Sill in July 1936 for an overseas tour of duty with the 57th Infantry Philippine Scouts based a few miles east of downtown Manila at Fort McKinley. His Philippine Islands assignment ended in November 1938, at which time he was transferred to the 7th Infantry Regiment at Vancouver Barracks in the state of Washington.

Though Gavin was still only a lieutenant after graduating from West Point ten years earlier, his star was finally beginning to rise. Recently, he had come to the attention of the army's top brass for quite successfully serving in what officially was a captain's capacity as a company commander in both the Philippines and at Vancouver Barracks. And so it was that, even though all officer promotions were excruciatingly slow in the peacetime Depression-era army, he was promoted to captain on June 1, 1939. Exactly one year later he was ordered to West Point for duty as an instructor in the tactics department.

Gavin and his small family remained at West Point until August 1941, when he requested and received a transfer into the army's paratrooper program, which was then just beginning to take shape at Fort Benning, Georgia. At the time he submitted his request for that hazardous duty assignment, America was not yet at war. (Japan's devastating attack at Pearl Harbor was still four months away.) The army's entire airborne force at Benning consisted only of an understaffed Provisional Parachute Group Headquarters, the Parachute School, and three parachute infantry battalions, two of which existed in skeletal form. Though he had no way of knowing it at the time, by war's end there would be five airborne divisions plus several separate regiments and battalions, bringing the airborne force strength to more than 100,000 men.

On their arrival at Benning, Gavin and his family were billeted on the second floor of a recently refurbished World War I barracks known as Officers Quarters 23. The following day he reported to the Parachute School to begin the arduous four-week course that ended with him being awarded the coveted silver wings of a paratrooper. In recognition of his demonstrated aggressive brand of leadership both on and off Benning's jumping fields, Gavin's superiors placed him in a number of challenging command and staff assignments. As all of his bosses and contemporaries expected, he performed each of them with remarkable ease and efficiency, which resulted in his being catapulted up through the senior officer ranks at dizzying speeds.

Gavin was promoted to major on October 10, 1941; to lieutenant colonel only four months later, on February 1, 1942; and to colonel seven months later, on September 25, 1942, by which time he had been appointed commanding officer of the 505th Parachute Infantry Regiment. One of his more outstanding contributions to the success of all rapidly expanding airborne forces at Benning occurred while he was the S-3 (plans and training) staff officer at the Provisional Parachute Group's Headquarters. There, in record time, he wrote Field Manual 31–30, a prodigious U.S. Army training guide titled *Tactics and Techniques of Air-borne Troops*, which detailed everything an airborne unit commander would need to know and do to achieve success on the battlefield.

During total darkness on the night of July 9, 1943, Gavin's 505th Parachute Infantry Regiment, then an integral part of Major General Matthew B. Ridgway's 82nd Airborne Division, jumped onto high ground behind the beaches to protect dawn landings of American amphibious troops at Gela, Sicily. In September he and his regiment made another successful night jump to reinforce the Allied beachhead at Salerno on the Italian mainland. Promoted to brigadier general (one-star rank) the following month, Gavin was appointed deputy to Ridgway.

On D-Day, June 6, 1944, the 82nd made massive predawn parachute and glider landings six miles behind German lines in Normandy, fighting for thirty-three days without relief or replacements while stopping all enemy attempts to reinforce their shattered coastline defense units. Gavin succeeded Ridgway in August, becoming, at age 37, the youngest airborne division commander in the war. On September 17, he led the 82nd in another huge airborne assault, this time in broad daylight and fifty miles behind German lines in Holland. His division was still fighting in Holland the following month when he was promoted to major general (two-star rank). In December the 82nd played a decisive role in halting the German tank thrusts during the epic Battle of the Bulge. Early in February 1945 the division pierced the Siegfried Line, marching deep into Germany. Three months later his airborne troopers linked up with Russian tank units advancing from the east. Gavin and his 82nd were on occupation duty in

Berlin until January 1946, at which time the entire division was returned to Fort Bragg, North Carolina.

Though just back from Berlin, Gavin now had to come to grips with an extremely serious matter. Ever since well before the war had even begun, he and his wife Irma knew their marriage was fatally flawed and they had been discussing divorce. They agreed to remain married for the duration of the war because a divorce would have resulted in great hardship both for Irma and their daughter Barbara. Still unable to resolve their longstanding differences now that they had been reunited at Bragg, the couple first separated and finally divorced in 1947. The following year Gavin married Jeanne Emert Duncan of Knoxville, Tennessee.

Between the emotional turmoil of his separation and divorce from Irma and then the pressures of commanding his division at Bragg, Gavin managed to write his first book, *Airborne Warfare*. In it he reviewed successes and failures of American airborne missions during the recent war and also expressed incisive views concerning how to manage large-scale parachute and helicopter airborne missions deep into the future. Published in 1947, it met with considerable success, instantly establishing him as the most forward-thinking tactician within the burgeoning worldwide airborne community.

On completing six years of distinguished service with the 82nd Airborne Division in 1948, Gavin became chief of staff at Fifth Army Headquarters in Chicago. In June 1950 he received an overseas assignment to Naples, Italy, as chief of staff at Headquarters Allied Forces Southern Europe. Two years later he received a prestigious field assignment to Stuttgart, Germany, as commanding general of VII Corps. In February 1954 he returned stateside to take up new duties on the Army General Staff at the Pentagon. Following his promotion to lieutenant general (three-star rank) in March 1955, he was appointed chief of the army's vast Research and Development program, remaining there until his retirement in January 1958 at age fifty.

Gavin wisely used his spare time as an unemployed civilian by putting finishing touches on his second book, *War and Peace in the Space Age*, a scathing appraisal of the American military's strategic planning and its recent downgrading of conventional weapons systems. His book had been on the market only a few months when he accepted a lucrative job offer as vice president at Arthur D. Little, Inc., an international consulting firm in Cambridge, Massachusetts. He was promoted to president of the firm in

1960 and to chairman of the board in 1961. In February of that same year, President John F. Kennedy appointed him ambassador to France, a post he held until resigning in October 1962 and returning to his previous position at Arthur D. Little. Gavin retired from Little in 1977 after twenty years with the firm.

For the next several years, full-time retired life greatly agreed with Gavin. There were long walks with his wife Jeanne along the beach at their seaside home on Cape Cod, Massachusetts, plus a return to his two favorite hobbies, golf and painting. Also during these happy times he wrote his wartime memoirs, *On to Berlin*, published in 1978. But shortly after celebrating his eightieth birthday in 1987, he began suffering from a combination of old and new ailments, which included the effects of too many bone-jarring parachute landings during his eight years on jump status (including his roughest landing, during the 82nd's combat assault into Holland, where he fractured his spinal column yet remained in command of his division); the wound he sustained during close combat with German tanks on Sicily; the gout; a weakening heart; and increasing problems with Parkinson's disease, which had been diagnosed when he was in his mid-seventies.

James Maurice Gavin, soldier, businessman, diplomat, and author, died February 23, 1990, at the age of 82. His mortal remains lie buried beside the Old Cadet Chapel at West Point. On the day of his funeral he was sent off to the other side in grand style by an honor guard and large contingent of paratroopers, all flown in from the 82nd Airborne Division at Fort Bragg.

In this fascinating book, Barbara Gavin shares with us more than three years' worth of letters she received from her famous father during World War II, while she and her mother Irma were residing in Washington, D.C. This large collection of heartwarming and morale-building letters from a fighting paratrooper general to his daughter back on the home front is truly unique in American World War II history. Each letter provides us with a privileged public look into the thoughts and emotions of someone who was a very private man. Surely, they will become a valuable source of previously unknown wartime information to present and future generations of historians. But most of all, they will provide many hours of enjoyment to everyone fortunate enough to read them.

★

The General and His Daughter

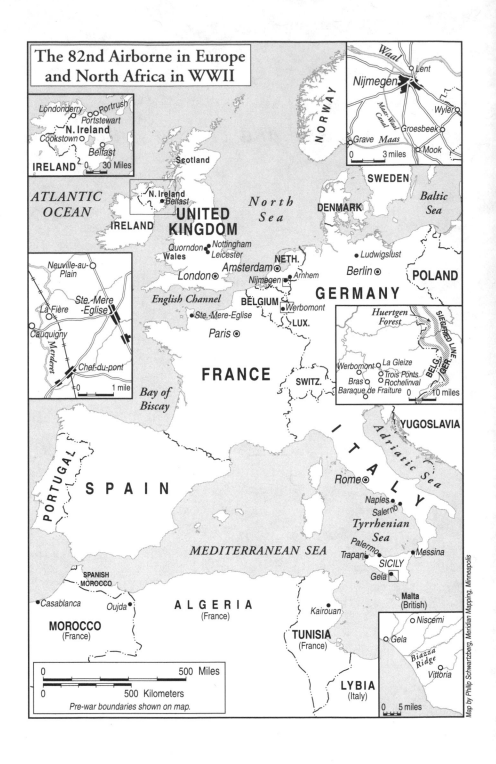

The 82nd Airborne in Europe and North Africa in WWII

Nijmegen inset:
Waal
Lent
Nijmegen
Wyler
Maas-Waal Canal
Groesbeek
Grave Maas
Mook
0   3 miles

N. Ireland inset:
Londonderry
Portrush
Portstewart
N. Ireland
Cookstown
Belfast
IRELAND
0   30 Miles

Normandy inset:
Neuville-au-Plain
Ste.-Mère-Eglise
La Fière
Cauquigny
Merderet
Chef-du-pont
0   1 mile

NORWAY
SWEDEN
DENMARK
Baltic Sea
ATLANTIC OCEAN
N. Ireland
Belfast
IRELAND
UNITED KINGDOM
North Sea
Scotland
Quorndon
Wales
Nottingham
Leicester
Ludwigslust
Amsterdam
NETH.
Berlin
POLAND
London
Nijmegen
Arnhem
English Channel
BELGIUM
Werbomont
GERMANY
Ste.-Mere-Eglise
LUX.
Paris
FRANCE
SWITZ.

Huertgen Forest inset:
Huertgen Forest
SIEGFRIED LINE
Werbomont
La Gleize
Trois Ponts
Bras
Rochelinval
Baraque de Fraiture
BELG. GER.
0   10 miles

Bay of Biscay
PORTUGAL
S P A I N
MEDITERRANEAN SEA
ITALY
Adriatic Sea
YUGOSLAVIA
Rome
Naples
Salerno
Tyrrhenian Sea
Palermo
Trapani
Messina
SICILY
Gela
Malta (British)
SPANISH MOROCCO
Casablanca
Oujda
ALGERIA (France)
Kairouan
MOROCCO (France)
TUNISIA (France)
LYBIA (Italy)

Gela inset:
Niscemi
Gela
Biazza Ridge
Vittoria
0   5 miles

0   500 Miles
0   500 Kilometers
Pre-war boundaries shown on map.

Barbara Gavin Fauntleroy

I was nine when my father left for war. He sailed from the harbor of New York City aboard the troop ship *Monterey*, a former Matson ocean liner. Just nineteen years earlier he had run away from home to New York to find a new life for himself. This time he had "his boys" aboard with him, the entire 505th Parachute Infantry Regiment of the 82nd Airborne Division.

After he left, I missed him terribly. I missed his Irish face and his sense of humor, but most of all, I missed his hugs. He had been the parent with whom I could share all my thoughts and dreams. Knowing how much I would miss him, my father wrote more than 200 letters to me while he was away. It wasn't until later that I understood how remarkable it was that he had taken the time to share so many of his experiences and thoughts with me, often writing from devastated locations and at the most emotional of times.

I believe that he wanted me to feel the security of being wanted and loved that he had never known as a child. He was born in Brooklyn in 1907 to a young Irish immigrant woman named Katherine Ryan. Hardship forced her to place him in an orphanage, and at the age of two he was adopted by Martin and Mary Gavin. Life in the coal-mining town of Mount Carmel, Pennsylvania, was hard for a miner's family. At the end of the eighth grade, the Gavins considered his education complete and sent him out to earn whatever money he could to help support the family. He sold shoes, pumped gasoline, and, most successfully, cornered the newsboy business in Mount Carmel. But life at home was increasingly difficult, so on his seventeenth birthday he caught a train early in the morning and ran away to New York City.

After days spent walking the streets looking for a job, my dad approached an Army recruiter who promised him an education as a payback for enlistment. The resourceful sergeant even provided a surrogate father to certify that my dad, who was underage, was indeed eighteen. On April 1, 1924, he was sworn in to the U.S. Army and began his new life.

The young private, Jim Gavin, was sent to the Panama Canal Zone. He quickly earned his corporal's stripes and became a clerk in an artillery battery, where a sergeant noticed the young soldier who enjoyed reading history at the post library. He encouraged my father to take the tests that would allow him to enter the school where he would be prepared to take the entrance exams for West Point, the United States Military Academy. After long days of studying, he passed the exams and was offered an appointment to the class of 1929 at West Point.

The days weren't long enough for all of the academic catching up he had to do. He once told me that at West Point he had to study at night in the latrines, the only place that was lighted after "lights out." (One day when I was in high school, I opened his old chemistry textbook, looking for help. Out fell some pieces of toilet paper with formulas written on them! I had to smile, and I determined to work harder myself.)

He loved being at West Point and referred to the Academy as his "Spartan mother." It is an indication of his character that he was selected to be the honor representative for his company during all four years there. He graduated in June of 1929, and in September, he and my mother (Irma "Peggy" Baulsir) were married in Washington, D.C. They had met two years earlier on a blind date.

As a young officer, he was sent to Army schools and posts in Texas, Arizona, Georgia, and Oklahoma. I was born in Washington, D.C. on Armistice Day, November 11, 1933. My earliest memories are of our time at Fort McKinley in the Philippines, where we arrived in 1936. It was the peacetime army then, and among my father's tasks was training the Filipino Scouts to defend the Islands in case of war. We took vacation trips to Baguio in the mountains, where we could hear the chants of the headhunters echoing from a mountain ridge across the valley. I know they were headhunters because my amah (nurse) told me they would come and get me if I didn't behave. One evening, my amah picked me up from my bed and ran from the nursery, screaming for my father. Before I knew what was happening, Daddy was holding up the long body of a snake, which he had separated from its head with a machete. That night I saw my father as the hero who would always protect me.

After two years in the Philippines, we returned to Vancouver Barracks in Washington State. There was war in Europe and Asia, and my father took part in massive military maneuvers at Camp Ord, later Fort Ord, California, as America prepared for the possibility of entering the war. My dad wrote from the maneuvers, "Unlike the spit and polish of garrison training, this has been rather exacting and for a complete period of six months, a good indication of what one can do. If the Army expands and we ultimately enter the war as now appears likely, I want an opportunity to command troops and I know I will go places with them."

In the summer of 1940, we moved to West Point, where my father had been assigned as an instructor in the Department of Tactics. The German juggernaut was moving across Europe, and my father would be teaching the young cadets who would do the fighting when the time came. As a seven-year-old, I wasn't aware of what was going on outside of my small world. My dad was reliving some of his happiest years — those spent as a cadet. We went to football rallies and games. We attended movies and concerts and watched the cadets parading on the Plain. We made dough-nuts and picked wild blueberries on Storm King Mountain. Cadets, includ-ing a handsome young John Norton, came for tea on Sunday afternoons.

At my mother's request, my dad began Saturday inspections of my room, with a nickel deducted from my allowance for every breach of order-liness. Since my twenty-five-cent allowance was quickly gone, he had to give me a raise. Into my life came a bicycle and a dog. Daddy hadn't had a dog as a boy, so he made sure that I had one — for both of us.

This idyllic life changed when my father asked to be released from his post at West Point. He had been talking to his friend, Lt. Bill Ryder, a member of the Parachute Test Platoon, about airborne troops, or para-troopers, a new way of going to war. He had decided that parachute train-ing at the Parachute School at Fort Benning, Georgia was the best way to be part of these innovative and elite army forces preparing for the coming war. In August 1941, he started jump training at the Parachute School. At the age of thirty-four, my dad was one of the older members of his class and he found it physically demanding. (Our converted barracks quarters were full of fumes from Absorbine Jr.) He graduated and proudly wore his parachute wings and jump boots. He also took me through my own special jump training — riding with him on the seat rigged on one of Fort Ben-ning's four jump towers for just such Sunday afternoon occasions. It was still the peacetime army. After three rides, he presented my miniature silver wings to me.

After a company command in a parachute battalion and a position on the battalion headquarters staff, he was assigned to the top parachute headquarters in the army—the Provisional Parachute Group at Fort Benning. We were at the movies in Columbus, Georgia, on Sunday afternoon, December 7, when the theater manager stopped the film and stepped in front of the curtain to announce that Pearl Harbor had been bombed. My father was on his feet instantly, pulling us through the door, saying that we had to get back to the post. America was at war, and our lives would never be quite the same.

My father was sent to the Command and General Staff School at Fort Leavenworth, Kansas, and then returned to the Provisional Parachute Group (renamed the Airborne Command) to start work on the formation of an airborne division. From Washington, he wrote that the War Department was entirely sold on airborne forces, but that it would still take a lot of work and planning. He was quickly promoted (as compared to his having spent ten years as a lieutenant) to colonel and given command of the 505th Parachute Infantry Regiment, activating it at Fort Benning on July 6, 1942. He always referred to the paratroopers of the 505 as his "boys."

Early in 1943, my father received orders to move the regiment to Fort Bragg, North Carolina, for more training before going overseas. My mother wanted me to finish the school year at Fort Benning, but, with my father no longer living there with us, we were ordered to vacate our quarters. In April we moved to Washington, D.C., my mother's hometown, to be near family and friends for the duration of the war. Washington was bursting at the seams with "new" people there for the war effort. Until we could find our own apartment, we lived with my grandmother Rosie and her sister, my aunt Lillie.

The 505 had been assigned to the first airborne division activated by the War Department—the 82nd Airborne Division (known as the "All Americans"). My dad wrote to me in April, and though he couldn't tell me when he was leaving or where he was going, he did tell me exactly how to address my letters to follow the wartime regulations by leaving out the word "Parachute" before Infantry and using an APO (Army Post Office) number, in care of the New York City Postmaster, from where mail would be forwarded to him. Mail and packages often took weeks to reach him.

I wrote to him every Sunday. Every day, I ran down the stairs to the bank of mailboxes looking for a letter from him, hoping one would be there. When my own children reached the age at which they were curious about their grandfather and World War II, I gave them the letters to read. The first question I heard was, "He called you Babe?" Yes, and Butch, Barbara, or Garbo, whichever fit his mood of the day. He always signed them as "Pappy," a name from the popular cartoon strip "L'il Abner," a favorite of mine and his 82nd Airborne "boys."

His letters arrived from all the places where battles were fought on the western front — North Africa, Sicily, Italy, England, France, Holland, Belgium, and Germany — though censorship didn't allow him to tell me exactly where he was writing from. His letters were handwritten or written on captured typewriters, and many were on the wartime writing paper known as V-mail. He wrote while he was on ships and planes, from fox-holes, bombed-out buildings, and sometimes luxurious villas and palaces. His signal to us, just before a combat jump, was a reminder that his insurance policies and magazine subscriptions were paid up and books from the Book-of-the-Month Club had been ordered and prepaid.

He sent me foreign stamps and invasion currency, military insignias, photos, and small gifts — anything he thought I would find interesting. I didn't care if he sent anything with the letters; just receiving a letter meant that he was still alive, and that was all I cared about. He reminded me regularly that he had "the luck of the Irish," promising me that no harm would come to him. Our letters were a strong bond between us that continued until the end of his life.

I believe that at this time I owe the reader an explanation of the fact that I was the only one in the family to receive letters from my father. Just before my dad went overseas, I was surprised to discover and gradually had to accept the fact that my parents were not happy together. They had simply arrived at a place in which incompatibility was constant. There was no shouting, and there were no battles. I know that my dad wrote one letter to my mother during the war, asking for a divorce. She asked him to wait until the war was over to make a decision about their future.

My dad returned to the U.S. in December 1945. He moved, with the 82nd Airborne, to Fort Bragg, North Carolina, and we joined him there at the end of the school year, in the summer of 1946. It was a difficult time for everyone, but the problems remained inside our home. My parents arrived at a divorce agreement, and my mother and I returned to Washington, then moved to Florida to obtain the divorce. My father offered me the opportunity of living with him, which I wanted to do. But I felt so very sorry for my mother that I decided that I should continue living with her.

I knew that my father would be able to build a good, new life for himself. He assured me that I would be part of it. During school vacations, I spent every possible moment with him and his new family. And, yes, I have another wonderful set of letters from father to daughter, written from Fort Bragg, Fort Sheridan, Naples, Stuttgart, and all of the places he was stationed after the war. After his retirement, until Parkinson's disease took away his ability to write, he wrote from Boston, Cape Cod, and Paris, where he served as President John Kennedy's ambassador to France.

For the longest time I couldn't bring myself to share his letters with anyone except my children. Then, after my father's death, as I read excerpts from his letters to 82nd Airborne veterans in after-dinner talks at their reunions, I realized that these wonderful men had cared as much for my dad as I had. They encouraged me to publish these letters. I hope that the reader enjoys reading them and is able to understand the enormous pride that my father took in the heroism of his boys of the 82nd Airborne, and the pride that I feel in being his daughter.

chapter one

THE CALL TO WAR

On November 8, 1942, the Allies invaded French North Africa, resulting in the capitulation of the Vichy French colonial forces.[1] Expecting complete victory over all Axis forces in North Africa by early spring 1943, plans were formulated for the Allied invasion, staged from North Africa, of the Italian island of Sicily. Invading Sicily — sandwiched between the northeast coast of Tunisia and the southwest tip of the Italian mainland — might induce the war-weary Italians to surrender and sever their alliance with Germany, thereby weakening Axis control in the Mediterranean. Code-named Operation HUSKY, the combined Anglo-American invasion plan called for supportive airborne operations: during the predawn hours prior to the amphibious landings, British and American troops would be dropped and air-landed inland to seize key terrain and block enemy movement toward the invasion beaches.

Selected to protect the American beachheads, Major General Matthew B. Ridgway's untried 82nd Airborne Division — America's first airborne division activated by the War Department in August 1942 and based at Fort Bragg, North Carolina — received orders to deploy to a training area in North Africa. The Division's table of organization included one parachute infantry regiment and two glider infantry regiments; however, to meet the plan's operational requirement, one of the glider regiments would have to be replaced by an additional parachute regiment — Colonel James M. Gavin's 505th Parachute Infantry Regiment at Fort Benning, Georgia, got the call. Fourteen years after graduating from West Point and determined to repay his "Spartan mother" for all that she had given him, Jim Gavin — the orphan from the small coal-mining town in eastern Pennsylvania — would now have the opportunity to cancel the debt.[2]

Assigned to the 82nd, Gavin moved his "boys" of the 505 to Fort Bragg. From Bragg, Gavin sent Barbara the first letter of their nearly three-year wartime separation, obviously determined that life remain as normal as possible for his nine-year-old daughter.

★ ★ ★

[Undated]

Dear Barbara,

I am sorry that I forgot to send your allowance. I liked your Valentine very much. I have it on my desk now.

I am enclosing $1.00, your allowance for the last two weeks and 50 cents extra for being a good girl. I am glad that you are buying a war bond. It is wise to save and it is patriotic to buy bonds. If everyone buys enough bonds the war will be over soon and all of the soldiers can come home.

It has been very cold here [at Fort Bragg]. I live in buildings close to McKellars Pond where you went swimming last summer. There is ice on the pond now.

Write to me again when you have the time.

XXX Love,

Daddy

★ ★ ★

April 11, 1943

Dear Babe,

I have finally after much looking about managed to get a typewriter so my letters from now on should at least be more readable. In addition, my letters from now on will very likely be exposed to an extra reading since the censor will be reading them too. That may ultimately cause some double talk and misunderstanding but it is all for the best.

I am enclosing a check for ten dollars which includes your allowance, plus the cost of "Never Call Retreat," and sufficient balance to get me a copy of "Lee's Lieutenants," Vol. II, by Douglas Southall Freeman. Please get it as quickly as possible and mail it to me at my present address. *[My dad relaxed by reading and especially enjoyed books about the Civil War. — BGF]*

I have been swamped with work and consequently haven't had an opportunity to send the radio, books, etc. I plan on getting it off tomorrow, or at least part of it. I have to send it express collect, let me know how much it cost.

Max was prop blasted last night.[3] He did very well. He had a big bowl of milk and seemed to like it very much. *[Max was the mascot of the 505, a handsome boxer dog who loved to jump. — BGF]*

Love XXXXXXX,

Pappy

The 82nd Airborne Division departed Fort Bragg on April 20, 1943, for Camp Edwards, Massachusetts, where it would make final preparations for deployment overseas. Traveling by train under strict security and thereby keeping secret their move to war, America's newest elite soldiers were also directed to cover or remove their telling airborne insignias and badges and were further instructed on the wartime censorship regulations governing all correspondence.

★ ★ ★

April 23, 1943

Dear Babe,

I have a new address now as you have probably noticed [by the enclosed APO card]. Be sure to address your letters to me exactly like that, notice that the word "parachute" is omitted, that is important.

I have been very busy or I would have written you sooner. After this letter it may be some time until you hear from me again. I will write you whenever I can. Sometimes letters may get lost or end up in the drink so you must expect that. In addition, any or all of my letters may be censored. That means that I will not be able to tell you very much, if anything, about where I am or what I am doing. If you follow the newspapers though, sooner or later you should find mention of our activities. Everyone is fine and very anxious to catch up with some nazis and japs. At present, as I said, we are very busy.

I saw some ceagles today. You remember them. It has been very cold and I miss the dogwood and cherry blossoms like I saw last time we took a walk together. *[I once confused a seagull with an eagle. Realizing my mistake, I then called it a "ceagle," much to my dad's amusement. — BGF]*

I was glad to get the candy that you sent to Fort Bragg. I received the Martha Washington and it was best of all. It should have been I suppose. Anytime you are wondering if there is anything you can send, send candy. I have about everything else that I can use. If you try to send anything it might be necessary for you to have this letter containing a request for a specific item, hence the request for candy.

I would like to tell you more about what's going on but I am particularly unable to right now. Perhaps later I will be able to be more newsy.

Love XXXX,

Pappy

On April 29, the three troop transports carrying the 82nd to North Africa sailed from the harbor of New York City in a well-protected convoy — the 505 on board the converted liner "S.S. Monterey." Though the assistant division commander, Brigadier General Charles L. Keerans Jr., also traveled on board the "Monterey," the less-senior Gavin was made commanding officer of troops.

★ ★ ★

May 1943

Dear Girls,

I thought I would let you know how things are going while I still have the time. This letter is to probably be mailed in New York. The permanent transport commanding officer, one Lt. Col. Truscott, is going to take it back with him and mail it upon arrival. If all goes well you should get it much more quickly than you would by the regular channels. Incidentally, I understand that the V-mail is now operating in you-know-where [French Morocco].

This is our fifth day at sea, maybe the sixth, and it is a very nice day. We are in quite dangerous waters and yesterday sighted our first sub. Fortunately it went right ahead minding its own business and we paid it no attention, so other than having to get up too early it caused no inconvenience. Our escort seems, to a landlubber, quite sizable. Except for losing some sleep and having to wear our water wings [life preservers] at all times, they cause no trouble. We will probably get a warm reception at the straits of you-know-where [Gibraltar] but no one seems concerned about it.

I have an interesting job. Being the senior officer aboard ship outside of General Keerans, who is not traveling in a command capacity, I am commanding officer of troops. The entire 505 is with me fortunately. In addition, I have an assemblage of 4,000 additional spare parts [replacement troops not yet assigned to a unit], casuals, and diverse nondescript forms of soldiery.

These parachute soldiers are tops and they are doing about all the work on this ship right now. Most of the people who joined have to be taken care of rather than helping. We have a grand ship, a big Matson liner. It is all quite an experience. Not the least interesting, Charlie is redoing his weekend in Tulsa, without accompaniment this time. I have been too busy, too much responsibility.

There has been nothing particularly exciting happening. We lost a big part of our air force yesterday. A ship was catapulted from one of our accompanying battleships during the passing visit of the sub, and when the pilot tried to land (this is an airplane I am talking about), the ship kept going into the ocean, busted a pontoon and disappeared. Too bad. A few more days and we may get within support of land-based aircraft. That will be much better.

We have no idea what is going on in the outside world. We have no way of getting the news. Radios are not permitted. No one on the ship receives news.

We have had the usual round of band concerts, physical training, care of weapons (which we don't have to caution them about anymore), boxing, inspections, etc. Starting today we are going to have language classes for everyone aboard ship simultaneously. We have records: Arabic, French, etc. After a brief introduction and explanation of what is to happen, they are played over the ship's public address system. At the same time officers have classes with the troops, each soldier has a text which follows the exact lesson being broadcast. Quite a system. Keeps them out of trouble. They don't learn much Arabic.

We have had no seasickness to amount to anything although the sea has been rough at times. This is a grand ship. The best ship in the convoy. I can look out and see the old "Chateau Thierry" at any time, she has been bouncing around like a cork since she left you-know-where.

I will give the V-mail a try as soon as I have an opportunity after debarking. It may get back before this.

The 505 is going to give a good account of itself in any capacity anywhere. Everyone is anxious and looking forward to what is coming. They have been outstanding in everything they have put their hands to since leaving Fort Bragg.

Love XXXXXXX,

Pappy

[On back of above letter]

We are now out eight days and things are pretty much humdrum. I thought you would be interested in the enclosed [*Pocket Guide to North Africa*]. Each soldier is to receive one before landing.

There has been no particular excitement. Passed Swedish prisoner of war exchange ship, or something like that, last night. Everyone was alerted and stood by for trouble. It stood out like Times Square in 1929. Lights aglow, we could see it for a long time. Our ship cannot be seen even a few feet away at night so we were quite suspicious. Since nothing has happened, I guess it was OK.

I finished "Lee's Lieutenants." Thanks very much. The purser aboard ship wanted to borrow it so he is taking it back with him, and if all goes well, he will mail it upon reaching the States.

Hope the allotment is coming through, I haven't been paid in a long time. If I can get some money wherever I am going, I will send it to the bank. I am sure, however, that your allotment is getting through.[4]

Lots of seaweed floating around these days. Must be near the Az-r-s [Azores].

Love,

Pappy

★ ★ ★

May 1943

Dear Babe,

Thought you might like to have this table assignment ticket. Although there have been but two meals per day, there is food enough on those occasions to last longer than the next meal.

This will probably be my last letter aboard. We are nearing the end of our voyage. The sailors call this area "submarine alley," so far it has not lived up to its name which has been a bit disappointing and reassuring both. Of course now after coming so far we are anxious to get where we planned on going even though a little excitement would relieve the monotony.

The past few days have reminded me of the trip across the Pacific [traveling between San Francisco and Fort McKinley in the Philippines]. The days are getting warm and the sea is calm. Most of the poor sailors are over their initial spell of seasickness. I have been very comfortable and am enjoying all of the comforts while I still have an opportunity.

I hope you are getting good use of the radio. We are not allowed news of any sort. It has been very interesting under these circumstances to hear the fantastic and highly imaginative rumors that are circulated throughout the troop areas. Usually they are accompanied by some authentication to the effect that a member of the ship's crew got the straight dope from the ship's radio operator. Actually, no one gets any news but if it would be possible to do so, some authentic news should be sent around.

Our first land-based friendly plane has just appeared over our area. Everyone is very glad to see it. From now on we should get good protection and it also means we are getting close. As you probably know, submarines can be spotted from an airplane better than by any other means, and best of all, the airplane can bomb the submarine but the submarine cannot retaliate.

I hope you are doing well in your studies. Work hard and be honest with yourself as well as with others. I will send your allowance as soon as I can get some money. It may not be negotiable in the States but it will be your allowance and it will be money. Let me know how your grades are in school as soon as you can.

I am enclosing an "invasion arm band" [a strip of canvas with a stamped-on small American flag] which I thought you might like to have. They were worn by all American troops in the initial landing in Africa. You probably saw them worn in the newsreels.

Note the correct APO number: 469

Love XXXXX,

Pappy

chapter two

OPERATION HUSKY —
NORTH AFRICA

Reaching the coast of North Africa on May 10, the convoy carrying the 82nd sailed into the harbor at Casablanca, French Morocco. While in North Africa, the Division fell under the administrative command of Lieutenant General Mark W. Clark's Fifth Army, headquartered at Oujda. Within days, the 82nd's units were bivouacked nearby, not far from a former French airfield selected as the base for the Division's partnered troop carrier wing.

HUSKY was scheduled for the early morning hours of July 10. American forces, commanded by General George S. Patton Jr., were to land on the island's southwestern coast, while the British and Canadian forces, commanded by General Bernard Montgomery, were to land on the southeastern extremity. The operation's final objective was to be the quick capture of Sicily's coastal town of Messina at the northeast corner of the island opposite the Italian mainland, preventing the enemy's escape across the narrow Strait of Messina.

Due to a shortage of transport aircraft, the airborne missions preceding the amphibious landings were scheduled piecemeal. Shortly after arriving in North Africa, General Ridgway informed Gavin that his regiment would be reinforced with parachute artillery, engineers, supporting elements of medics and signal personnel, and, exceptionally, one battalion from the 504th Parachute Infantry Regiment. Together, this regimental combat team would form the American vanguard.

Responsible for the first large-scale combat airborne operation in the history of the U.S. Army, Gavin had only two months to properly train his team of over three thousand paratroopers in a desolate region of less-than-perfect training and living conditions. High winds that swept the area drastically curtailed the required jump training with the troop carrier wing; moreover the terrain, baked hard under the hot African sun, was strewn with large jagged rocks, making

*selections of suitable practice drop and landing zones almost impossible. Con-
suming food and water rations contaminated by the wind-borne sand that was
infested with animal dung, the men soon became ill with dysentery so severe
many were unable to train, let alone exist comfortably. Making life even more
miserable for the men were the African flies that attacked them "as one dark
and horrible force" without mercy, determined to destroy them "body and soul."*[1]

★ ★ ★

May 11, 1943

Dear Babe,

Some place. The only difference between Pappy and the Arabs is that
the Arabs are a bit hungrier. We are both very dirty right now. In addition,
this is my first letter by candlelight, this is North Africa. *[It was also his first
letter written on V-mail.*[2] *— BGF]*

So far I have used a combination of French, Spanish, and Tagalog [the
official language of the Philippines] and it works OK. The Arabs don't
seem to understand anything except "Scram" and "Here is a cigarette."

Hope we don't have to stay here too long. It could easily become unpleasant. The climate seems like summer in Arizona but the place is dirty,
dusty, unsanitary, and infested with louse-ridden Arabs.

Let me hear from you. I understand that I am not permitted to send
XXXXs.

Love,

Pappy

★ ★ ★

May 17, 1943

Dear Babe,

I thought you would like to have these stamps so I am sending them
along. I had a hard time buying them. They are Moroccan (French) and I
am learning that my French is none too good. The francs you may like to
have. At the present rate of exchange they are fifty for a dollar. There are
all kinds of them, Moroccan, Algerian, Tunisian, etc.

It is very hot here in the daytime, like Oklahoma in midsummer and
very cold at night like midwinter. I used three blankets last night and was
quite cold. It should be very healthful and should be except for the insects,
Arabs, etc.

I have been very busy and had a night jump the other night. The ground was very hard. It is also hard to sleep on. I finally improvised a rope net that keeps me a little above the habitat of our friends the asps, bugs, etc.

By this point we have gotten beyond the canned ration stage and our rations are good, better than in the States. The dehydrated foods like potatoes, onions, etc., are surprisingly good.

I will be glad to hear from you, I never have since leaving Fort Bragg. Continue to work hard at school and be a good girl. These francs are part of your allowance. Do you want your allowance in foreign money or American?

X — I just remembered these are not permitted.

Love,

Pappy

★ ★ ★

[Undated]

Dear Babe,

I should be getting a letter from you soon. Some mail came in today but none for me. *[It was frustrating to hear that the letters I sent my dad weren't reaching him. Sometimes they took a week, sometimes a month. Bunches of letters arrived at the same time. Sometimes, of course, they never arrived at all. — BGF]*

Today was a big day. It was ration day. Every soldier gets a box of gumdrops, a couple packages of gum, and about a half-dozen packages of cigarettes. I traded my cigarettes for francs and more gumdrops. This is just about the only kind of candy that will keep here. This may not sound like a momentous occasion but it takes on all of the aspects of one living under these conditions.

Yesterday I met Gen. Clark and talked to him for a few minutes. We had a review for him and in the afternoon he had a number of us in for tea. That must sound funny to you, for us to be having tea. He has a rather nice villa, such conveniences are a necessity for diplomatic reasons if no other. As a matter of fact, I would have much preferred to have a bath instead of tea but he didn't give me a choice.

This must be the dry season here. It hasn't rained since we arrived. There are a lot of grain fields, barley, etc., that the Arabs are harvesting when they are not stealing from us. They are rather interesting people. Very hardy, dirty, lousy [lice-ridden], and unprincipled. On the other hand, they evidently have some personal religious tenets that they abide by very closely. They are all descendents of the Berbers, one-time overrunners of Spain, Italy, and a lot of southern Europe. They would still be a powerful race if their existence depended upon their ability to live on little and wield a sharp kris.

We were very disappointed yesterday to find out that Max did not make the trip. Everything was all set until about an hour before takeoff at Pope [the airfield serving Fort Bragg] when he could not be found. The people taking care of him thought that he was stolen by someone from Camp Hoffman [an Army installation (later renamed Camp Mackall) near Fort Bragg]. It may be just as well. There is a great deal of rabies here.

I understand that these V-mail letters go by microfilm airmail now, you should try it out. The other day I sent you some francs and postage stamps by regular mail.

We have been very busy. The work has been most interesting. We lose all track of time and days.

My French is improving and I haven't tried Arabic. A combination of French, Spanish and English gets one by most anywhere.

Have you ever been able to bring Toughie up from Georgia? [*Toughie was our cocker spaniel. Not knowing what kind of living situation we would find in Washington, we left Toughie behind at a boarding kennel near Fort Benning. To my great disappointment, my mother never felt that we could bring her to Washington. My dad and I were very attached to her. — BGF*]

I don't believe I told you that I received your Easter card sent to Fort Bragg the other day. I was very glad to get it and know that at that time you were well.

Love to everyone and write me when you get the time.

Pappy

★ ★ ★

May 24, 1943

Dear Babe,

How about a letter? I just received a deposit slip from the bank so Mommie's allotment is coming in OK.

I got a treat yesterday. I found a hotel where I could get a bath for twenty francs, hot water too. I am going back again if I get a chance.

You would like these Arab horses. They are smaller than American horses but very good. Some outfits that are able to have them for pets.

We are slowly becoming acclimated. The ration is good, at times better than in the States. What I miss most is a light at night to read by and music and news.

Love,

Pappy

★ ★ ★

May 25, 1943

Dear Babe,

It is about time you wrote me a letter. How about it?

I have just come back from town. I went in to get another twenty francs bath, pretty good too. Capt. [Al] Ireland [the regimental personnel officer] went with me.[3] Afterwards, we went to the Mess De Officiers for dinner which appeared to consist mostly of French-fried eggs and tomatoes, dry bread, and much vin rouge. It was rather delightful for a change. Besides, I beat the flies to most of it.

I hope that you are getting along well in school. I talked to Catherine's namesake yesterday for a few minutes. *[To pass censorship, this was a veiled reference to General Patton. Cathy Patton (no relation) was my best friend. — BGF]*

I was up at the sea and it was wonderful. Very cool and clean, at least so it seemed to us. This is the dry season and it is much dustier than anywhere that I have ever seen. The annual rainfall here is only twelve inches which is about the morning's rain in the Philippines. After May 1st it doesn't rain until November 1st. Sooner or later water will be rationed I suppose. Later I hope.

About all that could be done is being done to keep us comfortable. It is difficult however to do much with some of this environment. We receive many dehydrated foods from the States, like potatoes, cabbage, sweet potatoes, onions, and they are all very good. Unfortunately there is no dehydrated ice cream. Most everyone is slowly becoming acclimated and accustomed to the heat.

I have just received your letter telling of your game of cops and robbers. The time when the cave fell in. Sounds like a great game.

This information is really for Mommy. I have a two-year subscription to TIME, NEW YORKER, and READERS DIGEST. They should expire in mid-1945. In case anything unpredictable should happen to me you should know of these so that you can have them sent to you. I also have four books from the Book-of-the-Month Club due me; and in addition, they may continue sending them to me regardless of my whereabouts if I do not notify them to stop. Just in case the Adjutant General notifies you of any change in my status other than being just wounded notify these companies right away so that you will receive the magazines etc.

Love,

Pappy

★ ★ ★

May 30, 1943

Dear Barbara,

Your letter telling me of Uncle George's visit just arrived yesterday. It must have been very nice for him to have gotten home for a while. *[Uncle George was my mother's younger brother who had joined the Navy. — BGF]*

Your letter sounded as though you have been going to a lot of movies. You have never told me how you want your allowance.

Yesterday was gumdrop ration day so it was very nice. To our delight and surprise we also got a package of Life Savers. I haven't opened mine yet. I am saving them for some big occasion. Like a prop blast if we have one. We may have one, we have some novices.

I had my first opportunity this morning to use my reserve chute thru necessity and it was pleasantly exciting. I was making the first jump with a new type chute, free fall [manually deploying the chute rather than jumping via a hooked static line] and as usual didn't bother counting. Before I realized it, I was getting quite close so I pulled the main [chute] and to my chagrin it seemed to help me along a little faster. I pulled the reserve and it opened nicely and then the main followed. After landing, I found out that the suspension lines in the main had binded in their retaining bands and finally ripped out. It was a lot of fun [living up to the unofficial nickname of "Jumpin' Jim"]. The spectators seemed to have gotten a little excited.

I wanted to jump at an affair this coming week but the General [Ridgway] grounded me. Said he can't afford to lose me yet. He really isn't going to lose me. As you know, this is perfectly safe when you know what you are doing.

Is Uncle George going to sea or is he returning to Arizona? This place reminds me very much of Arizona except that now it is getting much more warm than it gets in Arizona. The dust is quite bad, so are the Arabs.

I will continue to write to you regularly as long as I am able to. Do not be surprised however if a long spell occurs during which there will be no letters. You probably know a lot more about what is going on over here than we do since we never see any newspapers. You will recall I told you to watch the papers when I left. We really know little except what happens in our own backyard.

You had better go easy on all of those Xs or the censor will get after you. I do not believe they are permitted.

Love,

Pappy

★ ★ ★

June 3, 1943

Dear Babe,

Busy day today. Had a review for Gen. Patton and a lot of dignitaries.[4]

I received a letter from Mommy today telling me of your new house. It sounds pretty good. Will you be able to bring Toughie up from Georgia? I know you would like to do that. What will you do during vacation when Mommy is at work? It might be a good idea to go to a girls' summer camp. I believe you would like that. *[My mother and I had finally moved out of my grandmother's apartment into one of our own in a building right next door to hers on Columbia Road in Washington and lived there until my father returned from the war. Because these were years when polio struck in the summer, especially in cities, I was sent to a girls' camp during the summer. — BGF]*

Everyone was very complimentary about the appearance of our troops today. They are looking fine these days. We have been training and working very hard. I have always thought that these parachute soldiers were very good and of a special cut but I am more than ever convinced now as I see them reach a peak in training. During the past few weeks their training has been very realistic and there have been several casualties. Those we have left are the very best.

After seeing the experienced troops and combat-seasoned troops here, I am sure that we have exceptional people. They [the "boys" of the 505] are going to do unusually well. Whether they do or not, and if they do not, it will be because of impossible circumstances way beyond their control. I will always think that the parachute private is an unusual guy. The saying now is that the AA [All American] in the Division insignia means "Awful Anxious."

The battalion that had Max for a mascot now has a native burro. I do not believe I will permit them to jump him although they would like to. I am afraid that he would kick the side of the plane out. They want to jump him and then use him to haul ammunition, food, etc. We will probably sell him or give him away.[5]

I saw a bottle of Coca-Cola at a short distance today. It looked wonderful. I almost forgot there was anything like that. There was some for the visiting firemen [general officers and dignitaries].

Mommy said something about sending Velatis. It would be best to wait awhile. I don't think that she will need a permit. *[Velatis were delicious caramels sold at the Velatis store in Washington. They were also known as the "dentist's friend" because they were famous for removing fillings as they were chewed. — BGF]*

Love,

Pappy

★ ★ ★

June 7, 1943

Dear Babe,

Today I had several letters returned by the censor because I had not signed the censorship certificate in the proper place. Since these were the first returned, and I have written you many letters and all of my letters V-mail since arriving here, I am wondering how many have gotten through. I'll try to sign this one properly and I hope it gets through.

Some time ago I wrote stating that I had received the deposit slip from the bank indicating that Mommy had received her check OK. Today I received a letter from her telling about having difficulties. Checking up, I find that the deposit slips that I received were for the month of April. For May, the allotment was raised to $400.00. It has been taken from my pay here. Perhaps because of the increase that month there was a misunderstanding and the entire thing was stopped. The place to inquire about it is the "Office of Dependency Benefits, 213 Washington St., Newark, N.J." If it did not come in this month, and if the May amount has not yet been paid, Mommy should write without delay.

It has been deducted from my pay and should be paid. I would like to have it settled while I am still in a position to do something about it, if there is any necessity for me to take action. It is important that this be cleared up promptly. Although my checking account had some money in it, I have cashed some checks on my balance as I keep it. I also have a monthly payment to make on the car and another to an Xmas fund. By draining the account clean without the allotment being deposited puts me on a spot. Some record should be kept of what is happening. At present, my own accounts show a monthly deposit and withdrawal of $400.00.

In case you have missed any of my letters, I again want to remind you to immediately upon notification of any change in my status that would indicate that I have no further need for reading material, to change the address of TIME, NEW YORKER, READERS DIGEST, and the Book-of-the-Month Club. Don't give a second thought to my welfare. The General has grounded me until the real McCoy.

The new apartment sounds rather good. Hope you can have Toughie.

Love,

Pappy

★ ★ ★

June 11, 1943

Dear Babe,

I thought you would like to have this [banknote] for your collection. I am getting along fine. Losing a bit of weight perhaps but it is only what I gained on the boat on our trip over.

Love,

Pappy

★ ★ ★

June 13, 1943

Dear Babe,

I haven't written for some time. I have been on a rather long trip [on a reconnaissance flight over the planned invasion drop zones]. It was a lot of fun and of course I am not allowed to tell you where I have been. I will be able to, however, next time I see you. My longest record, that of having been in the Army nineteen years and never having heard a hostile shot, was broken by a close, too close, bomb hit [during an enemy air raid against a British airfield].

Mommy mentioned something in her letter about me sending permission from my commanding officer in order to get a package. I believe that has been changed now and that packages of a certain size may be sent.

Anyway, there is little that I would like to have that can be sent in a package. Like a bath with hot water, clean underwear, or music, or a movie or something.

I sent some laundry to a nearby French [colonial] family and after about three weeks it was returned. It was not mine. It cost two hundred and forty francs for just a few pieces and I had to give her a cake of soap with it. If you give your laundry to an Arab that is the last ever seen of it. If you give it to a French family they wear it a month or so and then charge more for laundering it than the stuff was worth in the first place. So you see, you can't win. I am doing my own, if and when I have the time, however it quickly gets dark brown. Not from me, from the dust. It penetrates everything.

About the package, candy would be most welcome. I would suggest that it be sent without delay and then no more be sent until I mention it again. I have hoped to get you some more insignia. Censorship regulations however will not permit sending many of them. Yesterday I sent some banknotes that I got on a recent journey.

I hope Mommy gets the bank account straightened out along the lines I recommended. I would like to continue paying for the car, etc. Mommy should cash her allowance check only. Otherwise I am unable to keep any account or cash a check. This could become serious. I have talked to other people and they tell me that many times the allotment comes in around the fifteenth [of each month]. If this really happened, I would like to know. That will work OK.

I was talking to Bill Cunningham's commanding officer the other day. I understand that he got a chest wound [in the invasion of North Africa] and took a trip back to the States. You probably do not remember him. He was at Fort Sill with us.

I like my work very much. It is very real, never a dull moment.

Hope you like the new house. Are you going to camp?

Love,

Pappy

★ ★ ★

June 18, 1943

Dear Babe,

It's about time I get a letter from you, how about it?

Today is a hot quiet day with little wind and consequently no dust for a change. Unhappily on a day like this the flies become particularly aggressive and offensive. Any orifice is a haven of retreat. When you open your mouth to talk they fly in by the dozen. It's a nip and tuck affair, with you usually on the tuck end; you tuck yourself away where the flies can't get at you, if this is possible. I have found it difficult. These are stealthy and determined flies endowed with an inordinate degree of intelligence. You can't be elusive when an African fly is looking for you.

By now, however, we appear to have weathered our period of acclimation with little loss and probably considerable gain. We were early stricken with the plague of combat areas, dysentery. We have practically none of it now. It came in for many of the "Chic Sale's" type stories. *[Chic Sale, a former vaudeville actor, had written a popular, very funny "outhouse-humor" book, and this letter proved to my delight that my dad's sense of humor was still intact. — BGF]* Our ability to run 100 yards taking down a pair of coveralls on the way came to be the measure of military attainment. This required speed, prowess, and a versatility that could not be acquired overnight. Lacking these attributes of military accomplishment meant being caught en route and many befell this unhappy and odoriferous fate. To be so stricken was most unpleasant, so I have been told. One's nonchalance wilted quickly when you came from a gallop to a dead stop with everyone around promptly giving you a wide berth.

Soldiers call everything associated with the Army "G.I." To their delight, the medicos referred to this ailment as the "GIs" meaning gastrointestinal disorder. To have had the GIs came to be a mark of accomplishment of "having been there." A campaign ribbon should have been awarded the individuals rugged enough to have withstood its rigors. It may be yet.

Incidentally, I have another ribbon now, the multicolored one with the brown ends [European-African-Middle-Eastern Campaign Service Medal]. It is a saying among the soldiers that the brown ends are awarded the survivors of the GIs. If I should continue to acquire ribbons at my present rate by the time I retire, and I have no doubt that I will, slightly shot perhaps but otherwise intact, I should have exactly two more, making a total of four. That should be one line straight across, geometrically and artistically, leaving little to be desired. *[When my dad retired in 1958 (with the rank of lieutenant general) his ribbons required seven rows. — BGF]*

I do not know if you particularly like these letters, but as I said before, I like to write you while I still am able to. The things that I write you about are the things closest to the soldiers here. And that is not the enemy or his weapons. Instead they are the banal problems of food, sleep, and the simple things that we miss most from the homeland. Our contacts with the enemy are, and will be, few and spasmodic, our lack of an abundance of ordinary comforts are every day things.

Love,

Pappy

★ ★ ★

June 18, 1943

Dear Barbara,

I received a letter from Rosie today telling me that you had received my first V-mail letter. [Rosie was my maternal grandmother. — BGF] I have often wondered if you have ever received a letter or two written on board ship. They should have been mailed upon the return of the ship to the States and by now you should have received them. I also loaned "Lee's Lieutenants" to the purser of the boat. He promised me that he would mail it upon arrival in the States, did you ever receive it?

Conditions here continue to be as interesting and as busy as ever. We are all working hard.

For the past few days our mess has been favored with some native-grown fruit and vegetables. Unfortunately after it is stewed it just about all tastes alike. Cherries are just appearing. This seems hard to understand since it has been hotter than Hades for weeks. They must be boiled however. There are local ground rules on the consumption of most everything. Even oranges must be scalded before eating since presumably they have probably been handled by diseased Arabs. Prices are exorbitant but the troops have little to spend money for so that makes no difference.

I am beginning to think that the news about the easy money spreads quickly. During the past several days, a number of new Arabs have arrived in the vicinity of camp. They appear to have come some distance. They have an interesting method of hobbling their camels. Instead of tying the forefeet together as we do with American horses, they tie the hoof of one leg back against the upper leg, thus making him a three-legged quadruped. It is very effective for which we are thankful since it keeps them from wandering thru camp.

Camels incidentally can be much meaner than American mules and their proclivity for biting, combined with an enormous mouth, makes them formidable opponents under any circumstances. The Arabs use them and small burros as beasts of burden, both evidently more efficient in this part of the world than American mules would be. They require little or no forage or water. As a matter of fact their only rival, and the thing the Arab envies most from the lowest sheep herder to the local Pasha, is the American jeep.

A jeep can do anything a camel or burro can and an awful lot better. The Arabs never cease being amazed at finding jeeps back in the hill country where burros travel only with difficulty. Occasionally finding myself perched upon these jeeps, I am surprised to be there myself. *[One day at Fort Benning, he arrived at our quarters driving the first jeep I had ever seen and gave me a ride around Miller Loop. — BGF]*

By the way, I was up where "Uncle" Frank used to be the other day and he wasn't there. He no doubt has moved by now but I rather expected to find him there since it was the same outfit. *[Our family had known Frank Greer at West Point, and he had commanded an infantry regiment during the invasion of North Africa. — BGF]* Many of the older officers, unless they have a high command, seem to have left units they were with in the States. This is a rather rugged existence anyway.

Love,

Pappy

★ ★ ★

June 19, 1943

Dear Barbara,

Today is another one of those days of event. Candy-ration day comes but once a week and today it is two Tootsie Rolls apiece. In case you do not know what they are, Tootsie Rolls are like filet mignon in the event you haven't had anything sweet for a week, otherwise they are Tootsie Rolls.

I had a letter from Major Barney Oldfield [public relations officer with the U.S. First Army and a former 505 staff officer] the other day. Since the days of our early friendship in Georgia he has been my Ivy Lee and super-plugger. Knowing his propensity for the unusual and his flair for showmanship, any information he would furnish news agencies would be certain to be a bit hopped up. I suspect that he has given some yarns, as he calls them, to several different news sources just in case anything breaks. It has just occurred to me that you may not understand the reference to Ivy Lee, about any public relations person can tell you who he was [an early pioneer in the field of public relations]. I have considerable regard for Oldfield and I am sure his stuff is not too bad.[6]

I wonder sometimes if these letters come to you with the regularity with which they are written. Probably not, I suppose they come in batches. Well, I will not have time to write you so much very much longer. My time now is filled up, just about everyone works from daylight until they are tired, about nine or ten p.m., with occasional night problems. There is not, in this particular sector anyway, much in the way of reading material or music. For recreation one can always go back to work. Under these circumstances I find writing an occasional letter gets my mind off my work, for a few moments anyway.

At times things seem rather humdrum. I have had at least one delightful air raid experience. These slit trenches are very inviting at such times. They can, however, be a source of many amusing incidents and some misunderstandings. At one a.m., the yawning black can be particularly inviting, but to dive in like a Stuka [a German dive bomber] only to land on someone's head who was a bit more fleet of foot and got there ahead of you results in some confusion. For some years now the night-time view of the standard Army latrine and the current slit trench have been quite identical. To end up prostrate in the latrine, however, is not at all like being in a slit trench. In fact, there is considerable doubt as to whether or not it wouldn't be better to be bombed.

I happened to get into a Command Post the other day (British), I don't suppose it is a secret that there are British in Africa, where they had methodically placed signs at all slit trenches indicating the correct occupants just in case. "Visiting Officer," "American Officers," etc. It would tend to minimize the traffic problems at such a critical time but I know lots of people who would not stop to read signs.

The British incidentally are OK. I would perhaps be the last to boost their stock but I think their soldiers are fine, well-trained, well-mannered men. They are rugged and tough and all of the officers and headquarters with which I have come in contact with are most pleasant to work with. For ordinary every day cooperation [in fulfilling the requirements of the combat team], I prefer them to Americans.[7]

Love,
Pappy

★ ★ ★

June 20, 1943

Dear Barbara,

I am enclosing a few Italian stamps that I thought you would like to have to complete your collection. Their history is rather interesting. Someday I will be able to give it to you. Did you ever receive the Moroccan stamps?

I am also enclosing an insignia patch of an Italian colonial unit. Since arriving here I have been unable to send you any organizational patches of our own units for obvious reasons. This I thought was a rather attractive one. Since time immemorial it has been the barbaric if interesting custom of soldiers away at war to send to the folks in the homeland captured trinkets which are worn with pride as an indication of the military prowess of the warrior. I can claim little personal credit for having this but you might find some way to wear it anyway.

In recent weeks I have learned a great deal about foreign insignia. For example, at first I thought that there was a possibility that this could be a British insignia with the British Lion. They promptly informed me that the British Lion always wears a crown and never has wings. The lion herewith is the Lion of Venice.

This may be some time in reaching you but I would like to know when you do finally get it. I have sent you some other stamps, as I said above, which I would like to know if you have received.

I hope you are enjoying your summer camp. I am anxious to know where it is and what it is like. I will probably hear by airmail long before you receive this.

Love to everyone,

Pappy

★ ★ ★

June 20, 1943

Dear Barbara,

Your "school is out" letter just arrived and I am very pleased with your grades, Einstein. I rather think you did well in French too. My own French has been none too good. Too many people here speak Spanish, and worse, insist on speaking it when they hear my French.

I want to know all about your camp, Camp Matoaka. Where is it? What group are you in? What do you do? I am sure that you are going to like it very much. There will no doubt be many activities of an athletic nature, some perhaps a bit vigorous. Do not get hurt, be careful swimming and on hikes. If I were you, I would give the horses a wide berth, there are few horses or instructors in equitation nowadays who are "safe." *[When my dad was a cadet at West Point, he had spent his last two summers as a counselor at Camp Chippewa at Lake George, New York, so he spoke from experience. — BGF]*

I have frequently written you of the poor quality of the native Arabs. They are certainly that, in addition they are most interesting. As a racial group they are like no other people in the world, perhaps it is their religion that so sets them apart. The evaluation of a people is made in the last analysis in two ways: by the world at large and by the people themselves. To the world at large, the measure of worth of a racial group is evaluated in terms of their contributions, creative, to the arts, sciences, and welfare of the human race as a whole. To the people, their race is measured by their own happiness and contentment. For this they do not need material things like cars, movies, etc.

I will always remember that the Mexicans were extremely contented with their lot whereas we were sorry for them. *[One of my father's early postings, Camp Jones in Arizona, was very near the Mexican border. — BGF]* The Filipinos were the same way. And here, in an entirely different manner and way of life, the Arabs are a totally satisfied racial group who want nothing from us other than to be left alone.

If one learns anything from travel I suppose this is it, that grandiose international schemes do not enter into the thinking of human beings as much as their everyday comforts and necessities. So despite all that I have said about these people, they are in their own way seeking "life, liberty and the pursuit of happiness" and not doing a bad job of it at that. This is a rather weighty paragraph, muchacha.

I am sending you some stamps that should prove rather interesting for your collection. They were taken at Bizerte. I would like to have sent you some insignia to add to your collection but for obvious reasons I am unable to send you insignias of units in this theatre. Frequently of late I come across captured cloth insignia. If it is possible to do so I will try to send you some.

Love,
Pappy

★ ★ ★

June 22, 1943

Dear Barbara,

I received a letter from the United Services Auto Insurance, San Antonio, Texas, today regarding the car insurance. It expired June 19th. However, in view of the circumstances I would imagine Mommy could renew it if she so desires, it was only to cost $15.33 because of savings. Otherwise it would have cost $31.35. I would certainly like to know if Mommy has received *any* allotment check since my departure from the States.

Today is the first day of summer, a trifle belated in this climate but nonetheless it stirs our memories of cool summer mornings in early June at West Point. *[In the summer, my dad and I picked wild blueberries for pies and breakfast pancakes. He made a circle with his forefinger and the base of his thumb, and those berries too large to go through the circle had to be eaten and not put into our berry pail. — BGF]*

Although by now it is quite warm, the Arabs do not seem to change their garments to conform to the climatic change, if anything, they seem to wear more the hotter it gets. They bundle up from head to toe. Over their heads they wear a hood or turban and about their bodies they wear a number of unmentionables topped with a heavy robe. The females show only the tips of their toes (they always walk around barefooted) and a small triangle at one eye of about one square inch, otherwise they are completely clothed. In theory they completely cover their faces out of modesty. In practice, however, their modesty varies inversely with their curiosity. If something goes by that they really want to see, taboos and customs go out the window. It is amusing to see them peep more and more at something they want to see. To accomplish their desires and yet not displease Allah becomes a feat.

One [Arab] blew up the other day playing with a dud. They are rather childlike in their curiosity. They can and will steal anything that is not nailed down. I realize now that there is a great deal to the saying, "He could steal from an Arab." Upon our arrival in this sector, they had a field day stealing simple things like target dummies, etc. We placed booby traps in several and that stopped it instantly and unfortunately it stopped a couple of Arabs also.

The local tribes, including the Pasha, are in a bit of a tizzy today because the Sultan of Morocco is due in tomorrow. At least his resplendent if rather anachronistic vanguard arrived today. They were mounted on beautiful horses, riding saddles inlaid with silver, etc., and they wore flowing colorful robes on the order of "The Arabian Nights." Their rifles were muskets of the vintage of about 1825 or thereabouts, muzzle-loading flintlocks. I believe they carried them as a symbol rather than a utility weapon. They were of highly polished silver, etc. Seeing these people in their native habitat leads me to believe that Hollywood has not overdone it. By our standards little of what they do or wear makes sense. There is lots of color, fanfare, and the unexpected.

Incidentally, you would probably appreciate the news dispatches [from North Africa] more if you knew that "djebel" means mountain, "oued" means river, "sobkra" means lake.

Hope that you are enjoying your camp.

Love,

Pappy

★ ★ ★

June 25, 1943

Dear Babe,

I have been a bit too busy to keep my usual regularity in letter writing. Most soldiers like to write letters; it is a form of self-expression otherwise denied them. They can talk shop, etc. all day long but they can talk to no one as they can their own kin. Letters mean a great deal to them. I had a letter to you returned the other day. I had failed to sign it in the correct place. I hope that not too many more have fallen by the wayside. *[Every soldier needs to know that someone at home is thinking of him and praying for him, that someone cares whether he lives or dies. — BGF]*

I was talking to a lieutenant from the regiment today who may return to Walter Reed [army hospital in Washington, D.C.]. He experienced a bad jump injury a short while ago that has finally necessitated his evacuation to the States. I gave him Rosie's name to look up in the phone book so he may call, etc.

I rarely see a newspaper. We have a local mimeographed sheet that we look upon with suspicion. Since it is GI it is generally referred to as the propaganda sheet. It has, however, contained a brief reference to a riot in Detroit, and Mr. Lewis [the president of the United Mine Workers] continues to have his troubles keeping the government in its place. It makes us feel uneasy. Everyone knows that one of the things that we are fighting for is the right of everyone to do and say as he pleases, as long as it is not contrary to the public interest. But that stuff doesn't seem right. To the soldier mind, a respect for constituted authority must be a cornerstone of our social structure if it is to continue to exist. These things all evince a lack of such respect, so as I say, it makes us feel uneasy that they are tolerated.[8]

As our training goes on and on, I find my thoughts focusing more and more on things that are closest to me. These are of course censorable, even the thoughts, so it is at times difficult despite the enjoyment I derive from writing you to be circumspect. You will understand more in due time.

I received a nice letter from Aunt Lil today offering me the blessings of her shower. *[Aunt Lil was my great-aunt, Grandmother Rosie's sister. My dad had a close relationship with both of them. — BGF]* We have finally improvised one of a sort here. Wonderful. Biggest difficulty is that if one gets caught in it during one of the frequent dust blows you come out dirty brown. Still wonderful. Although we complain of the many discomforts, I believe that by now we are all in better health than we would be in the States. This life does have some things to recommend it. It is exhilarating and exciting, and for a parachutist doubly so.

When this war ends I think that I would like to be a curate in an out of the way parsonage with nothing to do but care for the flowers and meditate on the wickedness of the world. I have had more than enough excitement and danger to do for a lifetime.

Love,
Pappy

★ ★ ★

June 27, 1943
Dear Barbara,

This will probably be my last typed letter for some time. I think I'll move along and pack up my typewriter. If and when I have an opportunity, I will write longhand.

I was very glad to hear in your last letter about the camp, that is that you are going to one. I still want to know what it is like. I received a nice letter from Rosie telling me that you were going to a camp. I know you must miss Toughie. Her home in Georgia is very nice though.

It seems to be getting warmer here all of the time. I occasionally think of how nice and cool it was up at Cape Cod [prior to embarkation] when we were there. You probably didn't know about that. It was very nice, spring on Cape Cod is much nicer than spring on Cape Bon [North Africa], although I don't know about the latter.

I find on packing what remains of my effects that I brought along much more than I needed. I am getting down to bare essentials now. I don't know what I'll do if I need a lot of things that I finally threw away. What I have is in rather poor condition. It will be nice when the Army issues GI OD [olive drab] underwear then all of mine will look alike. It is impossible to get things white, perhaps I don't use LUX or Soapy Suds.

This afternoon we are, among other things, having a sniper contest. Fun. These youngsters are getting to be good shots. Regrettably, in the past few days they have practiced on some menacing looking parasitic Arabs. It makes them mad to get shot and we should stop it. It is difficult to sell international goodwill to a private soldier.

Hope you enjoy your camp.

Love,

Pappy

Beginning two weeks prior to the invasion date, Gavin and his combat team, along with their aligned troop carrier wing, were relocated to Tunisia — closer to Sicily. In Tunisia, near the area of Kairouan, airfields had been constructed from which the airborne assault phase of the invasion would be launched. At this final staging area, equipment was readied, orders issued, and briefings held.

With Sicily in Allied hands, shipping in the Mediterranean — of vital importance to the war effort — would be better protected. Moreover, if Italy surrendered, Germany would then be burdened with the sole defense of its occupied territories in the Mediterranean, and regardless of Italy's position, Allied occupation of Sicily would provide the necessary airfields and staging areas for an assault on the Axis-controlled Italian mainland. Gavin expected every paratrooper to jump and "fight to the last man and last round of ammunition" to achieve victory.[9] At stake was also the feasibility of future U.S. Army airborne operations, as HUSKY would test the Army's concept of an airborne division.

★ ★ ★

June 29, 1943

Dear Babe,

This is a luxury finding a typewriter here [in Kairouan]. I thought that I gave up all of those comforts long ago. I thought that it would be a good idea to drop you a line while I had the opportunity. It is highly probable that you will hear less and less from me for some time.

If I don't get some V-mail stationery, I will not be able to send you any V-mail letters. I would suggest if from all of the reports that you have when you receive this I am still able to write letters that you send me some V-mail paper. You will need a request.

This is quite a place. There is a thick pall of dust over all. It gets in your eyes, between your teeth, and in your ears. Doesn't seem to be anything that one can do about it.

The troops are getting along fine. Of course they are having the usual parachutist difficulties with drinking and fighting. This wine occasionally leaves them mesmerized. I think that is the word, it sounds good anyway. If it isn't that, it raises them in their own esteem to stratospheric heights of self-appreciation. Any sign on the part of anyone encountered during this inflation that may be considered derogatory is the sign to fight and they are off. MPs [Military Police] also have the same effect on them. I hope they fight as well in combat as they fight around barrios. I believe they will.

This is a poor typewriter. It still beats writing longhand and I hope it is more legible.

Met a Jack Thompson, columnist of a Chicago paper, Chicago Tribune I believe. His stuff may be interesting. Incidentally, good or bad, you will probably never hear anything of me or my doings. There is a local taboo in this theatre against mentioning people of the rank of colonel [or above]. The 505 should probably do something noteworthy sooner or later and of them you may hear.

What is the news about the camp? Has Toughie come up from Georgia yet?

Do not be surprised if there are longer and longer intervals between my letters. I'll always be okay even if you do not hear from me. You know, the luck of the Irish. I may get bumped around a bit but I have had too many hard landings and knocks to be concerned about any that may come. Like all parachutists, I have limitless confidence in my physical capabilities so share this with me if you will.

Love,

Pappy

* * *

July 5, 1943

Dear Babe,

I suppose that by the time you receive this you will be a bit concerned for my well-being. I will be, I am sure, in the best of health.

This is a bit different where I am now. Much hotter, which I hardly believed could be. Besides, the camels are vicious. They are big and mean, stand in the runways and won't let the ships land, stand in the roads and won't let cars by, bite anything including jeeps that come in reach of their long necks, and generally make a nuisance of themselves. The Arabs are much better than in the last place, there are none.

I was so glad to hear of your final arrangements for camp. I know that was a grand idea and I hope that you did not get too homesick and that you had a lot of fun. Camps always are fun. Rosie sent me the nicest picture taken downtown of you and Mommy. I was very glad to get it.

By now I have seen a great deal of this place, the northern portion of the continent I mean. Quite a place. The Romans were wise to give it up when they did. It isn't so bad really, extremely dry, and in the summertime very hot. The coastline and the cities along it like Algiers, Oran, Tunis, Sousse, etc. are quite cool, at least that is the way it seems to me although the residents there swear they swelter. In the interior the temperature rises considerably and, I hear, goes down once a year in midwinter. The Arabs wear considerable clothing. Why, God knows, unless they are to keep the flies off them, although I can't imagine a few folds of wool stopping an African fly. The soil varies from soft to hard, the hard always being where one decides to spend the night. There are a lot of olive trees where I am at present (I suppose the censor will permit this), they provide nice shade as well as cover.

There are quite a few doves flying around rather insolently. I can't get a shotgun anywhere. They would be wonderful to add to the menu. In the States we were always told that the good rations were being sent to the troops in the combat zone, then we were told that they were being sent to the troops at the front. Very interesting and I will tell you about it sometime.

I saw the loneliest sight in the world yesterday. Driving along a dirt road in the desert, I came to a lone Britisher's grave marked with a plain cross and a rusty helmet. Isolated graves are still around although most of them have been concentrated in larger groups. I heard a soldier suggest that would be a good job for the strikers back home.

The 505 is doing well, as you can be sure and no doubt know. They are all in extra fine fettle. A wonderful bunch. They are going to do very well. Their morale is unusually high. I have lost a half dozen or so over here from assorted injuries but what remains is tops.

Let me hear about camp [remainder of line blacked out by censor].

Love,

Pappy

On July 6, Gavin treated his troopers, now forged "lean, hard, and mean" by their strenuous life in North Africa, to a barbecue celebrating the one-year anniversary of the 505th Parachute Infantry Regiment's activation. Afterward, hoping to boost their morale, he spoke to them of better times at Fort Benning where it had all begun and when they thought nowhere could be hotter than Georgia in summer. Remembering Gavin's speech that night, one trooper later wrote: "We'd follow him straight to Hell, if he asked us, and plant our color over Satan's Command Post ahead of schedule."[10]

★ ★ ★

July 7, 1943

Dear Babe,

I have felt for some time that at this time I would have neither time nor means to write but to my surprise I have both.

Yesterday was organization day for the 505, the regiment's birthday. We were all anxious to celebrate the occasion in fit style but in these parts that is not easy. We finally managed to obtain a few gallons of local vino and some bulls and sheep for barbecue. The officers have been carrying around some of their ill-gotten gain from the slot machines [in the bars and roadhouses] in [Phenix City] Alabama [near Fort Benning] and so it was decided to have the Officers Mess contribute. Through the cooperation of the local kahib [qâid, North African functionary], some bulls were located and it all made for quite an occasion. It is the first beef that we have tasted as long as I can remember and it came in at a good time.

Many of us are beginning to have sore gums or receding gums that get sore from eating all canned soft food. Fresh vegetables seem to be about nil around here and it is too hot for anything like fresh food, especially meat, to keep. I am not complaining, of course, because those of us here realize more than anyone else the difficulties of getting food into here.

We had our first experience with a local seasonal phenomenon known as the sirocco. It is exactly the opposite of a Texas "norther." The winds suddenly shift and blow from the Sahara and it is time to burrow a hole. It is extremely hot. Yesterday in Maj. [Mark] Alexander's [Second Battalion] area it was 142 degrees and in Art Gorham's [First Battalion area] 136 degrees. Things like pencils, ammunition, weapons, get too hot to pick up and water exposed to its effects is far too hot to drink. Yesterday I put my hand in a can of water I had in the shade of an olive tree near where I was sleeping and I had to take it out because of the heat. Fortunately, there are available from the local Arabs earthenware jugs, quite thick and of all sizes. Water placed in them, sunk in the ground, stays rather cool.

This may give you the impression that living conditions are unbearable. On the contrary, everyone is in the best of health. Most of us have lost a bit of weight that we could probably afford anyway. As a matter of fact, today the 505 is in better health than it ever has been, I was just checking the sick rate this morning.

I have had time recently to take more than a passing interest in the Roman occupation. It is evident that they, in their centuries as rulers, made more economic and agricultural progress in the development of this promising country than anyone else. The signs of their establishments are still about and in many instances in active use, particularly wells.

Yesterday we adopted Jack Thompson of the Chicago Tribune into the regiment. You may enjoy reading some of his stuff. I do not know what he writes, I never see it but he asks a heap of questions.

By the way, wells over here aren't holes in the ground big enough for the old oaken [bucket] to slide up and down. They are enormous openings big enough to lower a car into, frequently they have a couple of camels raising large containers of water simultaneously, tell you more about it some other time.

Love,

Pappy

P. S. The camels *do not* climb up the wells that would be too good.

Pappy

★ ★ ★

July 8, 1943

Dear Barbara,

I thought that you would be interested in this ["Soldiers of the 505th Parachute Combat Team" (reproduced in full following this letter)] having known the 505 and many of its members. Although this is highly secret at the moment, I am arranging to have it mailed to you after we arrive at our destination. I suppose that it will not even be news to you then.

They have come a long way since the Frying Pan [a training area at Fort Benning] and they will turn in a good performance regardless of adversity or good luck. They have a healthy respect for their opponents but they are very confident of themselves.

Love,

Pappy

SOLDIERS OF THE 505TH PARACHUTE COMBAT TEAM

Tonight you embark upon a combat mission for which our people and the free people of the world have been waiting for two years.

You will spearhead the landing of an American Force upon the island of SICILY. Every preparation has been made to eliminate the element of chance. You have been given the means to do the job and you are backed by the largest assemblage of air power in world's history.

The eyes of the world are upon you. The hopes and prayers of every American go with you.

Since it is our first fight at night you must use the countersign and avoid firing on each other. The bayonet is the night fighter's best weapon. Conserve your water and ammunition.

The term "American Parachutist" has become synonymous with courage of a high order. Let us carry the fight to the enemy and make the American Parachutist feared and respected through all his ranks. Attack violently. Destroy him where ever found.

I know you will do your job.

Good landing, good fight, and good luck.

James Gavin/s

COLONEL GAVIN

chapter three

OPERATION HUSKY — SICILY

Winds strong enough to put the airborne missions at risk began blowing over Sicily during the early hours of July 9; in spite of this, HUSKY had to go on as planned. By late afternoon, the paratroopers of Gavin's combat team were ready. As they waited beside their assigned planes, each paratrooper received a slip of paper. On it, they read Colonel Gavin's reassuring words of encouragement: Every effort had been made to "eliminate the element of chance," they were "backed by the largest assemblage of air power in [the] world's history," and they had "the hopes and prayers of every American."[1]

Gavin held a last-minute briefing for the paratroopers, including war correspondent Jack Thompson, who would jump with him from the lead plane. Sergeant Jack Foisie, a reporter with the army newspaper The Stars and Stripes *and an eyewitness to the briefing, saw "a sacred huddle" with "the generals and staff officers who had come to wish them luck [standing] off to the side" while the men "with their faces blackened, the American flag freshly sewed on their sleeves, gathered at the feet of their commander . . . the tallest of them all, his lean face more liberally smudged with blackening, the darkest of them all." The men listened as Gavin spoke with "words that were calm and cool and direct." After the briefing, Foisie asked the enlisted men gathered around Gavin's plane how they felt about the upcoming jump; one sergeant confidently told the reporter: "We're going in with him so everything is going to be alright."[2]*

The serial formations of C-47s took off as dusk fell over the Tunisian airfields. As the planes neared Sicily, the high winds — the one element of chance no one could eliminate — proved disastrous to the tight pattern. Planes were blown off course and out of formation, forcing some pilots to climb to higher altitudes to avoid midair collisions. Adding to the confusion, the pre-invasion bombings of the island, coupled with the high winds, created dust storms that obscured many of the landmarks that were to have aided in navigation and orientation. With many of the transports lost or at incorrect altitude and speed, Gavin's paratroopers were not dropped as planned over the designated drop zones, but instead were dispersed, scattered over a sixty-five-mile area all along the southern coast of the island.

Gavin, true to his leadership axiom of "first out of the door of the airplane," led his men out into the dark night, landing several miles from his objective.[3] Although disoriented and only able to locate a few of his troopers, he followed one of the first battle axioms he had learned as a West Point cadet—he "marched them toward the sound of the guns."

By the afternoon of July 11 Gavin was able to make contact with forward elements of Patton's troops that had come ashore. He had also assembled a portion of his combat team—a small diverse force of infantry, artillery, engineers, and medics. Before the day ended, he deployed this small group of untried warriors in an attack against a large enemy force of tank-supported infantry moving toward a spur of high ground (Biazza Ridge) that commanded the junction of the American beachheads. If the enemy controlled Biazza Ridge, they would be able to split and flank the landed American force, pushing them off the beaches and back into the sea. Knowing that the ridge had to be held—at all costs— Gavin led his men in a fierce and bloody battle, with a count of "many dead and wounded," before their heroic "victory beyond question" was achieved.[4]

Elsewhere on the island, doing as they had been trained to do and as he had urged, the rest of Gavin's scattered combat team was also victorious. Though misdropped, Gavin's paratroopers had carried the fight to the enemy, attacking violently and destroying him—wherever found.

★ ★ ★

July 16, 1943

Dear Babe,

Well it was a good fight but the censor will not let me tell you about it. I didn't miss a minute of it. Believe I got a Purple Heart [for a minor wound to the leg]. Never felt better in my life. Tell you more about it some other time.

Love,

Pappy

★ ★ ★

July 17, 1943

Dear Babe,

I wrote you a short note yesterday which I hope by now you have received. As I understand this censorship, I will be unable to tell you anything about this recent fracas for at least two weeks. I am fine. Lost a bit of weight, been shot at a lot, had a wonderfully exciting time and everything is going well.

The 505 was wonderful and we are all extremely proud of its accomplishments. I do not know what, if anything, you hear back home but the 505 did things hardly short of miraculous in many instances.

That's enough about them. This is a very pretty place, climate is delightful although a bit hot in midday. All the civilians are most hospitable, insist on refusing money for anything and generally do everything to make us most welcome.

The enemy has been doing some very good fighting but the parachutists love it. Art is gone, so is Charlie. Hard on Corrine and Margaret. [Art Gorham was killed valiantly leading an attack against enemy tanks. Corrine Gorham was my first piano teacher; they lived across a grassy court from us at Fort Benning. Charlie Keerans was missing and presumed dead after the plane from which he was observing the combat jump was shot down by the "friendly fire" of our own Navy. We knew both of the families. — BGF][5] Bill Ryder should be back soon. He may call you up.[6]

Don't worry about me — luck of the Irish but there have been some close calls — too close.

Love,

Pappy

On July 19, the 82nd was attached to a provisional corps assigned to clear the western part of the island of the remaining enemy. By now, Gavin had accounted for most of his scattered troopers and led them westward, marching 150 miles nearly nonstop. On July 23, the 505 reached the Italian garrison at Trapani, where after a brief skirmish several thousand Italian soldiers surrendered. With the end of combat for the 82nd Airborne Division on Sicily, Gavin and his troopers assumed occupation duties.

Though the Italian government chose to maintain its alliance with Germany during the battle for Sicily, it did depose its fascist dictator, Benito Mussolini, in concert with clandestine overtures of surrender to the Allied high command.

★ ★ ★

July 22, 1943

Dear Babe,

This is as much of a surprise to me as it is to you. Fortunately these Germans and Italians do not destroy everything in their wake, a clerk in my regimental headquarters captured this one, this typewriter I mean. I have written you two regular letters as soon as I could. You have probably not received them yet. I am really fine.

So far I have been fired at by everything and at all ranges but the luck of the Irish is holding out. It has been extremely interesting and exciting, especially the first few days and nights. The latter were spent behind the enemy lines. I don't think the censor will permit me to tell you about it at this time. Our losses have been not light but the 505 has made an enviable name for itself. Everyone without exception fought wonderfully well.

Perhaps some mention has been made of it in dispatches to the States. If you come across anything of particular interest to the regiment, I would appreciate it if you would send it along. We get no news and really know little of what goes on outside of our own little world. At the moment however that is intensely interesting in itself.

Other than getting little sleep and rather irregular rations I have been doing fine. I have had a chance to pick up some sleep the past few nights, but the seam squirrels that I have acquired since arriving here were intolerably persistent in their pursuit of something to eat off my carcass. Several days ago I made the unfortunate error of checking an abandoned dwelling too thoroughly. These Sicilians do not live too cleanly. I came out of the place quite populated. They are fleas I believe, but they are awfully hard to get rid of and they seem to multiply.

I had just about gotten rid of them, and then the other morning I came over the top of a ridge in a jeep to try to find a way into a private war another outfit was having when an artillery piece decided apparently to obliterate me and the jeep. I am getting extremely agile in moving from a sitting position in a jeep to flat as a pancake on the ground. My agility came in good stead and I made it except that I dove into an abandoned Italian gun pit. When I came up for air later, I found myself alive with seam squirrels again. So you see, you just can't win.

This is a delightfully attractive place, especially compared to Africa. There are many fruit trees, lots of olives and almonds. Regrettably they are not ripe yet. There are tomatoes, cucumbers, etc. Anyway, compared to Africa it is a Garden of Eden.

The civilians have been extremely hospitable. Some towns have actually turned out to welcome us with flags, flowers, and cheers. This is normally preceded by a rather tough fight in which some lives are inevitably lost. As warriors the Italians have been entirely unpredictable. Sometimes they fight intensely and are capable of inflicting heavy casualties, again for un-explainable reasons by our standards anyway, they knuckle under with little struggle. It keeps us wary and mean anyway.

Don't worry about me, as I am doing fine, even if I can't write very often.

Love,

Pappy

★ ★ ★

July 23, 1943

Dear Babe,

I have the nicest captured typewriter today. Yesterday I received a letter from Rosie and one from Aunt Lillie, for both of which I am very apprecia-tive. I hope that they read your letters and understand that they are for them also, it works better that way. When things are very warm around here [in combat], I really do not have much time for letter writing.

Rather quiet at the moment, spent some time this morning looking for dwellings out in the country quite a distance. They of course harbor guer-rillas, stolen equipment, arms, etc. As I have mentioned before, these Sicil-ians have been very hospitable but I still am a poor contact man to work with them. Our first few hours or days at this place were a bit hectic and some of our youngsters' memories are too good to fully accept the present plaudits as being genuine. I am afraid that the impression of Americans that they get from me is not entirely a friendly one.

The sirocco of Africa that I mentioned in one of my former letters even gets to here, we are discovering to our intense discomfort today. It has been blowing a gale of hot dusty wind all day. Today the local civil adminis-trator told me that crimes committed during a sirocco are to some extent condoned, or at least clemency is granted the criminal. If a climatic condi-tion can be considered maddening, this is it.

Tonight with the evening meal every soldier will be given a half canteen cup of wine. These people, despite the great shortage of food, all drink wine instead of water. Although they can be, and at present are, without bread or meat, they do have wine from their own grown grapes.

We all read of conditions of these Axis-controlled countries but none of us really appreciated how deplorable things were until we encountered conditions here. The state and the local fascists took everything. Most of every crop and just about all meat goes to the individuals in the inside of the local political circle. There appeared to be no way for the people to beat the system. They are about all pinched-faced and hungry.

We have had only a form of hardtack since our arrival and several days ago a nearby town baker agreed to sell us some bread. When we went to get it, it turned out to be flour that he kept solely for the Italian army and politicians. At that very moment there were crowds of hungry civilians outside asking for bread. We ordered the baker to give it to them, much to his dismay. It is a dark brown bread, they would consider your white bread cake.

Love,

Pappy

★ ★ ★

July 26, 1943

Dear Babe,

By the time that you receive this I suppose that your camp for the summer will be over. I know that you have had a good time. I would like to hear about it. I am in a lull at the moment.

Had a busy day before yesterday and now am billeted in a rather nice villa formerly occupied by Germans. They left in a hurry and left a great deal of reading scattered about but it is all german and a little Italian. They were not very popular around here, evidently the Sicilians did not like them. Perhaps they just tell us that now but I am inclined to believe my observations of the Sicilians.

Much to our surprise, many Sicilians formerly lived in the States, places like Detroit, Hackensack, etc. They came back here during the Depression and Mussolini wouldn't let them out. The civilians welcomed us apparently but the troops fought well, especially the Germans. I had the good fortune to tangle with both of them at close quarters and they meant business. I am having to leave some of my boys here [in graves] but that was to be expected.

We all like the climate and find it much better than Africa. My most distressing discomfort at the moment is that I am still wearing the same clothing, underwear, shoes and socks, etc. that I wore in the jump. Several times when the opportunity presented itself, I took them off and washed and put them back on wet to dry but that doesn't quite get them clean. It does, however, discourage visitors. My seam squirrels have departed for more luscious fields. I managed to get some catnip they didn't like.

Several days after landing I captured a blanket and a mess kit, so now it is really the life of Reilly, well almost anyway. Myself and my staff have a rapidly disappearing cake of soap among us. Rumor has it that there is some soap down the coast about fifty miles. If I can, I am going to send down for a cake. Unfortunately, also my razor that I jumped with (in my pocket for weeks) was thrown away by a zealously industrious, but somewhat erratic, striker [an enlisted soldier acting as an officer's field orderly] a day or so ago. I'll get another somehow.

I wouldn't dare grow a beard, wow, what a haven for homeless squirrels. I have enough trouble discouraging them as it is. They are most difficult to cope with and, really, the successful seam squirrel hunters are endowed with an inordinate versatility. They usually track them to their lair, this is normally an inner seam of the jumpsuit, there with an agility that is a delight to observe, they pounce upon them with either hand depending upon their intended direction of escape. This is not as simple as it sounds. The other day during a quiet spell I hunted for at least one hour without capturing more than two. So you see, in the final analysis our pursuits turn to simple things like seam squirrel hunting.

I am, however, very grateful to our opponents for abandoning without destroying such a good typewriter. They destroyed about everything else.

Love,

Pappy

★ ★ ★

July 29, 1943

Dear Babe,

I understand that in a day or so V-mail letters are to be photoed and shipped microfilm, this may make the schedule. If it does it should get to the States in a few days.

We are notified today that we can now tell exactly where we visited in Africa. It makes little difference in my particular case since I spent a bit of time in many different places: Casablanca, Oujda, Oran, Tunis, Algiers, Tripoli, and Kairouan. They were all very interesting even though not pleasantly habitable. Kairouan, "the second most holy city in Islam," especially so. Spent about a month there. That money that I sent was from a place I visited in my travels. It really wasn't all travel though, there was a lot of work. These affairs must be carefully planned.

I suppose you know how things are going here from the papers. Since I do not know what you read *and* the censor, there is little that I can tell you. News would be well received here. It is very scarce, except the rumor variety. If I ever had it to do again, I certainly would bring along a lot of radios. Of course, we could not have jumped it anyway, too many more important things to take along.

I am still doing well with my one suit of underwear and jumpsuit. Tonight if I get the time and opportunity, I am going to boil them. Can't seem to get them clean, not that I object to my clothes being dirty but I have found that it pays to make the seam squirrels most unwelcome. Lots of bathing does it.

Today I got an overseas issue of Time dated June 14th. It made very good reading. Nothing around here but German and Italian. By now my mixture of languages is fantastic. The dictionaries have helped.

The civilians around here seem to be getting back to normal. They are, I am convinced, genuinely pleased with Il Duce's abdication. With a little luck with crops and being left alone for a while, they will probably soon have enough to eat. That is a big thing with them. They are evidently always hungry, or at least they were under the old regime.

How was camp? Did you ever get Toughie? Since I arrived in Africa I have never been able to find out whether or not Mommy has ever received an allotment check. This is very important and I do not know what to do about it.

Love,

Pappy

★ ★ ★

July 31, 1943

Dear Babe,

This is some typewriter. They are hard to get around here so I shouldn't complain.

I have been rather busy. For the past few days I have been what I suppose you would call a military provincial governor. I'll tell you about it sometime.

Today I received my Purple Heart officially. Although I was wounded July 10th and entitled to it at that time, it just caught up with me. I was very glad to get it as I particularly wanted that decoration. Tomorrow the

505 will receive about 125 of them. Of course, all of the badly wounded have been hospitalized and received theirs there.

We have all been very busy and although the work of the past few days has been a bit different, it has been unusual and interesting. I may as well tell you that I have been recommended for the DSC [Distinguished Service Cross] so that just in case anything ever happens to me before I got it, that you know that Pappy has been getting around. At present it is merely a recommendation having been made by the Division commander. It may take a long time to arrive if approved by higher headquarters.[7]

We have been doing well recently, both rations and sleep having improved. The greatest impediment to sleep at present are the Sicilian mosquitoes. It is not that they are large in size, but like the Stuka compared to the bomber, they make up for lack of size by incredible maneuverability. They rarely fly singly like American mosquitoes, instead they come in, in formation, and peel off for the attack in close proximity to their objective. They are evidently equipped with flaps that enable them to come into attacking range with remarkable accuracy. Slowing down just in time to attack and be away, they leave little opportunity for retaliation on the part of the befuddled victim. Occasionally they precede their attack formations with reconnaissance flights that instantly, and with no lost effort, find means of penetrating the deepest blanket folds and the smallest hole in a mosquito net. After one night of combat with them by daylight you are ready for a good day's rest. This is a lot of time to spend on mosquitoes.

I expect to hear any day now of your summer camp. Rumor has it that there is some mail up the coast. We have only received one mail delivery since jumping which was over three weeks ago. But don't misunderstand me, several times in the past few weeks I would much sooner have had ammunition than a letter.

Love,
Pappy

⋆ ⋆ ⋆

August 1, 1943
Dear Barbara,

I thought that it would be a good idea to drop you a line as long as I have the time. As I have said before, the time may and no doubt will come again as it has in the past when I will not be able to write for weeks at a time.

My work the past day or two has taken me through some of the local dwellings and I have found them extremely interesting. One I went through this morning dates from before Christ, a number of them date that far back. There are many interesting local Roman ruins. This island has been the stepping stone in the conquest, or counter-conquest, of Italy or Europe since recorded time. The oldest city of Syracuse was a Greek settlement long before Rome was settled. The last great wars fought on the island were fought in 238 B.C., the Punic Wars. A couple of weeks ago I captured a Roman history so I really don't carry this stuff around in my head. I have found reading the history in snatches to be a form of relaxation, much worthwhile and not unpleasant.

The streets of the cities are very narrow, winding, and filled with steps and stairs. Jeeps negotiate them readily. When a jeep goes through, however, it is necessary for all of the pedestrians to hug the walls. This condition of narrow streets is common throughout the Mediterranean basin.

In this locale to add interest to one's travels along such venturesome passageways there is the local plumbing problem. As you no doubt well know, sanitation and plumbing as we know it in America is non-existent here. One of the daily chores of the local housewives is to pour the slops and garbage into the streets from the upper balconies. Frequently while we are zooming along a native street, a housewife appears above with a bucket and a menacing look. Accustomed as she is to the local horse-drawn traffic, she times the release as well as she can, but the speed of a jeep is deceptive and as likely as not, the jeep and the contents of the bucket arrive at the same point at the same time. It does serve to keep one on one's toes anyway, and you will never be caught by snipers if you observe in all directions at all times.

Incidentally, a sniper fired at me yesterday. It is an exasperating problem. I went right back, mad as a wet hen and armed to the teeth, and couldn't find him.

It is hard to believe that August is here already, soon it will be fall and winter. This is a beautiful place and the climate is ideal, especially near the sea. I would like to know what winter will bring. I never did like soldiering in too cold a climate but now is the time for likes and dislikes to go out the window.

Let me hear about your camp.

Love,

Pappy

★ ★ ★

August 3, 1943

Dear Barbara,

Warm sunshiny day today. We have been blessed with good weather. Hot and dusty but that is rarely as discomforting as rain and cold. That will come next month or whenever winter starts. The vegetation here would indicate that they have a mild winter, lots of palms, etc.

I may as well tell you this because it will be of interest to you and anything could happen before it materializes. I have been recommended for promotion and with a little luck it should go through. It seems like a hard way to get it but once it is here it is probably the most satisfying way.

[His first star! I was so proud of him but I remember crying, because I felt sure that his boys of the 505 had helped keep him alive. Being a brigadier general meant that he would have to leave the 505 for Division Headquarters, and I was afraid that without their watchful care he might be wounded or worse. — BGF]

Jack Norton is the new S-3 [regimental plans and operations officer] and just by chance he missed being under any enemy artillery fire. He has been into about everything else. The staff has him all prepared now, and Al [Ireland] told him that the best way to get under fire in this outfit is to get on the staff. (I started to tell you a different story or the same story in a different manner but I realized halfway through that I was probably running afoul of the censor.)

It is surprising the number of these Sicilians who have relatives in America or who have been there themselves. Quite a number of them made a lot of money before October 1929 and then when the Depression hit they packed their kit and came over here. They remember many of our slang expressions, especially of that time or earlier and must, I am convinced, feel that they have got to use them to speak American. Instead of saying "Good Morning," they say on first meeting, "Hi ya, Kid." They always insist on doing a lot of hand-shaking and then the war must stop while they tell you of their brother in Hackensack. That we are fighting and that death is sometimes imminent while they bat the breeze is most difficult to get across. With Mussolini's denouement they seem pleased, but I still suspect that they are pleased with anything that is supposed to please us.

We do manage to get from them for a proper number of lira a few grapes, melons, etc., for all of which we are grateful. We missed some form of greens or fresh food in Africa more than anything. Despite the conditions under which we live the boys are much healthier and of better morale than they were in Africa. They didn't like that place very much, especially the 142 degree temperature, but like it or not there is a job to be done and they are doing it.

Love,

Pappy

★ ★ ★

August 5, 1943

Dear Babe,

Big day yesterday, I received two letters from you. It was the first mail in goodness knows when. I was so glad to hear about your camp. From your description of it I think that it must be a very nice place to spend the summer. When you get the time, tell me some more about it.

I received a nice letter from Aunt Lillie from which I surmised that you all had either read or heard of the 505's part in the current affair. Since we do not get to see any papers or have radios, I must leave to conjecture any idea of what you know. I did tonight see a clipping that Chaplain [George] Wood [the Protestant regimental chaplain] received from a Syracuse [New York] paper. It was written by Sgt. Jack Foisie of The Stars and Stripes. The night of the takeoff he was present when I had my final briefing with the boys in my ship and I didn't realize that he was taking the stuff down.

Two days later, Jack Thompson of the big-eared Thompsons was present in the middle of an awful mess of the fight when it looked like some big German tiger tanks were going to run us back into the ocean. There was some plain talk being kicked around and I understand that he got some of it into his column. As long as he did not quote me too verbatim, it is OK. Incidentally, he should have some interesting dope on our affairs. I know him quite well and have spent a lot of time in discussions with him. He knows of what he writes and knows our business better than anyone over here. Whatever he wrote about our first days' activities must have been OK because he just recently showed me a congratulatory cable and five hundred dollars that he received for a bonus.

The Syracuse clipping seemed OK except the inference that the losses were light, not that they were anything to get scared about, but I do not believe that parachutist losses ever have been or ever will be "light." Anyway, I suppose when they are your best friends and they die beside you and it may have been yourself, and you help bury them, and you help evacuate the wounded, it can never seem light even if it is from a journalistic viewpoint.

The 505 performed beyond our fondest expectations. They love to fight and they learned some grim costly lessons the hard way in this affair. They should be that much better in the next. The current one is enough to keep them occupied, for the time being anyway.

I was glad to hear that the allotment is coming through on schedule. No Velatis to date, I will let you know when it catches up with me. Everything is going fine.

Love,

Pappy

★ ★ ★

August 7, 1943

Dear Butch,

It certainly was nice to hear of how well you were getting along in camp and how much you liked it. Swimming 200 yards was quite a feat. Soon you will be able to swim farther than Pappy, then when we go swimming you will have to watch me. It would be nice to go swimming up to Delafield [West Point's swimming pond] again, perhaps next summer.

The horses that you ride sound very safe, not like the horses that Pappy had at Fort Sill. Every Sunday you would go down to the stables with me and feed your favorite, "Sunshine," sugar.[8] These people have nice horses here. They seem to have part of the Arabic tradition regarding the care of their horses. They have many horses and they are used by everyone. There are practically no private cars.

Did you ever receive the book "Lee's Lieutenants" that the purser of the transport I came over on was supposed to send you? Did you ever receive the banknote from Malta or the lira note from here? I also sent you a silk map that I carried in the jump on July 10th that I am rather anxious not to lose.[9] Let me know if you have received any of those things so that I can decide accordingly whether or not to send anything else. Living under present conditions, it is very easy to have things lost or stolen.

I do not know how much you know of what is transpiring in these parts and as a matter of fact, I am not sure how much I can tell you. Suffice to say, everything is going well and soon we will have those jerries swimming to the boot [of the Italian mainland].

We are all fine and thriving on the somewhat precarious existence we seem to wheedle out. I realize more than ever how much it helps to have sympathetic natives about. We manage to do pretty well in supplementing our issue ration with some local fruit and vegetables.

Before you realize it, it will be time for school to start again. That is the plan? Are there any schools suitable nearby?

Love,

Pappy

P.S. Thank Aunt Lillie for her very nice letters

Pappy

★ ★ ★

August 13, 1943

Dear Babe,

I have been rather busy of late, a little too busy to write much. I do not know if you have been receiving all of my letters. I heard through the grapevine that one of my letters was stopped in Africa for violating the censorship regulations. Seems like we have a different set of rules here, but if one was stopped, possibly all of them could have been. I am not going to say much in this and see if I can get it through.

I am fine and in the best of health. I am very lucky. I just received the DSC, the order came through yesterday.

Hope you are ready for school and that you have a school to go to.

Love,

Pappy

★ ★ ★

August 17, 1943

Dear Barbara,

I haven't written for a few days. I have been rather busy. I suppose the capture of Sicily [with the fall of Messina on August 16] is well received in the States. Understandably it is but a small step, and a very small one at that, in the right direction. There will be many graves between here and Berlin and Tokyo. What few papers I have seen from the States are surprisingly optimistic.

Our mail here is not so regular as it was at our last stop so I have not heard from you for a long time. By now you must be back from camp. I know you enjoyed it.

Love,

Pappy

In analyzing HUSKY, critics of the airborne missions labeled the operation a SNAFU (situation normal, all fouled up). Gavin preferred the label SAFU (self-adjusting foul-up) because the supporting airborne missions had successfully allowed the Allies to gain a firm foothold on the island of Sicily — they had not been thrown back into the sea. Operating without a command structure in place during the first critical hours of the operation, the small groups of his widely dispersed and disoriented paratroopers successfully improvised, preventing the movement of German reserves headed toward the landing forces on the beach. Gavin praised his combat team: "The accomplishment of the missions is a tribute to the courage and skill of the pilots and crews of the 52nd Troop Carrier Wing, who flew them in, and the fighting heart, individual skill, courage and initiative of the American Paratrooper. Here, in Sicily, he proved the hard way that vertical envelopment at night was feasible and almost impossible to stop, that the American trooper has the mental and physical courage to try anything, asking and expecting no odds."[10]

chapter four

OPERATION
AVALANCHE — ITALY

While still battling on Sicily, Allied command finalized plans, once the island was in hand, for the invasion of the Italian mainland — Operation AVA-LANCHE. In a two-pronged attack, General Bernard Montgomery and his British Eighth Army would cross from Sicily onto the southern tip of Italy, with Lieutenant General Mark Clark's U.S. Fifth Army (and attached British troops) following a few days later as the main assault at Salerno on the western coast. The Italian government's anticipated capitulation announcement (secret negotiations were ongoing), which would reduce the risks of the invasion, was to be concurrent with Clark's landing at Salerno. Fifth Army would push northwest from Salerno to capture the port city of Naples while Eighth Army moved up to join them; upon linking up, Clark's and Montgomery's armies would continue to push north. After capturing the great prize of Rome, they would continue to advance until all of Italy fell under Allied control.

The 82nd Airborne Division, made available to General Clark if needed, returned to North Africa from Sicily to quickly refit; it had to be ready to deploy on short notice.

★ ★ ★

August 21, 1943

Dear Baber,

Judging from that error, one would never guess that I had my own typewriter. The Italian and German typewriters were not bad but they had the letters in a different arrangement.

Africa is very hot at this time of the year but like everything else we can and will get quite accustomed to it. About the only ones who seem to like it are the Arabs and they wear long hooded nightgowns even in midday.

One of your recent letters seemed to show some concern about the Purple Heart. I should have long ago set you at ease about it. It was merely a case of a stone wall, a Sicilian stone house, a tree, and me moving along at about 30 mph meeting in the middle of a very dark night. When the holocaust came to an end I seemed to have come out the winner. Even if the house and wall are still there.

Anyway I was too busy, etc., to know that anything had happened until a day or so later, included in that period was the rather interesting interlude [at Biazza Ridge] that Jack Thompson wrote about. When things began to settle down for a while, I had what amounted to quite a toothache in the leg. The Doc said it was a sprained knee and ankle and a lacerated right leg, all of which is now entirely a thing of the past so it could not have amounted to much. I am in fine fettle and didn't miss anything.

About JT's [Jack Thompson] doings, I spent a few days with him about two weeks ago. He has taken over a big broadcast from —— and does a daily stint that keeps him there. *[Following censorship guidelines, my father did not disclose Thompson's location. —* BGF*]* I have not seen much of him lately and probably will not for a time. He normally does his stuff for the Chicago Tribune. I have come to know him very well and like him very much. He is a fine chap and couldn't be beat for nerve in combat. We like to have him around.

The Velatis arrived and was enjoyed by all of the staff. Jack Norton is my S-3 and wanted to particularly express his thanks. Better not send any more for a while. Not that it was not great to get but you'll understand later.

[When my dad was a tactical officer at West Point, one of the cadets he met and admired was John (Jack) Norton, First Captain of the Corps of Cadets. When Jack graduated with the class of '41, he went through airborne training and was soon assigned to the 505. When my dad became Commanding General of the 82nd Airborne Division, Jack came with him to Division Headquarters as G-3. Many years after the war, Jack told me that it was my dad's intelligence and great good luck that had kept my dad alive — I still believe that it was the 505. My dad mentions Jack in several of his letters because my mother and I had known him as a cadet. We were happy to receive positive reports about him. Lieutenant General John Norton is buried just a few feet from my father in the cemetery at West Point. — BGF*]*

I will be glad to hear all about the camp. I really haven't received a letter from you for a week or two but by now I am sure camp is over. You must have had a wonderful time. Rosie has been writing to me and telling me all about it.

If you do not hear from me for a time or as regularly as you have in the past, be not disturbed, it is just a case of being very busy.

Love,

Pappy

Working with the 82nd staff as airborne task force commander for Operation AVALANCHE, *Gavin was kept busy by the "avalanche" of proposed supporting airborne missions—as quickly as plans were made, they were changed, only to be made again and changed yet again.*

★ ★ ★

August 28, 1943

Dear Babe,

I have been rather busy of late so have not had much of an opportunity to write. I particularly enjoyed your last letter from camp, and I can imagine how much you regret having it end. It continues to be as warm as ever here with the usual galaxy of Arabs, camels, heat and hard work to absorb our interests.

This morning we had a formation to receive the awards from the last Sicilian affair. I was very fortunate to get a DSC. Our memories of our losses will stay with us however. There were many to be decorated who were not there.[1]

Art Gorham was recommended [posthumously] for the DSC. Well, you may in the not-too-distant future be particularly concerned for my well-being, but I can give you every assurance that I am and will continue to be well, regardless of the hazards in which I may become involved. So do not worry regardless of what the newspapers may say. Most of us are pretty well able to take care of ourselves now.

Love,

Pappy

★ ★ ★

September 2, 1943

Dear Barbara,

A man I know in public relations gave this to me the other day and I thought that you might like to have it. It was taken at a time when I had just moved back a short distance from a very hot fight [Biazza Ridge] to get some of the boys. Upon returning, we had a clambake that went on into the night and we finally started them on the way to Berlin. The man that I am pouring my troubles out to is Jack Thompson.

For some reason or other, the conventional concept of the "soldier compleat" is a guy neat as a pin, spotless in appearance, and flawlessly clothed. Having been the "piece de resistance" in some of these photographic forays, and having on those occasions emerged feeling more like a military clotheshorse than a soldier, I am peculiarly attached to this particular snapshot. I feel that for once I looked like a soldier. I know that at the time I felt like one after many years of coming close but never quite making it.

One sees some screwy pictures of people in the papers that manage to find their way over here these days. If anyone ever wants a picture of me give them this. That is, if the War Department does not suppress it in the interests of "good order and military discipline."

I am glad to hear of your progress in riding. Camp must have been lots of fun.

Love,

Pappy

P.S. Do let me know if and when you receive this.

★ ★ ★

September 4, 1943

Dear Barbara,

I have received the V-mail stationery which will be enough to do for a long time. The Velatis was very good and came through in fine shape. In a recent letter Rosie asked about Xmas. Since the future is so uncertain that seems a long way off. There is little that can be sent to the environment to make it seem more like Xmas. I would recommend candy, something like peanut brittle, chocolate does not survive the trip.

I have finally started to receive the bank statements and know that the account is straightened out. Tell Mommy to discontinue deducting the Xmas fund deposits because I have deposited more than enough to cover those up-to-date and for some time in the future. Those $30.00 deductions should be totaled up and Mommy should draw that amount for whatever use she sees fit, as I said, I have deposited enough to more than cover them.

Prior to the Sicilian jump, I "cleared the decks" by sending about every cent to the Highland Falls Bank to the joint account. In the event of anything unusual in the way of becoming a casualty ever happens to me, that is either killed or missing, Mommy should inquire about the bank account right away, and I would recommend draw the entire account. In this connection, such an eventuality would necessitate shipping all of my effects back to the States. In due time they would be shipped to Mommy but to expedite their return, and perhaps obviate their complete loss, inquiry should be made of the "Effects Quartermaster, Army Effects Bureau, Quartermaster Depot, Kansas City, Mo."

Since through accident more than design I have become inadvertently somewhat of a character in this clambake, any quick change in my status would promptly be reported by the Germans or our own troops. I mention this because I know that due to unavoidable reasons many deaths are not reported for a long period.

Incidentally, this is just a lot of planning that does not infer a thing. I do expect to be quite busy for some time and may not get an opportunity to write as much as I would like to. You can be sure, however, that I am getting along fine. I will write as soon as I can.

I do not care what Mommy does with the [silk] map. Might be a good idea to frame it. Glad Mommy talked to Col. Norman, Africa hasn't changed since he left. Today is a hot day but we expect the rains soon.

Love,

Pappy

Fearing an aggressive German retaliation to their betrayal, the Italian government insisted that Rome and the Italian heads of state be protected. Negotiating the terms of their capitulation, the Italians proposed an airborne drop of at least division size on Rome timed with their surrender announcement — offering assurances that they would secure the drop zones and provide logistical support to the landed troopers until a main Allied force could reach the city.

Elements of the 82nd Airborne Division, with only a few days to prepare, were quickly moved to airfields in Sicily. But the drop on Rome would not happen — two American officers covertly sent into the city to meet with government officials discovered that the Italians had grossly underestimated not only their ability to support such a risky drop, but also German troop strength in the city. Anticipating an Italian defection, the Germans had reinforced their positions in Italy, withdrawing a large force from Sicily to the mainland while still battling for control of the island, and were prepared to seize and disarm the Italian forces to retain their foothold in Italy. Gavin simply wrote in his diary, "It was well that we did not jump."[2]

Landing on the Italian mainland as planned on September 3, Montgomery's Eighth Army met little opposition. The Italian government did capitulate, and timed with this announcement Clark's Fifth Army landed at Salerno on September 9. Though no airborne missions preceded the landings, the 82nd Airborne Division waiting in Sicily remained at General Clark's disposal.

★ ★ ★

September 10, 1943

Dear Babe,

Well, the Italians signed an armistice last night. It ended a very busy ten days for me. Sicily is lovely. At this time of year there is a twinge of autumn in the air. I am not looking forward to winter. The ground is a bit cold at night even now.

The civilians here in Sicily received the surrender very enthusiastically. The war has been an unpopular one with the Italian people. To our own troops here it made little impression. They about all feel that there is too much grim work ahead to be elated over this. Elation is a luxury they do not feel like enjoying yet.

Have you started school yet? It is hard to believe that another fall and winter are on the way. I do hope you do well in school.

Love,

Pappy

★ ★ ★

September 12, 1943

Dear Babe,

I have been too busy lately to write you a long letter. The other day, after all of the rushing about in connection with the armistice subsided, I sent you a short note. Letter writing conditions are very uncertain these days.

I am permitted to tell you that I am in Sicily and it is quite nice again after Africa. Conditions are evidently improving rapidly. Having seen the place in pre-invasion condition, well pre by a few hours anyway even if we weren't very observant, it looks much improved now. The crowds demanding bread have disappeared although everyone always wants "mangiare," something to eat. None of the masses of people appears to have had enough to eat as long as they can remember. It is a condition with which they are entirely unfamiliar.

The towns are very unusual, being built generally on hilltops of native stone and plaster. Streets are narrow, winding, and very dirty. A custom coming down from the Middle Ages causes everyone to sleep in town despite the fact that the sole industry is farming and everyone has a farm. On the farm they generally raise olives, almonds, and grapes. A little wheat is grown. Everyone would be much better off if they would raise something of immediate food value, like corn, but custom again seems to work against their best interest. They do not have much to do with corn and seem to consider it horse food.

Strangely enough, they do not keep their animals or chickens on the farm. Instead, they keep them on the ground floors of their town abode. This is particularly true in many of the better type of homes where they can afford an elaborate dwelling including a ground floor menagerie. The "padrone" lives upstairs and the sharecroppers who work for him live with the animals on the ground floor.

Recently to my acute discomfort I learned that this causes a bad lice condition even in the best of homes, besides it smells frightfully. The odors, however, are taken for granted. There is, of course, no sanitation system as we know it so that the odors of the animal waste are a small part of an odiferous cloud that seems to hang over all.

Judging by the extensive and in many cases rather remarkable architectural remains of the Roman and later buildings, it is evident that the island at one time was a show place of international renown. Poor government and poorer people accelerated a decadence that must have set in centuries ago. Now all that remains of many beautiful gardens are masses of rubble cluttered with guides who offer to escort you about and give you a quick liberal education on the greatness of Rome, all for ten lira.

Since your camp has come to an end, I am anxious to hear more about it. Now about school, has it started yet?

Love,

Pappy

Fifth Army was in danger of being pushed back into Salerno Bay; German intelligence, having determined that the Salerno area would be the most likely target for an Allied invasion of the mainland, prompted the German forces to prepare accordingly. By September 13, Clark realized that without help he might be forced to abandon the beachhead. Sending a letter to General Ridgway "as an order," Clark requested "an immediate drop" within his lines on the beachhead that night. "Can do" was Ridgway's succinct reply. With a drop on the 13th and 14th to supplement Fifth Army's forces, Clark was in Italy to stay.³

★ ★ ★

September 21, 1943

Dear Barbara,

This may take some time to get to you but at least it will let you know that I am fine and getting along well. I am "somewhere in Italy," this is all I am permitted to say at present. After the Sicilian imbroglio, I "sweated this one out" a bit as the boys say but it turned out to be the easiest jump for some time.

You probably know a lot more of what is going on here than we do since we only know of our immediate vicinity. Generally things are looking up after a very rough start.

I hope you are enjoying school. They do not appear to have schools for children here, they all work on farms. At the moment though they spend a lot of time with their parents hiding in cellars. Artillery and air bombing know no distinction.

Love,

Pappy

Rather than being withdrawn after the completion of their airborne mission as doctrine dictated, the 82nd remained as a reserve force of conventional infantry under General Clark's control. On September 27, taking advantage of their "can do" attitude, he employed them as the vanguard in the drive across the Naples plain and into the city. As the Allies pushed against them, the Germans fell back, purposely wrecking the city's port as they abandoned Naples. On October 1, Gavin and the 505 were the first American troops to enter Naples and the first to discover that what had not been destroyed by Allied bombing had fallen victim to the retreating Germans' malicious destruction. Assigned to occupation duty by General Clark, Ridgway set up Division Headquarters in the "Questura Di Napoli" (Naples police department) and began the arduous tasks of restoring order, cleaning up the city, and securing its port.

After losing General Keerans in Sicily, Ridgway had been, more or less, running the Division without an assistant commander. Having recommended Gavin for brigadier, a rank that usually necessitated a change of station from regimental command, Ridgway appointed him as the Division's new assistant commander.

★ ★ ★

[Undated]

Dear Babe,

After a very active two weeks the 505 had the privilege of capturing Naples. It is a lovely place although at the moment rather badly off. The Germans destroyed all water and lights, opened the prisons, destroyed all docks, food stores, etc. On a city of 700,000 that is pretty hard.

I have just been transferred from the 505 to Division Headquarters where I have the job of Assistant Division Commander. I do not particularly mind since it entitles me to a very nice room in an excellent hotel. For the first time since May 10th [the last day on board ship], I slept in a bed last night. Really didn't sleep well, it was too soft.

Everything is going well and I am getting along fine. Col. Robert Aloe [an old friend from Airborne Command] who will deliver this can give you all of the dope.

Love,

Pappy

P.S. I am sending along some insignia of the Italian army taken from Granité Barracks, City of Naples, when the 505 captured it several days ago. You have mentioned some trinkets in one of your letters and I will try and get some for you. I really have been very, very busy as Col. Aloe can tell you. The people who have time to buy trinkets have not been doing much fighting. I may be in that bracket myself for a few weeks. If so, I should be able to pick up a few things around here.

Love,

Pappy

P.S. I am also enclosing some invasion money you may like to have for your collection. Note my new address.

Pappy

★ ★ ★

October 2, 1943

Dear Babe,

Well I took off my jumpsuit for the first time in two weeks last night and today I found a sheet of V-mail paper. I have been on the go since my last letter and I am afraid that last letter may not have been passed by the censor. I said I was in Italy at that time which I was not supposed to do.

I have received some letters from you telling of entering school, etc. I am very glad that you got into Friends School. *[I had passed some competitive exams and was accepted at Sidwell Friends School. — BGF]*

Gen. Ridgway told me yesterday that my name went to the Senate. You probably know if it did. *[Lists of officers whose names had been submitted to the Senate for approval of promotion to general officer rank were published in Washington newspapers. — BGF]*

This is a beautiful place. This morning I accompanied the Division Commanding General to a special mass the cardinal held at the cathedral. The mayor and Marshal Badoglio's [the new head of the Italian government] ministers attended. It was quite an affair. I'll tell you about it sometime. *[During the celebration of the mass, the priest held up a glass vial containing red crystals for all to see. The crystals were believed to be the crystallized form of the blood of Christ. The cardinal announced that the crystals would change into the liquid blood of Christ, if the coming year was to be a good one for the city of Naples. And so they did. This ceremony has been performed in times of crisis as part of the mass in the Cathedral of Naples up to present times. — BGF]* I expect to have more time to write from now on.

Love,

Pappy

★ ★ ★

October 10, 1943

Dear Butch,

They finally took those chickens [colonel's eagles] off my shoulders [and pinned on the single stars of a brigadier]. It was made official with a bit of a ceremony this morning.[4]

Please note the change in address. I have been very, very busy and even if the time were available, the means to write a letter were not. I suppose that you get all of the latest information from the papers. We really do not know a great deal except what goes on in our immediate sphere. They [the 82nd Airborne Division] are doing a great job although we continue to lose a lot of our best.

This opportunity to write came as a result of the promotion I suppose. Several days ago I was given my new job and, at the time, ordered to stay out of the immediate front. All parachute commanders continue to have a fatal weakness of spending most of their time in the front lines and chasing me back was, for the moment anyway, a good idea. Anyway, I found myself in Division Headquarters with all of the niceties like V-mail paper, a typewriter, etc.

This morning being Sunday, I again visited the cathedral that I went to last Sunday. It is a lovely place. The interior, paintings, statues and sculptured pieces are things to behold. The outside of most of the cathedrals here remind one of the ones in Manila, but the interiors were in many cases many centuries old when the Manila churches were founded.

If I understand the present censorship regulations correctly, and I had better, I am not supposed to tell you where I am. You understand then the vagueness of this letter.

This being a general has some nice things about it I have been told but in my case, unfortunately, it means a reduction in pay. There is an administrative technicality that takes away my jump pay [additional pay for hazardous duty]; there is not supposed to be a parachute general in an airborne division. It seems sort of silly since I will continue to jump anyway but red tape is red tape.[5]

About the medals of which you asked in a recent letter, I have to keep them with me so I will not be able to send them back. I would like to since I will probably lose them in all of this moving about. Needless to say, I do not jump with them so for weeks at a time they are with a lot of other stuff back in the hills somewhere.

I did send you some Italian insignia and invasion currency recently. Col. Aloe took them back with him and he will get them to you in Washington. With the assistance of an aide, with which I am now blessed, I should be able to get something in the way of stamps or jewelry. As soon as I do, they will be on the way.

I have slept in a bed every night for the past five nights, some softie. Hope that you do well in school, Butch.

Love,

Pappy

★ ★ ★

October 14, 1943

Dear Butch,

Since the receipt of your last few letters, I have been on the prowl for some stamps, coins, etc. Rather my aide has. I should take no credit for it. Both stamps and coins are hard to get.

I did get in some Xmas shopping, the package should reach you shortly. When it does, save it until Christmas unless you need the gloves very badly. It is most difficult to shop. After all, no one can stop in the midst of all of the fireworks and make a few small purchases. Generally speaking, anything the "tedeschi" [Germans] left around here is not worth much anyway. This was quite a leather and glove manufacturing center prior to the war, you will believe that after your Xmas package arrives, and during the reign of the tedeschi many of the firms hid their wares. They are just getting them out now, but just about as fast as they get them out they are gobbled up. To the 505 fell the dubious honor of being first into this hamlet, consequently we knew about where everything was.

At the moment I have the good fortune to be quartered in a villa that exceeds in charm, originality of architectural design, functional efficiency and sheer beauty, anything that I had conceived of. That is quite a sentence and probably sounds like the old malarkey but anything short of colored photographs or the real thing would do the place an injustice.

Twice this evening, entering my room and looking out the floor-to-ceiling and room-width glass doors, I thought that I was seeing a picture. A full moon was just coming up over a bay, on the far side some distance away a beautiful symmetrical volcano [Vesuvius] towers to the sky. From its top a plume of smoke constantly flows. After dark, spurts of flame and lava shoot skyward. The bay itself is lovely, surrounded by beautiful dwellings, palms and citrus trees, among which are not Arabs wending their way to the Moslem Holy Kairouan, which was OK but the Arabs can have it; this is a bella, bella place.

Perhaps these people know how to use marble or maybe it is because it is so readily available here, but the interior of this place is trimmed or surfaced with marble in such manner to be very attractive in its effect. There is not a light to be seen yet there is more than enough light at all times, all of it indirect. A colonnade and striking architectural designs become apparent when the lights go on that are not apparent in the daytime. The colors throughout are unexpected yet in entirely good taste, refreshingly bright after drab Africa. Maybe that's it, I was too long in Africa. As I understand it, a princess lived here.

I am sending you some insignia that should be along a week or two after you receive this. I am trying to get some local trinkets also. You will have to of necessity consider this Xmas since one can never tell where one will be at Xmas.

Incidentally, I hope you are enjoying school. Soon you will start on the round of English literature. It will no doubt include that Dickens tale containing the character Scrooge. To many, the locale of that tale has always been the setting for a traditional and typical Xmas. Plum puddings notwithstanding, that does not strike me as being the sort of place to spend Xmas. What do you think?

[By giving me the clue of a story set in London, my dad was letting me know that he might be going to England. — BGF]

Love,

Pappy

★ ★ ★

October 17, 1943

Dear Babe,

Slowly I am accumulating all of the refinements of civilization, now a typewriter.

I actually had to go out and run for exercise yesterday, I have been doing so little. Around here it was not easy to find a place. I finally found a street not far from our villa that did not have many houses on it and was comparatively free of traffic. *[At Fort Benning when my dad was home for the evening, he would go out for a run before dinner. He was the only person I knew in those days who ran for exercise. Once he took Toughie with him but came home carrying her. — BGF]*

This morning, glancing at the news from the States, I noticed a war "communiqué" from Florida. There appears to have been some "accidental" bombing. This sort of thing could get entirely out of hand and become a rather serious situation. It may not be unwise to get everyone on their toes and informed of the merits of a good deep slit trench to have handy on such occasions. While you cannot carry one around with you, you can accomplish practically the same effect by rugged and intensive training of the proper type.

Our experience has been that the average soldier fresh from the States takes, on an average, one to two hours to dig a rather shallow hole. The same man in the midst of a rough air attack can get completely underground in about thirty seconds. Of course if he doesn't, he is no longer a problem anyway. You will also find that carrying a small collapsible hand shovel, perhaps in your handbag, or some people might like to wear it for a hat, will work wonders when the time comes. With this problem, the experience has been that the average youngster comes from the States carrying just what he was taught to carry, a small shovel. If he emerges from his first fight intact, he rushes frantically around to find a bigger shovel *and* a pick to take into his next one. Finally, by the time he has been around awhile, he settles down to a combination of the small shovel and lots of speed in its employment.

I have managed to find some things that may be properly considered Xmas presents. It's awfully difficult to get anything like that around here. In addition, I found some Italian stamps that will no doubt in time be of considerable value to a collector since they are no longer in use. I will send them along shortly. I also located some Italian insignia which I will send as soon as I can find something to send them in.

Today being Sunday I again went to Mass. I find myself in an unusual situation in this respect. These people attach such inordinate significance to the Church, and it is such a politically potent instrument in control of the people, that it just simply cannot be overlooked. Too, we are in a sense under very close critical scrutiny and we must prove ourselves worthy of their confidence. To be effective we must have more than lip homage and mechanical obedience, the masses must believe in us Americans and our cause. Which all comes down to this, you gotta go to church every Sunday.

Love,

Pappy

★ ★ ★

October 20, 1943

Dear Butch,

Everything is going well outside of an occasional time bomb going off. As I understand it that cannot go on forever and the next few days should wind it up.

I am anxious to hear how Friends School is, do you like it, etc.

I am ashamed to admit that for the past week or so I have been living a very comfortable life. It is easy to do if the opportunity presents itself, knowing that any day it's back to the mud and slim rations. I have a very comfortable villa, a beautiful spot in fact. Things in this city are rapidly getting back to normal. Despite all of the charm of the city and comforts of living, I am ready to leave. Wanderlust is, with us, a normal trait by now — greener fields are always beckoning — beyond the horizon always a challenge.

Love,

Pappy

★ ★ ★

October 26, 1943

Dear Butch,

Thank you for your letter of congratulations. I hope that I can be a good general.

Right now I am grounded by bad weather [having returned to Sicily to witness a demonstration of an experimental-type parachute and glider landing]. I am about ten miles from the place where Jack Thompson wrote those stories [about Biazza Ridge]. It is raining quite heavily. Winter has started here I guess. I hate to see it come. Many people are going to be very cold. Those who have spent so much time in Africa have the chills already.

I sent you some insignia and a storybook. I have just learned that I am not supposed to send back postage stamps so I guess you will have to wait awhile for them. I have some good ones for you.

Italy is a very lovely place. Near where I have been staying there are beautiful mountains. One looks like Mayon. I wish now that I had gone to see it when we were at Fort McKinley. Well, someday we may go back.

Love,

Pappy

★ ★ ★

October 28, 1943

Dear Butch,

Yesterday I received your nice letter of congratulations, the one that had Mommie's and Coursey's in it. [Col. Dick Coursey and his wife, Billie, were among my parents' closest friends. — BGF] Thank everyone for me. I have also received a very nice letter from Aunt Lil. You will seem to keep guessing my whereabouts and, of course, I am in no position to tell you despite the revelations of the current press.

Incidentally, reading the latest Time that I have received, September 27th I believe, the Fifth Army had a very hard time in the Salerno Bay area; very, very interesting. It is if I may say so, gratifying to at last read news accounts from the States that have us met with something besides flowers and platitudes. I believe that I speak for many when I say that it is at times disheartening to read of how the peace is to be settled and of how certain American arms will triumph with ease when we (in our own hearts) know of the danger, heartaches, and graves yet ahead of us. Perhaps we should send over to our erstwhile kraut playmates the current issue of Time or the latest clippings from the New York Times or Washington Herald Tribune. They seem so unconvinced of our unquestioned superiority at times.

But don't let this all bother you, Butch. I am getting along fine. Yesterday I returned from Comiso, Sicily, where I wrote you my last letter. As I understand it, I can now tell you of exact places I have been in Sicily. I spent a day over there grounded by bad weather. The opportunity was not an unwelcome one since it gave me another opportunity to look over my landing area of that fateful night. There are still some boys missing and I always hope that I may find another one or so. For a while I did but by now it is about all cleaned up.

The picture that you have of Thompson and me was taken at a railroad crossing within a few feet of the caretaker's house. He was in the morning that I arrived there. With some trepidation he pointed out that some tedeschi were so and so, etc. I hadn't eaten for several days so he and his wife gave me a piece of native black bread and a glass of wine. It was wonderful. They had a child about the house so I showed them your picture which I had carried with me; the wife was particularly interested in the type clothes you were wearing, etc.

Well, a few minutes after they gave me the wine, I captured two germans outside the house and then the fun started. The house was badly bombed and they left. The other day I stopped by; at first they didn't know me, which shows how fat and sassy I must be getting but when I showed them your picture, I was back in good standing again and eligible for another ration of black bread and wine which I forthwith devoured.

Sicily looks a bit barren these days, even beautiful Trapani where I lived for a few weeks. Etna, by the way, had snow on it the other day, the first snow that I had seen since leaving the States. The volcano near my present dwelling does not have snow on it yet and I am not sure that it ever will. Snow would really look silly on a volcano that was steaming a mile a minute and that is just what this one is doing.

Glad to hear that you like the Friends School. By the way, Aunt Lil said something about me not being a jumper anymore; just to keep the record straight, Uncle Sam quit paying me for it but I jump just as much as ever, maybe more. It's too much fun to miss.

Love,

Pappy

★ ★ ★

October 31, 1943

Dear Butch,

I sent you some more insignia this morning. Let me know what you receive. I am always interested in what gets through. Several days ago I sent some insignia and a book.

I received a nice letter from Aunt Lil this morning. She told me of Uncle George probably getting a change of assignment. Tell him to be sure to look me up upon his arrival. Remember the reference to a Dickens tale? I am glad that he is on the road to recovery. Quite some time ago he and Aunt Jane [George's wife] wrote me a very nice letter. I received it during a several weeks stay [at Kairouan] a short distance south of Enfidaville [Tunisia]. In the hustle and bustle that ensued in preparation for the latest affair, I somehow misplaced it; consequently, I have been unable to answer it which I would like to do. Since I will see him in the not-too-distant future, it is not so important now.

Things are moving along on a rather fast schedule here. Tomorrow the electricity will be turned on and the area affected is to be vacated. The feeling seems to be that the tedeschi left everything wired for demolition upon his departure and as soon as the juice goes on, everything goes up. We'll see.

Incidentally, "tedeschi" is Italian for "german." Here among these people it has come to be a term of bitterness and hate synonymous with hun and vandal. We have come to use it a great deal, both in combat and out. My Italian is still a bit spotty, there are some gaps in the vocabulary, but what I lack in words I make up for in signs. Besides I really believe anyway that in the final analysis these people do most of their conversing with their hands.

Love,

Pappy

★ ★ ★

October 31, 1943

Dear Barbara,

I just came across these Italian insignia which I thought that you might like to have.

Several days ago while cleaning out some of my papers, I found a few copies of a send-off I gave to the Combat Team the night of the Sicilian clambake. In its inception it was rather hastily scribbled mid the dust and flies of Kairouan, and there was so much that had to be done that it didn't seem to be very important at the time. In the meantime, however, it has come in for some undeserved publicity and it may in time, particularly when you get older, be of interest to you. Each soldier was given one a few minutes before the takeoff, it was his first inkling of where he was going.

Love,

Pappy

As they slowly slogged through the winter mud and mountains toward Rome, a gap developed between Fifth and Eighth Armies that could easily be exploited by the Germans. General Clark once again requested the Division's help, and Colonel Reuben Tucker's 504th Parachute Infantry Regiment (with its supporting artillery and engineers) was released from occupation duties in Naples and sent to Fifth Army as conventional ground troops.

★ ★ ★

November 6, 1943

Dear Butch,

Your last letter that came yesterday showed much improvement in your writing. I am glad that you like Friends School. Your letter was waiting for me when I returned from a recent trip. I have been doing a lot of gallivanting around lately [visiting the 504 in their mountainous location and overseeing the activities and continuing training of the Division's other units].

At present I am back to the city beautiful [Naples]. Jerry came in right after me last night [with bombers], gave the place a good going over and jarred it about a bit. I was getting ready to take a bath upon his arrival and figured the bathtub was as safe a place to be as any so I went ahead, although he made big waves in the tub. Some fun.

I believe that I told you that we are not permitted to send postage stamps back. I had just managed to get you a good fathering of European stamps when I found out about the restrictions. I'll keep them for you.

Received a nice letter from Aunt Lil and from Rosie also. Had a letter from Cameron Knox in Lee and he is getting along fine. A letter from Jack Cornett also. Mommie probably knows of Jim Hite's recent death. Very sad, seems odd to meet death that way. With all of the difficult and unorthodox jumping that we do, we have practically none of that. Safest job in the world. *[Cameron Knox and Jack Cornett served with my father in the 503rd Parachute Infantry Battalion; however, I don't remember Jim Hite or the circumstances of his death. — BGF]*

Getting a lot colder around here, how it will be other places, wow, we're going to freeze. See a lot of Rube Tucker these days, he always mentions Mrs. Tucker visiting Mommie's apartment. There must be a lot of people around Washington whom we know.

You'll probably get this around Thanksgiving, hope that you enjoy the turkey.

Love,

Pappy

★ ★ ★

November 8, 1943

Dear Barbara,

I have been saving these stamps for some time because I thought that the censorship regulations would not permit me to send them. I found out today that I have been in error. I hope that you can use them for your collection.

Happy Thanksgiving.

Love,

Pappy

P.S. On second thought, Merry Xmas, you will probably not receive this until December.

Pappy

★ ★ ★

November 9, 1943

Dear Barbara,

Yesterday I sent you some postage stamps which you should find suitable to fill some of the gaps in your collection.

Things with us continue to move along in routine fashion. This morning about four a.m. the mud seemed very cold; what the coming winter will bring, I would rather not think about. Actually my present location should be, and I believe generally is considered, a delightful climate. There are palms, a few anyway, lots of greenery but judging by the present, the winter should be cold. Didn't I mention Xmas?

We turned all the electricity on in this hamlet the other day. I don't believe that I have told you about it, it was a bit out of the ordinary. Since the tedeschi left about everything about these parts "wired for effect," that is booby-trapped or mined, it was with considerable trepidation that the populace awaited the big day when all the electrical circuits got hot. They had been out for a long time, months.

During the interim, since our occupation of the city, we have had several places go up in a cloud under the impetus of a ton or so of well-placed TNT with a tedeschi timeclock. It makes for a hazardous and inordinately interesting way of life to never know when the ground will go up under you or the building collapse down upon you. Consequently these people "sweat it out" as the boys say, never knowing from minute to minute what is going up next. The day of the big event they were without exception on the edge of their chairs, figuratively speaking. Actually we deprived them of the comforts of their chairs by evacuating them to the outskirts of the town. Anticlimactically the juice surged thru the lines and nothing happened, but anticlimax or not everyone felt much the better for it. Now with electricity there are papers, cars will run, etc., etc.

It is interesting to see a city reborn. There are so many things that we take for granted. Imagine a city of the size of Washington totally without electricity, water, gas, automobiles. The health problem is first the most serious one. To get water, people from the outskirts haul it in and sell it. They sell anything that is wet. Garbage and waste remain in the streets. Everyone lives on anything edible, there is no bread of course. Where food is found there are long lines and prices soar way beyond the average person's means. Inevitably there is stealing and hoarding. One's life is always in danger. Exciting times but most unpleasant.

What do you hear from Lady Toughie these days?

Love to everyone and Merry Xmas,

Pappy

When the 82nd and 101st Airborne Divisions were activated — the U.S. Army's first airborne divisions — the original intent was to integrate them into the expected Allied cross-Channel liberation of Nazi-occupied northwest Europe.

Instead, the 82nd faced their first test of combat on the battlefield of Sicily while the 101st remained untried. Several factors, including the ensuing operations in the Mediterranean, had delayed any landings in force on the Continent; however, now the time had finally come for Operation OVERLORD *—the beginning of the end of Nazi domination and oppression.*

Receiving a request from the U.S. War Department for "an able officer with vision and combat experience" to serve as airborne adviser to the OVERLORD *planning staff in England, General Ridgway offered Gavin. Ridgway believed no one other than Gavin possessed the "vision, combat experience, professional knowledge and personality" to get the job done. However, Ridgway also offered a caveat to his recommendation: "I want him back."*[6]

★ ★ ★

November 14, 1943

Dear Butch,

The fruitcake just arrived. I was most anxious to save it until Xmas but you can well imagine how long it was saved. The staff shared it with me and enjoyed it very much. I have a little trip ahead of me so I really couldn't save it a day. It was most fortunate that it came today, otherwise it might have been the 4th of July when I received it.

Everything is going well. If anyone I know goes back to the States, I'll have him call or stop by. By the way, *what is* your phone number? Best to everyone.

Love,

Pappy

★ ★ ★

November 15, 1943

Dear Butch,

These coins are for your collection. The map is the one I jumped with into Italy. The cameo is a local product. It is of "The Three Graces" and I thought you would like it. These cameos are hand carved by local artists from onyx shell.

Love,

Pappy

P.S. The fruitcake was great.

★ *chapter five* ★

OPERATION OVERLORD/
NEPTUNE — UNITED
KINGDOM

With orders for the European Theater of Operations, General Ridgway arranged to move the 82nd Airborne Division to the United Kingdom, where the 101st Airborne Division, fresh from the United States and ready to begin training, was already in place. Still struggling to reach Rome, General Clark protested the release from Italy of the aggressive troopers and able commanders of the 82nd. As a compromise, Tucker's 504th Parachute Infantry Regiment (along with its battalion of supporting artillery and company of engineers) would remain under Clark's control. Ridgway, however, once again uttered a familiar caveat: He wanted Tucker's 504th Combat Team back in time to train for participation in Operation NEPTUNE, *the assault phase of* OVERLORD.

On November 18, the Division sailed from Naples without Tucker's troops and without Brigadier General Gavin. That same day, Gavin arrived in England by plane to report to COSSAC (Chief of Staff Supreme Allied Command) for his advisory assignment.

The massive Anglo-American amphibious landings, preceded by division-size airborne operations, were to take place on the Normandy coast of France's Cotentin Peninsula. With control of the peninsula, the might of the Allied war machine would then drive onto the Continent, push Hitler's armies out of the occupied countries, destroy the German military, and force Germany's unconditional surrender. The assault and its operational planning would be a huge undertaking. Evaluating the details of the proposed airborne missions, in collaboration with General Omar Bradley, whose First Army would hit the beaches, Gavin addressed his special assignment in earnest. After all, "nothing chastens a planner more than the knowledge that he will have to carry out the plan."[1]

★ ★ ★

November 19, 1943

Dear Butch,

First, note the change of address, that APO number is "887." Since it will be ages since I hear from you through the old APO, I would appreciate a word on how you are getting along. Would you please ask Mommie to send me my long overcoat if that can be done conveniently. If it cannot be found do not bother. It seems awfully wet here.

I am not certain, just yet exactly, what the censor will permit me to say in this theatre. I will give you some news of the locals as soon as I can. I have been quite busy for the past week but it looks now as though I will get to settle down, for a short time anyway. This is a very interesting place.

I will send you some coins for your collection as soon as I can. Let me know when you receive the last I sent you. I believe Capt. [Don] Faith [General Ridgway's aide] was to give them to you.

Last fruitcake certainly was good. Let me know how you are getting along in school.

Love,

Pappy

★ ★ ★

November 20, 1943

Dear Barbara,

I am becoming a bit more adjusted, although I have not been able to sleep nights. The bed is awfully soft, I wake up thinking something is wrong or I am in the wrong place.

You have never seen such fog. I thought the natives were very likely used to it but tonight an old lady inquired where she was of me on my way back to the hotel. I finally managed to get her to where she intended to go. There is even fog in the room.

These people are making the most genuine "all out" effort I have seen yet. Everyone is doing something, regardless of age or sex, to bring the war to a successful end. Wood is hard to get and carefully rationed and saved but everyone seems to be existing without too much discomfort. From an ardent Anglophobe, I am becoming a definite Anglophile. Of all the people I have seen, and I have seen many by now, these people are most deserving of the sacrifices being made for them on the battlefronts.

Love,

Pappy

★ ★ ★

November 24, 1943

Dear Butch,

I had a very nice long newsy letter for Capt. Faith to take back to Mommie and you but on second consideration I had him give it back to me. You should see him soon.

I hope to hear from you soon at my new address. I like it here. It is wonderful to come to after where we have been, nevertheless, I am looking forward to getting back to the boys. This sort of life was never cut out for me.

By now you should be getting lots of use for your ice skates. Can you skate well now? I'll bet.

Tomorrow is Thanksgiving. I do not know how it will be here. The British probably do not observe it. We are supposed to "work as usual" but work here is wonderful relaxation and a vacation compared to the Italian front. I've had a bath every day the past four days—it's wonderful. I sleep in a nice bed. I feel a bit ashamed of enjoying such luxuries but everyone here seems to take them for granted. Don't you do that, Butch, people are dying so you can have them.

Love,

Pappy

★ ★ ★

November 26, 1943

Dear Barbara,

Well, Thanksgiving came and went yesterday with little apparent change in the routine here. I stood in a queue (everyone seems to stand in those things around here) for a long time waiting for a turkey dinner but finally gave up. I then had to stand in a queue to get my coat to leave.

Capt. Faith should be in to see you very soon. Be sure to tell him that he left his scarf and gloves with me in the Grosvenor House [officers' billet in London]. I will save them for him.

When my typewriter comes, I will be able to write you more newsy and longer letters.

Right now I am quite busy getting to know my way around this place. It is quite a change from the Italian front. It is most interesting and rather nice to have clean clothes, beds, and hot water. I am afraid that I am becoming spoiled. Sometime you will have to come here; I will bring you, if and when I have the opportunity. It is much like America in many ways, certainly much more than Africa, Sicily, or Italy.

Love,

Pappy

★ ★ ★

November 26, 1943

Dear Butch,

Now that I am in a cold climate how about sending me some candy. Is it rationed in the States?

I had to get a new uniform so I got a ready-wear job at the PX [military Post Exchange] and took it by a tailor to have it altered. Can't get one made on account of clothing coupons. Well I found that I had to be formally introduced to the tailor. After he checked the fit of the uniform, before he would start work, I had to give him a banker's reference and a reference from one of his clients. I explained that I merely wanted an alteration for which I would pay when the job was done but it seems as though paying had nothing to do with it. To get an English tailor to work for you takes nothing less than a papal bull. Anyway, I am all set now.

Tell Capt. Faith that tomorrow I expect to go to our new home [in Northern Ireland] for a few days. I will send Gen. Ridgway an airmail report as soon as I get back. I talked to Col. [Paul] Turner [of Division Headquarters] and he thought the [Division's training and bivouac] area much better than expected.

Don't forget the boodle [West Point slang for candy and treats].

Love,

Pappy

★ ★ ★

December 2, 1943

Dear Butch,

It is about time I got a letter from you, must be a month now since the last. Hope Capt. Faith got to see you. Tell him everything is going well and I'd like to know when I can expect him and the General. *[When General Ridgway and his aide, Captain Faith, returned to Washington for conferences, they visited my mother and me. — BGF]*

Have been busy the past few days gadding about the auld sod. Lots of Gavins there. Lots of rain, cold, and fog too. For a full-time home I do not believe that I would like it. It is much nicer here, although by most standards this is supposed to be frightful weather, "beastly," as these people say.

Although the weather may be inhospitable, the people are not. They appear to be quite kind and thoughtful to American soldiers, although I can easily understand how they might resent the good rations, etc., of the Americans compared to this war-rationed bit.

Let me hear from you and tell Mommie to send some boodle.

Love,

Pappy

   ★ ★ ★

December 6, 1943

Dear Barbara,

When are you going to write me that first letter, Skipper? I have not heard from you for over a month. I expect to see Capt. Faith and Gen. Ridgway any day now and I hope to get some word of your well-being.

Have you had any snow yet, have you been ice skating? Did you get my birthday card from Italy? It was hard to get and more difficult to mail, it may not have gotten through. Just in case it didn't, Happy Birthday. Did you ever receive the cameo, I thought that you would like it. "The Three Graces." They are hand carved from onyx shell, a number of artists quite good at it are in Naples. *[I still have the lovely cameo. — BGF]*

I hope that you are getting along well in school.

I am kept quite busy these days but it is all very interesting, time flies. I feel a bit isolated since I do not get any mail of any kind, at least not yet. Is there anything that you would particularly like me to get for you here? I have not had much of an opportunity to shop yet. Let me hear from you soon.

Love to everyone,

Pappy

The 82nd arrived in Northern Ireland on December 9 and would remain there until mid-February when the troop carrier wings arrived in England and were assigned to their respective airfields in the English countryside. The Division would then join them in bivouac sites nearby.

★ ★ ★

December 10, 1943

Dear Beautiful,

How about a letter? I haven't heard from you for six weeks. Yesterday I received information that would indicate that Capt. Faith may see me soon. This should be a source of some information of your whereabouts and how well you are. I can't imagine what the mail trouble is.

I am still living out of one handbag which is at times a bit trying. Yesterday I went into a store to buy a pair of pajamas. He asked me to try them on, insisted that I'd no doubt want them to fit properly. When I flatly declined, he proceeded to measure the pajamas and then me. Funny people—about having things tailored.

I thought I'd go see all my boys in the morning so you may not hear from me for a while.

Is Uncle George coming for tea? I am looking forward to seeing him.

Let me hear from you when you can. I at least can use boodle or a good book.

Love,

Pappy

★ ★ ★

December 16, 1943

Dear Butch,

Another change [in the assigned APO number]. I'll never get a letter from you if I don't quit moving about. How are things going? Uncle George on his way to see me yet?

Merry Xmas, if not too late. I expect to see Capt. Faith in two or three days, he should have some news of you.

Love to everyone,

Pappy

★ ★ ★

December 26, 1943

Dear Barbara,

My aide came in town yesterday and brought four letters from you. These were the first that I had received in about six weeks. They were written in October and November. Better still, I met Gen. Matt Ridgway a few days ago and he had your snapshots and told me of visiting you. That was a wonderful trip that he had, I wish that I could have gone along. I was glad to hear of your good reports from school.

Lt. [William] Oakley, my aide, also brought your Xmas package. It arrived the day before Xmas and it was grand to get, everything was fine. Having it arrive when it did made this seem much more like Xmas. I had dinner last evening with a very nice British family, and being Xmas, it was done in traditional style despite the food restrictions. I believe that they had been saving bits for it for some time. They had a nice turkey, I have no idea how they got it. The plum pudding came from Canada and was brought in blazing in traditional style.

Incidentally, these British people are doing a wonderful job of regulating their lives and way of doing things towards winning the war. Everyone is doing something, and regardless of their station in life, everyone pitches in. Food is carefully rationed and clothing is on a coupon basis that seems to work quite effectively.

I believe that I will start using this type of writing paper. It may take a bit longer but I will feel that I am writing and not to the entire headquarters. V-mail can't be sealed anymore; consequently, it is handled by all of the clerks on its way out to the post office. I have been away gadding about on a training trip or I would have written you sooner. Write me when you can, note my new address, however things sent to APO 469 will get to me.

Love to everyone and a Happy New Year,

Pappy

★ ★ ★

January 6, 1944

Dear Barbara,

Yesterday I received your letter of December 19th so it is not taking so long now for a letter to get across. The news of Toughie was interesting and surprising. Where is she now, in Georgia or Washington? I always did want her to have a family.

Did you ever receive the cameo and map that I sent back?

I was glad to get your phone number. I have asked several people going back to call you or Rosie but I believe that they have had difficulty finding the number. Gen. [Elbridge] Chapman [the former head of Airborne Command] told me that he couldn't find Rosie's in the phone book.

Everything is going along fine here. We are kept rather busy. We don't get shot at as often as in Sicily and Italy but it is very interesting anyway. It is just as interesting to figure out how to keep from getting shot at next time.

Christmas was very ordinary. I had dinner at a civilian home. It was complete as Christmas dinners go. I missed not being with you, however, especially since this was the first Xmas that we were not together. Your box was most welcome. The Velatis came through fine.

I am certainly glad to hear of how well you are doing in school. A few doors away from me there is a Colonel Lash who has two, I believe, children in Friends School. Perhaps you know them. *[Sally and Peter Lash were at Friends with me. It was comforting to have army friends who understood about having a father away at war at this very civilian, "old Washington" school. — BGF]*

Today is an unusually nice day here with the traditional fog conspicuous by its absence. Although most Americans dislike England because of the fog, or no hot dogs, or no Coca-Cola, or something like that, all of the boys coming up with me think that it is wonderful. Even the cold and fog is much more like America than anything in the Mediterranean area. There are movies also, and shows, if one can get the time or opportunity.

Everyone here, all of the civilians here I mean, are doing their bit to help win the war. Compared to what I remember of the States, it is very marked here. If people through their own efforts are ever worthy or deserving of victory, these people certainly are.

Continue your good work in school.

Love to everyone,

Pappy

★ ★ ★

January 12, 1944

Dear Babe,

Sounds as though you had a nice Xmas, lots of presents. I am particularly glad that my things came through. Maybe next Xmas I will be around to help you celebrate, although the prospects of that are rather remote.

I continue to receive very welcome letters from Rosie and Aunt Lil. I am very sorry to hear of Uncle George's illness. I felt at first that perhaps it was something that would clear up quickly but it is evidently much more serious than that, terribly unfortunate, knowing how badly George will feel about it.

I guess that by now you have come across Col. Ryder's Saturday Evening Post story [about the battle at Biazza Ridge]. One way to make money. It is, however, quite true in most respects, much more so than a great deal that has been published about Sicily.

The picture of myself and [Jack] Beaver Thompson [nicknamed "Beaver" because of his bushy beard] has been my undoing. It is the pride and joy of the eight balls and sad sacks in the 505th, something to be pointed to with suppressed pride and obvious horror as an example of how lousy the Colonel gets to looking in a fight. This, after I spent over a year making them all scrub and shave daily regardless of where or what, I would get caught looking like that.

I met a classmate whom I hadn't seen for years the other day and he told me of an incident involving himself that you might enjoy. The locale is a local hotel-billet inhabited by both American and Scotch officers. The Scotch, of course, wear kilts and are grand people (although there are exceptions). An exception in this case came walking across the lobby on an evening recently when this classmate of mine stopped him and told him that he couldn't go out like that. Drawing himself to full height and exuding dignity and the grandeur of the Empire in a firm stare, he demanded to know why. Why, said my classmate, because your slip is showing.

Blows were barely averted and Anglo-American goodwill slipped back another notch. So it goes, but it is a great war. In actuality, we get along very well with all of these people, they are all right.

Where is Toughie and her family?

Don't bother about any coming affairs involving me, the letters of the family indicate some concern. Really quite needless, the job has got to be done and I am no more likely to get hurt than anyone else. The best thing that people in the States can do to save the lives of the boys over here, or on any other front, is not to worry but to work and save. Stop the strikes and give the youngsters the things they need to finish the job in a hurry and get home. Every strike and delay in production means more lives lost and more days of fighting. All of the Axis powers are playing for time. I know every correspondent tells the people the same story. Such things as the strike that I read of yesterday, when workers on invasion barges struck for more wages because they were given spray guns instead of paintbrushes, are pretty hard for soldiers to understand. I have found that writing letters to mothers of boys who have been killed in action is most difficult. There is a reason for everything but if some parents were given an explanation of their son's death in terms of strikes and production shortages, it would be sufficiently shocking to bring home the necessity for a continued all-out effort.

I am sure that Tojo [the Japanese prime minister] figures that too many Sicilys or Tarawas will cause the American public to demand a withdrawal from further fighting and too many losses. You can be sure, however, that the soldiery would want no part of such an idea. The job is to be done and will be done. I don't know how I got started on this. Anyway, the idea is that it is really not worthwhile to worry about me or anyone else; they all know the task that lies ahead and they are in the final analysis going to derive a great deal of satisfaction from a job well done. No sacrifices will be made in vain. We know that. We do want to feel, however, that everyone at home is back of us all of the way. Amen.

Love to everyone,

Pappy

★ ★ ★

January 20, 1944

Dear Beautiful,

Seems like a rather long time since I called you that or do you forget? I enjoyed your letter of January 2nd, the one in which you said that you write every Sunday. I think that is a good idea.

It is hard to say where my own time goes nowadays. I usually start work at about 7:45 or 8:00. The British on the other hand start at about 9:30 but they work until about 7:00 or 8:00 in the evening. The result is then that I usually plug away until about their time.[2] It doesn't leave much time for recreation of any sort and this makes little difference anyway. We have a long hard job to do so we might as well keep at it until it is finished.

I did manage to get to a show Saturday evening, "Arc de Triomphe." Quite good after the first act and a half. It takes that long to get accustomed to their accent. After that it isn't so bad if you have some tolerance for their odd, and to an American, decidedly dull sense of humor.

About a day after I arrived here, Barney Oldfield had a couple of tickets for "This is the Army," so we went to see it, afterwards we went backstage to meet Irving Berlin. It was a tremendous success here. It seems peculiar that the British enjoy our type of humor and slang so much but yet appear constitutionally incapable of imitating it in any of their dramatics or publications.

I am enclosing some stamps that you will probably be able to use in your collection. The large envelope contains 100 stamps, each from a different British colony; the smaller two New Zealand stamps are of recent vintage and at the moment some rarity. I went during lunchtime today and got those from a nearby stamp dealer. I intend to do more shopping than I have. Do you still save insignia and stamps?

The news in the papers from home is disheartening and depressing, all they seem to be doing is having strikes and slowing up production of things we need to carry on.

I had lunch with Walter McCallum of the Washington Post yesterday. He is a very nice individual and quite pleasant to talk to, it was most interesting to hear of present conditions in Washington. I expect Beaver Thompson up tomorrow, we should have quite a reunion. Seems like everyone is coming here.

Love,

Pappy

As D-Day — the date chosen for the cross-Channel invasion — drew near, the scope of NEPTUNE's final plan increased. The British Second Army (reinforced by the Canadian First Army) was to land on three beaches, code-named Sword, Juno, and Gold, near Caen on the Normandy coast. The U.S. First Army was to land on two beaches, code-named Omaha and Utah, to the west of Caen at the base of the Cotentin Peninsula, isolate the peninsula, and capture the port of Cherbourg at its tip. Thereafter, the U.S. Third Army would come into the American beachhead to capture Brittany and its seaports. Airborne missions preceding the amphibious landings would be mounted behind the British and American beachheads at Sword and Utah.

With its mission expanded, the 82nd needed to augment its fighting strength. The 504th Parachute Infantry Regiment was still in Italy; therefore, to fill the slot and bring the Division up to an enhanced force, the 82nd received two new parachute infantry regiments — the 507, under the command of George "Zip" Millett Jr., and the 508, under the command of Roy Lindquist. (Both Millett and Lindquist were well known to Gavin.) One additional battalion was also added to the Division's glider regiment — Harry Lewis's 325th Glider Infantry Regiment — giving it a total of three battalions, equal to the parachute regiments. (General Clark would eventually release Tucker's combat team by early spring, prior to D-Day, but when it arrived in England after months of arduous winter fighting, General Ridgway declared it too depleted and too beat up to participate in NEPTUNE.)

Having finished his assignment as airborne adviser to COSSAC, Gavin returned to Division Headquarters where General Ridgway had added an interim additional assistant commander to the staff—Brigadier General George P. Howell Jr. (whom Gavin had served with at Airborne Command). The new regiments brought to England had been organized into a brigade under Howell's command; with the brigade disbanded, Howell was assigned to the 82nd for NEPTUNE. Dividing responsibilities, Ridgway designated Gavin as the commander of the main force of parachute troops (Task Force A), himself as commander of the glider component (Task Force B), and Howell as commander of the Division's seaborne tail (Task Force C).

★ ★ ★

January 24, 1944

Dear Babe,

Please note the new APO, it strikes a familiar note I am sure. First I want to thank you and Mommie for the nuts and cookies, they were wonderful. I forgot, well almost, that there were such things.

Today is what I suppose you would call a bad day. It started with a two-hour session with the dentist. It took that long to undo the African and Italian harm. Another appointment or two and I should be ready for that Second Front the papers talk so much about.

The particular town that I am in is rather nice. I hope to be able to do some shopping. It has a nice bridge but it keeps falling down. If I can, I'll get you some insignia, that is if you are still saving them.

How is Lady Toughie and her family doing?

It is quite cold here now. I'll be glad when spring comes, winter was never for soldiers.

Have you ever met the Lash children in school, I know their father here.

Love to everyone,

Pappy

★ ★ ★

January 27, 1944

Dear Babe,

The Martha Washington has just arrived and it is wonderful. As you probably know, we are rationed to one candy bar a week. It certainly is good to taste some good candy again.

You have probably noticed the new APO. It will be good to rejoin the boys for all that's cookin'. I presume Gen. Ridgway told you of my stay here. Now it looks like back to the old preparation and work again. But after two combat jumps I like it, everyone is much more sober and steady about it now. Not quite as excited as much as grim and determined. I'll be glad when warmer weather comes.

The English people are quite nice to us. If I were they, I would be dreadfully tired of so many Americans overrunning their pubs, clubs, and cinemas all of the time. Americans have so much more money and are so unscrupulous about spending it for anything, regardless of scarcities. The English are, to Americans, strange that way. If the home government says there is a shortage of a particular item of food, for everyone to be careful in their purchase and use of it, they all stop buying it and as far as possible stop using it. Americans on the other hand all buy more.

Love to everyone,

Pappy

★ ★ ★

January 28, 1944

Dear Butch,

The enclosed was given to me yesterday by a British airborne brigadier. It is the shoulder patch insignia of all of their airborne troops, both parachute and glider. We have come to respect it highly, they are troops of quality. I'll get some more for you as soon as I can.

Love,

Pappy

★ ★ ★

January 31, 1944

Dear Babe,

I am enclosing a pair of RAF [Royal Air Force] wings and two pips. The pips are indications of rank in the British army, you may have heard of them. A lieutenant wears one, then two, a captain three, etc.

Shopping around, or trying to, I find that I can buy practically nothing without ration coupons, which are unobtainable. Books or something but not anything to wear. Do you still save stamps? Or did I ask you that before.

I haven't heard from you for some time, you haven't missed a Sunday?

Strange weather we have here, the past few days have been beautiful. It never gets as cold as it gets in the States. I'll know more about sleeping out in it next week. It will be nice to be with the boys again.

Love to everyone,

Pappy

★ ★ ★

February 10, 1944

Dear Babe,

I suspect that your last letter was written in school. I was very glad to get it. I did receive the candy that Mommie sent, also the nuts, they were great. Now that the weather is cold I particularly appreciate these things, they keep and are most welcome. How about sending me some and I'll send you a check. I know that you can't spend all of your money sending me things.

Yesterday I sent you a Scotch scarf, I hope you like it. I also sent you a short story, "The Snow Goose" [by Paul Gallico]. I would like very much for you to read it. The people here say that it is a true story.[3]

When I get another snapshot I'll send you one, better than the one with the beard. You know better than to ask me about the girls, you are my girl.

It's snowing and very cold, I don't think I'll ever be warm again. I spent most of the day in a jeep and almost froze.

Love to everyone,

Pappy

★ ★ ★

February 14, 1944

Dear Butch,

This being February 14th it is fitting and proper that you, the young lady of my esteem, should be inquired on the possibility of being my Valentine so I thought I would write you a letter.

I received a nice letter from you this morning written January 30th. Your writing has improved very much in the past few months. I am glad to hear that you are a full-fledged scout, certainly like to see you in that uniform. I am glad that you liked the stamps. I will get you some more as soon as I can. Next aide I get, I will put him on the trail of stamps.

I am in the process of changing aides. *[My father's new aide was Hugo Olson. — BGF]* Last one I had, despite a high IQ college background and all of the stuff, spent a great deal of his time getting lost in the woods; consequently, I found myself taking care of my aide instead of him taking care of me. The qualifications of a parachute aide differ somewhat from those expected of an aide in the heydays of peace.

We are very busy these days, lots of training, even expect to get in a jump any night now. I have almost forgotten how. Last two were combat jumps. I don't know how long this sort of thing can go on but it sure is fun while it lasts, exciting anyway. We have a tremendous amount of training to get done. It is surprising how quickly people forget many of their basic lessons.

Hope you have noticed my new APO by now. Aunt Lil's fruitcake has never caught up with me, either that or it caught up with someone else.

You would like this country, for a visit anyway. Very beautiful countryside. Where I am located there are many evidences of the old Roman occupation, foundations, tiles in the churches, etc. I never realized before the full extent and thoroughness of the Roman conquest of these islands. Without further study, it would appear as though their racial origins lie as much with the Romans as with the French, Angles or Saxons. The English wouldn't like that.

There are Italian prisoners all over the place, those "Roman warriors." They are pitching hay and picking Brussels sprouts now, if that is what one does with Brussels sprouts.

Will you be my Valentine?

Love to everyone,

Pappy

★ ★ ★

February 21, 1944

Dear Babe,

Your writing has improved a great deal in the past few months. Your last letter was particularly good.

I think that it is well that Toughie is still in Georgia. She would have a difficult time with her family around Washington, everything is so crowded now. Besides, she would have to stay locked up all of the time.

Where I am now it is quite cold. There is some snow on the ground and it is always very damp. The dampness is particularly bothersome, so everyone says. I soon expect to spend some nights in foxholes in training, and since it is so different from our last habitat, I am taking particular pains to be prepared for it. This morning I wore three pairs of wool socks and two pairs of wool gloves. Needless to say, my hands and feet were warm but I needed more than socks and gloves. The pressing problem is to figure out how many suits of wool underwear and how many pairs of socks, etc., can be worn and still not come down too fast [during a jump]. The point is reached when the rate of descent caused by too many clothes does more harm than the good effected by all of that extra padding.

Things have been rather quiet. Managed to be in the big city [London] for an air raid the other night. Papers said that it was the biggest since the Blitz. Seemed small compared to some of the goings-over Naples took.

Did you ever receive the Scotch scarf? I am trying to get you a kilt. It takes coupons and they are rather difficult to obtain. The clothing rationing system is very effective here and everyone saves their coupons for real necessities. As you no doubt know, each Scotch clan has its own distinctive plaid. They are described in a small book that I have seen but I have been unable to obtain a copy of it. You may be able to get it in America.

I am looking forward to the arrival of spring and better still, summer. Rumor has it that it came on a Wednesday last year. It only lasts a day.

Love to everyone,

Pappy

★ ★ ★

February 23, 1944

Dear Beautiful,

Xmas comes but once a year, except for me — it comes twice a year. Yesterday I received three Xmas packages, some surprise. One was a fruitcake in a cardboard container with six sides; very, very edible (that is, the fruitcake was). I describe the box so carefully because I have been on the trail of a missing fruitcake for some time. It has become the cause célèbre of the European Theatre of Operations. Every package I see I suspect contains Aunt Lil's fruitcake, was this it? It was addressed from Mommie. The other two were shoeboxes containing gum, candy, nuts, etc., all of which were most welcome. It isn't everyone who has two Christmases. I still receive stray letters that have chased us about the Mediterranean.

Nice day today, rained only half the day. Spent the day out in the nearby fields playing soldier.

The boodle is particularly welcome at this the end of the Brussels sprouts season. I hope that it is the end. But the troops here are very well fed. I didn't want to sound too much as though we were complaining but the rations in Africa were very poor. During the two weeks before Sicily we all lost considerable weight. It was no doubt one of those unavoidable things, everyone seemed to be trying but all that came out was Spam and more Spam.[4]

Two nights before the takeoff for Sicily, the officers of the 505 got together and donated about $1,000 for the purchase of cows, a sheep or two, and some wine. This was contrary to the theatre policy; that is, we are not supposed to buy food and so deprive civilians of it. But everyone was quite hungry for a square meal. It all worked very well, we tied it in with an organization day celebration. You remember the 505 was activated July 6, 1942. It was supposed to be July 1st but Pappy got too snarled in red tape to write the order.

This afternoon I am going to quit early and run a few miles. Might be a good idea, just in case I have to chase a couple krauts real fast or vice versa.

Love to everyone,

Pappy

★ ★ ★

February 28, 1944

Dear Barbara,

Thank you for the Valentine, although it may have been a bit late, I am afraid that mine was too.

I am sending to you today, two medals: the Distinguished Service Cross and the Purple Heart. Both are as I received them, except for the ribbons which I will keep for wear. I am rather certain now that I will have no occasion for needing the medals, and I am sure that I could lose them if I tried to keep them with my baggage. I have already lost my camera and numerous small articles. This is to be expected, however. Anyway, the medals are yours for safekeeping or to do with as you see fit in the event I ever become a casualty.

Today everything is covered with about an inch of snow. It is the first heavy snow that I have been in since West Point. That place certainly seems very far away. It would be nice to visit there sometime again.

We continue to be very busy, that is to be expected however otherwise we would all go home. There is so much to be done and so little time to do it in.

Most of these English people where we are now try to be very nice. It is somewhat of a truism however in our service that a general officer is pretty much alone. There are too many things that one is not expected to do and too many places where one should not be seen. Probably a good thing anyway.

I enjoy the letters that I receive from Rosie and Aunt Lil. I am interested in Uncle George's probable foreign assignment. It would be nice if I could see him over here.

Love to everyone,

Pappy

★ ★ ★

March 7, 1944

Dear Babe,

Thank you for your nice letter. Next time that I see Col. Lash I will tell him that you know his two children. I do not see him very often anymore.

I suppose that you are getting ready for Easter now, it is still very cold here, lots of snow. I had a new experience in it Sunday, my first jump in snow. It was rather cold and the ground was hard, being a bit frozen, but I had a very easy landing. I have been very lucky so far. A number of our old-timers, Col. [Walter] Winton, Capt. [Al] Ireland, Capt. [Harold] Swingler, all are off jump status until they get their knees repaired. I haven't had any trouble since I was a student [at Parachute School], remember how funny they got, my knees I mean.

This morning I had to have a picture taken for the local public relations officer. I'll send one to you as soon as I get one. I don't believe that I told you that I ran into Walter McCallum the other day. I had him and Barney Oldfield to lunch. He is a very nice person, most interesting to talk to.

About a month ago, Jack (Beaver) Thompson turned up and we had lunch together, it was nice to see him again. His beard is a bit shorter, he fell asleep in a barber's chair in Cairo. I expect him up around these parts any day now. His paper has grounded him so no more parachuting.

Everyone here tries to be very nice to our soldiers and they are all having a reasonably good time. I, unfortunately, am not in a position to give a firsthand report on the local brand of hospitality since for some reason or other there are too many things a general doesn't get a chance to do. My time is spent at work, usually until ten or eleven at night. Perhaps it is just as well, although after a taste of combat it is difficult to do nothing but prepare and plan.

I am so glad for Uncle George that he is going to see some action, a little goes a long way. [*Uncle George had received orders to the Pacific.* — BGF] He will be very glad to get back to America. Getting shot at loses its novelty with surprising abruptness. I really am very glad for him. I know how badly he wanted combat service, there certainly is enough of it around for him to get a share and it only takes a bit.

Love,

Pappy

★ ★ ★

March 9, 1944

Dear Babe,

This no doubt is a Valentine from one of your many admirers. It appears as though he chose a rather roundabout way of sending it to you. Or perhaps it was sent to me for censoring. Being rather uncertain about the whole affair, I am forwarding it to you exactly as it came to me. I suppose the censor will get at it now so I hope that its content matter is acceptable.

I would like sometime to get Uncle George's address, could you send it to me?

The receipt of the last letter from your Mommie definitely clears up the matter of the lost fruitcake. The cloak of suspicion has been lifted from the shoulders of the mail orderlies of the 82nd Division as much to my relief as theirs. Thank Aunt Lil for me, please. It was very good and very much enjoyed, actually much more than had it arrived at Xmas.

Our food here is much better than it was in Africa. That was really quite a place. Maybe that's why they fought so well when they got out, they were fighting mad to get out. Like some potential refusals who get so airsick that they jump anyway just to get out of the airplane.

They still refuse [to jump] occasionally, especially the replacements. Some of the older hands, I believe, regale the new boys with tall tales of the horrors of Sicily, et al. It scares them enough anyway so that they decided that they are in the wrong business. Should be a stop put to it. Perhaps it isn't as bad as I make it sound. There really aren't so many refusals.

By now you must be looking forward to Easter, seems strange, Easter in America is a very nice time. Spring is a bit later here, if it comes at all, I am not convinced yet that it does come.

Love,

Pappy

★ ★ ★

March 10, 1944

Dear Butch,

This is just a note to obtain some measurements that I need in order to get you a kilt. The enclosed is a sample of the cloth selected. The tailor is all set and is waiting for your waist and hip sizes. Also your height and weight. It should be very nice. As a matter of interest, it will cost six pounds ten shillings but what is of much greater concern is that it will take fourteen coupons. That really is a bit of a misstatement, the cost is of no concern actually but I thought that you would be interested. Send the measurements as soon as you can.

Love,

Pappy

★ ★ ★

March 21, 1944

Dear Babe,

It is about time that I wrote you a letter. I have been gadding about a bit lately in connection with training. It is frequently impossible to get a letter either written or mailed. I am enclosing a few snapshots.

Some time ago I was in the big city for a stretch of duty, while there I went out stamp shopping. I sent you the stamps at the time. When I came out of the stamp shop, a soldier from the old outfit was waiting and wanted to take a picture. The enclosed is the result which shows at least that I have acquired the habit of shaving again. The sergeant who was with him wanted a short-snorter bill autographed, as I recall.[5]

The fourth picture represents, rather portrays, a spring day in the United Kingdom. Taken about a week ago, it is typical of that particular time since we were having a snowy spell. Today being the first day of spring, it is hardly a bit warmer, but we have been warned to expect cold damp weather for some time.

I have seen a great deal of George Howell lately, daily in fact. Yesterday Col. Millett showed me a clipping from a Kansas paper purporting to be an obituary on him, his picture was included, allegedly he was killed. You must get some tall tales back in America. Everyone is kept very busy here which is really a very good thing.

You mentioned in your letter that I would be able to help you with your geography when I came back which is quite true. From a historical viewpoint England has proven most interesting. Africa seemed rather impenetrable; the languages, customs, and habits of the people making it impossible for an outsider to do much more than surmise, guess, and occasionally need a tourist's bromide. Sicily and Italy were both steeped in the lore of the past and the evidences of civilization back to the earliest known times are to be seen everywhere; but unfortunately, circumstances at the time confined our interest in geography to how quickly could one dig a foxhole in a certain spot. We rarely got above that. Much of it was beautiful country however, seemed to come right out of a storybook. Everything was so entirely different and untouched.

Here, however, everything worthy of note can be found. They are proud of their historical past and evidently they can well afford to be. Many of the things one learns about in school are readily to be seen. The countryside is most pretty and attractive, despite the weather. Sometime you will have to see it. I would like sometime to be able to bring you to some of these places for a visit. All of them in fact, including Italy and Sicily, I am sure you would like that.

Love,

Pappy

★ ★ ★

March 22, 1944

Dear Babe,

Since this is my [thirty-seventh] birthday I thought it a good idea to drop you a note. It bids fair to be a day of activity and even perhaps a bit of sunshine. The sun is peeping out just a bit. It is, of course, the second day of spring. There are a number of flowers about, allegedly spring flowers. The natives are having flower shows and things. This is entirely understandable. After being closed up all winter, the first flower and bit of color is greeted with exuberance unrestrained.

What is lacking in spring warmth is made up for by picturesque scenery. The town church, in a huddle of small dwellings sheltered by massive towering trees, is beautiful at times. The soldiers get around to see these things, regarding them with proper awe and respect, something that the average soldier would sooner not be caught dead with.

As a birthday so far it does not appear to differ from any other day. I have a suspicion however that there is something cooking at the mess and it isn't Brussels sprouts. I have been informed that I am not expected to let training interfere with my attendance at dinner this evening. These things are, I suppose, always shrouded in great secrecy. I'll let you know how it all comes out. Too bad I can't send you a piece of the cake.

And now I really must get to work, it is 9:00 a.m. and I have a busy day ahead. I am very proud of your fine grades at school. I have decided that in keeping with our past practice I should make some monetary reward, this I will send you in pence and shillings in a day or so.

Love,

Pappy

★ ★ ★

March 29, 1944

Dear Babe,

I wish that you would thank everyone for me for the nice St. Patrick's Day cards, also the birthday cards. It is nice this far away to know that someone remembers those things.

I am glad that you received the scarf. As soon as your measurements arrive, work on the kilt will be started so please don't take too long.

I am sending today a german beer mug and a german soldier's set of eating utensils. On a warm July day last year, myself and the "Irish Eyes Are Smiling" boys [of the 505] had the pleasure of running the krauts out of Trapani [Sicily]. It was quite a day and they left in a bit of a hurry. As dusk fell, we were looking for a suitable Command Post for the night when we came upon a very lovely villa that had been used by the krauts for a couple of years. It was rather complete, especially in view of the haste of their departure, kitchen utensils, a stove, iron cots, tables, chairs, etc., all of the refinements that we had long given up as being only for people in America.

Among other things, they left several beer mugs of which the one I am sending you is one. I kept it for a long time for use at prop blasts, we still have them, and now rather than have it lost in the bedlam about these parts, I thought that I had better send it along. You can do as you see fit with it. In future years if anything ever happened to me, it would be nice to return it to the commanding officer of the outfit. *[I gave this mug to the commanding officer of the 505 for placement in their museum in 1998. — BGF]*

The knife, fork, spoon set I picked up somewhere in the scuffle. It is a very neat, compact, handy set. In my own opinion, superior to similar equipment of our own. You may find it interesting. Keep it and I'll get another one, if and when I need one.

By the way the long overcoat did arrive and has been put to good use. I may have to return it in the next few weeks. But it has been fine to have.

About boodle, I would like to get some in the form of Martha Washington candy, or chocolate candy, and some nuts like were sent some time ago in glass jars. I will send you a check if you will let me know what it costs. Since I am a general officer and my own commanding officer, well almost anyway, I believe that this request is sufficient. If it is not, please let me know.

Glad that Uncle George is on the way.

Love,

Pappy

★ ★ ★

April 3, 1944

Dear Barbara,

Just yesterday I received a wonderful box of Martha Washington candy. It is very, very good and I am most grateful, please tell Mommy. Our weekly candy ration has been a roll of "Necco" wafers for so long that I am becoming allergic to them.

I also had a delightful surprise on my birthday when I received your cablegram. That *was* a surprise and an especially nice one.

I am enclosing with this letter some British coins, some colonial, that I picked up in a shop in the local barrio. I hope they add some interest to your collection. I'll send some more as soon as I can get my hands on them.

How about the kilt size? I am about to guess and you know how that would be. You must have grown a lot in a year.

Please let me have Uncle George's APO number when you get it.

Love to everyone,

Pappy

★ ★ ★

April 4, 1944

Dear Babe,

I am returning today my long overcoat. If it makes it, will you please ask Mommy to throw it away, or put it away I mean. It might be cold next winter. If I try to keep it with me, I am certain to lose it somewhere. My striker has just taken it out to be packed.

Incidentally, I have a fine striker, a Southern boy from the backwoods of the Carolinas. He has been with me since before Sicily. I soon learned there that it doesn't make much difference if a striker keeps things clean and orderly, or even if he keeps himself clean, provided he has a nose for food. Sgt. [Eugene Walker] Wood can always find food even when there just simply ain't any, and better still he can make most anything edible and this latter is the more important qualification.

Much to my satisfaction, I found out in Sicily that he has in addition to his culinary and thievery attainments an inordinate degree of personal courage. On one occasion Sergeant Weber, he still drives for me, was cruising up a road with Wood and myself perched in the jeep when an antitank gun opened up on us. Wood just did a somersault over the back of the jeep, landing on his head in the middle of the road. While admittedly a bit hard on the head, it is nevertheless the approved technique in such cases since the payoff is on speed and originality. That was Wood's narrowest escape to my knowledge. I must remain unaware of any scrapes he may have had with any United Nations gendarmerie while on his foraging safaris, but needless to say, he always does well. *[Sgt. Weber was my dad's driver again in Naples, Italy, in 1952 when I spent the summer with my dad and his family. Weber had a great memory for war stories, and shared those that were repeatable with me while riding in the car. Sgt. Wood lives in North Carolina with his wife Polly, surrounded by his wonderful family. My dad thought the world of both sergeants. — BGF]*

I am also sending you some British insignia in a day or so. By the way, did you ever receive my medals? I was afraid that they may have run afoul of the censors. After reading the papers the past day or so, I don't know whether to give them back or not, it seems as though too many medals have been awarded. It took twenty years and lots of shooting to get them but maybe they should be awarded to Lewis's [striking] miners or Petrillo's [union] musicians [who were squabbling over making recordings versus live performances]. I really don't know.

Love to everyone,

Pappy

★ ★ ★

April 11, 1944

Dear Babe,

Thank you for the snapshots, both of yourself and the bear. *[The photo was taken during a visit to the Washington Zoo. — BGF]* You are growing, quite a young lady. I am looking forward to taking you out to lunch to a nice place where usually grown-ups go. Anywhere, it doesn't matter where, just so you like it.

I am glad that you like the plaid, now how about the measurements? Nothing can be done until I can give them to the tailor. They just arrived, I just received your nice letter written on March 24th. I will get them to the tailor today.

I heard that Jack Cornett is around but I haven't seen him, probably will in the near future.

I am glad that you are planning on returning to the camp this summer. I am sure that it is a nice place for you and it is much better than Washington in the summertime.

I had read a review of "News of the Nation" in Time and I wished at the time that there was some way that I could get it for you; now that you have it that is fine. As you get older and further along in school, you will find that a complete and thorough knowledge of our country's history will be a valuable asset. Everyone should know our history, it is only with this basis that they can appreciate our aims and aspirations and intelligently plan our future, and someday you will be both a planner and a voter.

I am mailing to you a german glass that I had the dubious pleasure of "capturing" in a command post that we ran the krauts out of in a bit of a hurry. For some time it became the custom in the outfit to use it as the commanding officer's glass at prop blasts. I explained this all to you once before I am sure, anyway, I will lose it or break it if I try to keep it so it is coming along. Let me know when you receive it. Have the medals ever arrived?

Would you please send me a dictionary, preferably Webster's Collegiate Edition, also a thesaurus, Roget's, if that is not too big, probably you can get a small condensed one. I will send you a check for the amount they cost as soon as you let me know how much.

I can hardly believe that you are three inches short of five feet tall, you'll be as tall as Pappy.

Love,

Pappy

★ ★ ★

April 19, 1944

Dear Babe,

Well I am glad that you received the medals. There was some prospect of the censor stopping them, more because of what accompanied them [the citations with the account of combat, dates, and locations] than the medals themselves.

I am sorry that I cannot accompany you to Glen Echo [an amusement park in Maryland]. It would be lots of fun, maybe next year on opening day. When school is out, and if you have the time, I think that you should visit West Point. I would like to very much and I will whenever I get back to America.

There are several things that I want to remind you of again just in case I forget. I have subscriptions to TIME, NEW YORKER, and READERS DIGEST that you should have diverted to you just in case I find myself in a spot where I can't use them. I also am paid ahead to the Book-of-the-Month Club until about July, drop them a note and tell them to ship the books to you in case I can't use them. All insurance is paid up, including yours with Lincoln National Life and Mommie's with Travelers Insurance Co. of Atlanta, Georgia. The Highland Falls Bank is all squared away as a joint account and I don't think that there will be anything in the London bank. Any excess cash I am having transferred to the Highland Falls Bank.

Don't let this unduly alarm you, it doesn't mean a thing. I just have been thinking of these things, and I thought that it might be a good idea to get them off my chest.

As near as I know, the tailor is as busy as a bird dog on the kilts; it will probably take him a long time.

I thought that you might be interested in the enclosed photo since it is of our mutual friend George Howell. The occasion, unfortunately, was one of those times when things don't work the way they are supposed to. [*My dad and Gen. Howell were examining a parachute that had malfunctioned during a training exercise, resulting in the jumper's death. — BGF*]

I hope that you are enjoying the spring weather that must certainly be your lot at this time of the year. It is very nice here and we are, of course, very busy.

All of my love to everyone,

Pappy

★ ★ ★

April 21, 1944

Dear Butch,

I thought that the enclosed invitation would be amusing since I profess to be working so hard. Actually, it was the only party that I have been to in this locality and was very much of a "duty."

Spring is definitely here and I imagine you must be thinking of your summer camp. When do you go? And be sure to let me have your address.

Love to everyone,

Pappy

★ ★ ★

April 24, 1944

Dear Barbara,

I am sending you today a copy of "White Cliffs" which I believe in time you will enjoy. It is a bit mature at the moment for your tastes, Mommy may like it. I have found in it the essence of feeling that enters into many of our Anglo-American relations: the British aloofness, disdain and chill, and the American critical attitude towards the British in a reassertion of their liberty and independence. They blend to make a story that should have a happy ending but, unfortunately for me anyway, did not since another youngster off to war is hardly a "happy ending." But they are a good people doing the best that they are able under considerable adversity. And if this poem contributes in a small bit to a better understanding of our common problems in war and common heritage in peace, it deserves some reading. You may someday like it, I hope so.[6]

We continue to be rather busy, reminding me somewhat of old times in Kairouan. There is lots to be done and never enough time to get everything accomplished. The boys all look well and are fit and anxious. The Wehrmacht [German armed forces] expect a great deal of paratroopers and I hope that they will not be disappointed; I do not believe they will be.

As I believe I have told you on past occasions, never worry about my well-being. My jumps are somewhere beyond the fifty mark now and I am sure that I have a lot of bounces left in me. My past experiences have convinced me beyond the need of reminding of the great virtue of digging a deep hole fast. It will be a fleet-of-foot kraut that will catch Pappy, or vice versa.

This all sounds silly and I suppose it is. Actually I don't know what to say. As I recall, I didn't seem to be exactly inarticulate before Sicily or Italy. Maybe I didn't know any better then. Anyway, it will be a real clambake and I wouldn't miss it for anything.

Love to everyone,

Pappy

★ ★ ★

May 1, 1944

Dear Butch,

May Day and here we are. The other day we celebrated our first annual departure date. It hardly seems possible that time has moved along this quickly.

I received Uncle George's address from Rosie yesterday. I plan on writing him today. I am glad that he has gotten into things and I would like to get out his way. Perhaps I will, if enough good fortune comes my way.

I am enclosing two rather candid shots taken several days ago. They are of mutual friends of ours and I thought that you would like to have them.

We are as busy as usual. It is a good thing as there is more fact than fancy in "Idleness Breeds Discontent."

I will be very anxious to hear of your arrangements for the summer. Re the kilts, I have arranged, just in case, to have them shipped to you. They may be some time in the making and the way things happen nowadays there is no telling where I will be.

I am glad that you received the coat and medals. Has the kraut mug and glass ever arrived? I am a bit uncertain what to advise you to do with the insignia, just keep them until you collect more. Perhaps it would be best to keep them in a box.

From your letter I judge that you had quite an Easter, you received many nice presents. It is getting quite nice here now. The trees are all blossoming. There are evidently many more trees, fruit trees, here than in America. Many of them are along the streets and in front gardens. The gardens are very lovely.

Love to everyone,

Pappy

★ ★ ★

May 11, 1944

Dear Butch,

I have enjoyed your recent letters very much. I am sorry that I have not written more, I have really been terribly busy. Not since I was G-3 [plans and operations officer] at the Airborne Command at Fort Bragg have I kept such long working hours, seven-thirty to around midnight on an average, and I still can't seem to get everything done that must be done. The days are very long, it is broad daylight at ten-thirty, gets dusk now around eleven.

Thanks very, very much for the candy, it was great to get. Now that the headlines are getting larger, I would suggest that nothing more be sent to me unless I ask for it specifically. Those instructions should ring a familiar note.

I have written Uncle George and should hear from him come Michaelmas. We could hardly be farther apart. Well if everything goes well, maybe this time next year we will be closer together.

Thank you for the little picture taken at Glen Echo. I still have the one that you sent last year. You referred to a poem that you had written in school and that you were enclosing in your letter. From your description I am sure that it is a lovely creation, but Butch, you forgot to enclose it. Sounds as though you wrote the lyrics for your school song.

Did you receive the small German goblet?

For a while now my letters may be fewer and farther between and I hope that you will understand and don't worry about what is going on just because you don't hear, sometimes it is impossible to write.

Haven't had a school report in a long time, how are you doing? Are you going to camp? If so, when and what will your address be?

Love to everyone,

Pappy

★ ★ ★

May 16, 1944

Dear Butch,

Thanks for the candy, it was awfully good to get and was very much enjoyed. All things considered, it would be a good idea not to send anything more until I say so. And while I think of it, if under any circumstances you do not hear from me for a while *at any time* [as D-Day was rapidly approaching] do not be disturbed.

We are all quite busy and circumstances being what they are, it is not always possible to write letters. I believe that I explained this at some length to you last summer. I realize that you would like to receive more news from me in these letters but I have never had as much occasion to be more circumspect. Neither grade, position or interests permit even the most casually hazarded guess. Too many people are guessing about things they know nothing about anyway. Really all that most of us know is that we are very busy and that the days are never long enough. It is fortunate that the sun does not go down until about ten or ten-thirty in the evening, it gives us a good long day.

The days are warming up a bit but the nights are still quite cold. I have never liked combat in cold weather. In fact, the first thing most parachutists look for is a kraut with an overcoat or blanket, captured dead or alive. A mess kit is also nice to come across.

But to get back to our present way of life, everyone is in fine fettle. A few residual malaria and jaundice cases from down below [North Africa, Sicily, and Italy] but they are getting well quickly. These lads will give a good account of themselves. We are hoping that they [the replacements and new units] will be up to the performance of our parachutists in the past but short of shooting it is hard to tell. They look fine.

Had a phone call from Jack Thompson this afternoon. He expects to spend Saturday evening with me. Unfortunately his sheet has grounded him so the clambake is out.

Jimmie Bassett [a friend from Airborne Command] called this afternoon, I expect him in for lunch tomorrow. Maybe he'll stick around and I'll get a chance to push him out the door. The people I would like to push out the door are the strikers in the P-51 factory in Detroit.

Love to everyone,

Pappy

James Maurice Gavin at about five years of age in Mount Carmel, Pennsylvania. (All photos courtesy of Barbara Gavin Fauntleroy unless otherwise noted)

Gavin as a swimming counselor at Camp Chippewa on Lake George, New York. He taught swimming and hiking at the camp for two summers during his summer leaves from West Point.

Left: Gavin holding Barbara at Fort Sill, Oklahoma, 1934. *Below:* Toughie and Barbara, sitting on the front steps of the Gavin quarters at West Point, 1940.

CAPT. GA

Coach Gavin and the regimental championship basketball team of the 25th Infantry Regiment, Camp Harry J. Jones near Douglas, Arizona, 1930.

First squad, Company C, 503rd Parachute Battalion, ready for their third jump of the five required to qualify as a paratrooper, Fort Benning, Georgia, October 2, 1941. Gavin is standing, third from left.

Cocktail party at Fort Benning, 1942. *Left to right:* Lt. Col. Roy Lindquist, Lt. Col. Jim Gavin, Mrs. Millett, Lt. Col. Art Gorham (killed in Sicily), and Lt. Col. "Zip" Millett (captured in Normandy). (Photo courtesy of Lt. Col. Gordon Smith)

THE COLUMBUS LEDGER, COLUMBUS, GA., TUESDAY, DECEMBER 1, 1942.

MEET MAX, BENNING'S AIRBORNE CANINE

Parachutists' Mascot Makes Five Jumps, Qualifies, Gets Wings Without A Hitch

Max, a 90-pound rust colored boxer dog, as mascot of the 505th Parachute infantry at Fort Benning, is leading anything but a dog's life.

The dog has jumped the necessary five times from a plane in flight, made all landings without injury and has been mentioned in the regimental orders of the day as a qualified parachutist.

To top it off, a review was staged in his honor with Colonel James M. Gavin, the regimental commanding officer, pinning the silver wings on his jacket.

Max made the first jump without hesitating, but reacted humanly on the second jump. Parachutists invariably approach the door of their second jump with pronounced timidity.

However, the mascot made the second leap after considerable coaxing, and then knocked off the remaining three like a veteran, as other jumpers chided him with such quips as 'Watch it, Max, ain't that first step a daisy?" and "if all those girl dogs could see you now."

Newspaper article about Max, the "parachute-qualified" boxer mentioned in Gavin's letters of April 11, 1943, and an undated letter following one of May 17, 1943. (*Columbus Ledger,* Columbus, Georgia, December 1, 1942)

Cartoon of Gavin sitting at his desk at 505th Parachute Infantry Regiment Headquarters, by artist Pvt. Linzee Prescott. *Right:* Lt. Col. John Norton, West Point Class of 1941. He was as close to a son as Gavin had. See letters of August 3 and August 21, 1943.

Left: British foreign secretary Anthony Eden inspecting the 505 at Fort Bragg, March 1943. Gavin is walking just behind him. (Photo by U.S. Army Signal Corps)
Below: Standing on the hood of a jeep in Kairouan, Tunisia, Gavin gives his boys a talk a few days before the jump into Sicily on July 9, 1943. (Gift of the 505 RCT to Barbara Gavin Fauntleroy)

No. _____

To Miss Barbara M. Gavin

2022 Columbia Road

Washington, 9

D.C.

From
Col. James M. Gavin,
505th Infantry, APO 469
% Postmaster, New York
(Sender's address)   N.Y.

July 7, 1943
(Date)

(CENSOR'S STAMP)

Dear Babe
    I have felt for some time that at this time I would have neither
time nor means to write but to my surprise I have both.
    Yesterday was organization day for the 505, the regiments birthday.
We were all anxious to celebrate the occasion in fit style but in these
parts that is not easy. We finally managed to obtain a few gallons of
local vino and some bulls and sheep for barbecue. The officers have been
carrying around some of their ill gottengain from the slot machines in
Alabama and so it was decided to have the officers mess contribute.
Through the cooperation of the local kahib some bulls were located and it
all made for quite an occasion. It is the first beef that we have tasted
as long as I can remember and it came in at a good time. Many of us are
beginning to have sore gums or receeding gums that get sore from eating
all canned soft food. Fesh vegetables seem to be about nil around here
and it too hot for anything like fresh food especially meat to keep.I am
not complaining of course because those of us here realize more than anyone else the difficulties of getting food into/here.
    We had our first experience with a local seasonal phenomena know as
the sirocco. It is exactly the opposite of a Texas norther. The winds
suddenly shift and blow from the Sahara and it is time to burro a hole.
It is extremely hot, yesterday in Maj. Alexanders area it was 142° and
in Art Gorham's 136°. Things like pencils, ammunition, weapons get too
hot to pick up and water exposed to its effects is far too hot to drink.
Yesterday I put my hand in a can of water I had in the shade of an olive
tree near where I was sleeping and I had to take it out because of the
heat. Fortunately there are availabb from the local arabs earthenware jugs
quite thick and of all sizes. Water placed in them sunk in the ground
stays rather cool. This may give you the impression that living conditions
are unbearable, on the contrary everyone is in the best of health most of
us have lost a bit of weight that we could probably afford anyway. As a
matter of fact today the 505 is in better health than it ever has been,
I was just checking the sick rate this morning.
    I have had time recently to take more/ than a passing interest in the
Roman occupation. It is evident that they, in their centuries as rulers,
made more economic and agricultural progress in the development of this
promising country than anyone else. The signs of their establishments are
still about and in many instances in active use, particularly wells.
    Yesterday we adopted Jack Thompson of the Chicago Tribune into the
regiment. You may enjoy reading some of his stuff. I do not know what he
writes, I never see it, but he asks a heap of questions. By the way,wells
over here aren't holes in the ground big enough for the old oaken to slide
up and down. They are enormous openings big enough to lower a car into,
frequently they have a couple a camels raising large containers of water
simultaneously, tell you more about some other time,

Love Pappy

V - - - MAIL

V-mail letter
sent to
Barbara by
her father on
July 7, 1943.

Gavin speaking to Jack "Beaver"
Thompson, a war correspondent
for the *Chicago Tribune* who
jumped into Sicily with the
505 PIR in Gavin's plane.
He accompanied the 82nd
intermittently during the entire
war. See letters of September 2,
1943, and January 12, 1944.
(Gift to Barbara Gavin Fauntleroy
by James M. Gavin)

Photo taken in England and sent to Barbara by Gen. Gavin to use if anyone asked for a picture of him, and they did. See letters of March 7, 1944, and January 16, 1945.

Gavin loading on his equipment for the jump into Holland, September 17, 1944. (Photo by U.S. Army Signal Corps)

Gavin in a jeep in Holland with his junior aide Lt. Rufus Broadaway (*left*), a soldier, and Sgt. Weber, Gavin's driver. (Photo courtesy of Rufus Broadaway)

Photo taken in Holland during the visit of King George VI to the 82nd, which was serving under British command. *Left to right:* Gen. Brian Horrocks, King George, Gen. Gavin, Col. March of the Field Artillery, Col. Roy Lindquist of the 508, Col. Reuben Tucker of the 504, Col. Bill Ekman of the 505, and Col. Chuck Billingslea of the 325. See letter of October 21, 1944.

HEADQUARTERS 82ND AIRBORNE DIVISION
OFFICE OF THE DIVISION COMMANDER

Aug 28th

Dear Babe

I sure [...] to me that I write you at least once on the official stationery of the division since it isn't every day that one has a division commander in the family. It may look well in the family archives. It is most interesting and at times trying, enough to keep me rather busy. I hope someday that you will be able to see the division together. They are a rugged hearty lot and superb in combat.

Love to everyone

Pappy

When Gavin's promotion to major general was announced, photographers from several newspapers in Washington, D.C., came to the Gavin's apartment to take pictures of his wife, who was Washington-born and -bred, and daughter Barbara. It was an exciting time. *Left:* Letter written on official 82nd Airborne Headquarters paper, Office of the Division Commander.

The letter of March 12, 1945, from Suippes, France, describes this prop-blast ceremony held to initiate newly qualified paratroopers. At the head table are Col. Chuck Billingslea, Col. Bill Ekman, Gen. Gavin, Col. Reuben Tucker, Col. Wilbur Griffith, and "Jim's Jug," a champagne cooler obtained in Berg en Dal, Holland, containing the potent prop-blast drink.

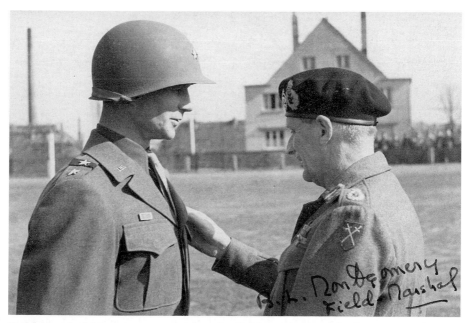

Field Marshal Montgomery pinning the British Distinguished Service Order on Gavin.

General Matthew Ridgway and Gavin in Belgium during the Battle of the Bulge. (U.S. Army)

Lt. John ("Jocko") Thompson, Gavin's aide, helping him prepare for a jump at Tempelhof airfield in Berlin. Tommie led the troops who captured the Grave bridge in Holland. In 2004, the bridge was named for him by the Dutch. In civilian life he had pitched in the minor leagues for the Boston Red Sox organization and after the war would pitch in the major leagues for the Philadelphia Phillies (U.S. Army).

Gavin, Ingrid Bergman, and Gen. Parks in Berlin, after the war in Europe had ended.

In June 1945 Gavin returned to the States for a war-bond drive. One of the events was the presentation of Hermann Goering's diamond-studded baton to President Harry Truman. *Left to right:* Maj. J. M. Wilson, aide to Lt. Gen. Lucian Truscott; Lt. Gen. Alexander Patch; Pres. Truman; Gen. Truscott; Maj. Gen. James Gavin. (Photo courtesy of Press Association, Inc.)

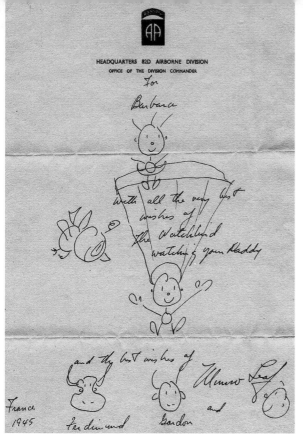

Munro Leaf, author of one of Barbara's favorite children's books, *Ferdinand the Bull*, visited Gavin in France in March 1945 and created this drawing for Barbara of "The Watchbird watching your Daddy."

Gavin leading the Victory Parade past the reviewing stand at the Metropolitan Museum of Art at Fifth Avenue and 82nd Street, on January 12, 1946. He returned to join Gov. Dewey, former Mayor LaGuardia, Mayor O'Dwyer, Grover Whelan, and Gen. Wainwright (who had served in the Division in Word War I) in the reviewing stand. (Photo by U.S. Army Signal Corps)

Mrs. Gavin and Barbara in the stands at the parade.

Gavin and his aide,
Maj. Derwood Cann,
with Barbara and her new
dog at Fort Bragg in 1946.

Gen. Gavin in 1984 at La Fiere near the Merderet River Bridge and Ste.-Mère-Église, talking to active 505ers about the fierce battle there in 1944. Veteran Bob Gillette stands behind him. (Photo courtesy of Bruce Gillette)

★ ★ ★

May 23, 1944

Dear Babe,

Time seems to be flying these days. I am glad that the glass arrived safely. I'll try to get some more, a bit difficult, but it all depends. If you hurry in the front door as they rush out the back and make a quick grab before the GI souvenir hunters, of which we have many most avid ones, can put the snatch on them, you have them.

Congratulations on the splendid report card. Seems as though I should send you something for it, what do you want?

I talked to Patrick this morning, also Jack Norton. I told him that you had asked about him. Jack Thompson (Beaver) paid me a visit today. Paper grounded him so he cannot go in. You will have to look to someone else for the red-hot dope. I'll let you know who to read later, we expect some volunteer scribes in sometime.

Everybody very busy, very well-fed and ready to go. Conspicuously better is the ration situation here than it was in Africa. We were about all a bit skinny when we got out of that place, perhaps for that reason it was an easy place to go to war from, everyone was so darn glad to get out of there.

Love to everyone,

Pappy

★ ★ ★

May 30, 1944

Dear Babe,

Today is Decoration Day, I just remembered. I always liked Decoration Day when I was a boy because of the parades, etc.[7] Later as a soldier I disliked it for that very same reason. Here there is no such thing as Decoration Day, either that or every day is Decoration Day, I am not sure.

I was very glad to get your address for the summer. Please send it to me again when you go to camp, I may lose it in the scuffle in the meantime.

We all continue to be very busy and well we might be I suppose. There is little that I can write you and still conform to the standards on censorship imposed upon us, and of all people, I should not be the one to violate the standards. Everyone is working hard and in fine fettle. I am certain that I have a few bounces left in me and looking forward with pleasure to any affairs that chance sends our way. If I survive this combat parachuting,

I will certainly have a storehouse of practical firsthand information. In a professional way it has been wonderfully informative and I have no doubt about surviving it of course. I even amaze myself sometimes with the speed with which I can get under a flat rock.

Anyway, these are fine lads, they are the finest in soldiers, and it is both a pleasure and an honor to take them in. Again, it is the thing for which I have spent years in preparation and it is the way of a soldier's life that the Academy [West Point] has taught us to live properly. I continue to hope that I can be a credit to the Academy and that my behavior in combat merits me a place as one of her own.

But enough of this, I will promptly put the snatch on anything that I would think of interest to you, perhaps some more glassware or cutlery. In the meantime, let's hope that I get back to see you before too long.

Love to everyone,

Pappy

★ ★ ★

June 2, 1944

Dear Babe,

Seems like a good time to get a line off to you. I have been thinking of some of the things that I may have forgotten about and remembered Mommie's insurance with the Travelers Insurance Co. in Atlanta. Be sure not to lose track of that policy.

Mr. [William] Walton of Life and Time and Sgt. [Phil] Bucknell of The Stars and Stripes joined me yesterday. Mr. Walton I will personally push out and Sgt. Bucknell will be a short distance away. You may hear from them. Unfortunately Jack Thompson has been grounded.

Everything is going along fine. I have never known our lads to be in finer fettle. Much, much better than before leaving Kairouan. We were in sorry shape in some respects down there, due entirely to the climate and environment and not lack of care or management on anyone's part. We were quite under-fed when we got out of there. This has been just the opposite and perhaps too soft a life.

I hope that you enjoy your summer camp, let me hear from you from camp from time to time. I would like to know what it is like and what you are doing. I will write you when I get an opportunity; if you do not hear for a spell, do not be disturbed, we will really be kept quite busy.

Love to everyone,

Pappy

Moving onto the airfields, the troopers were confined behind guarded fences and barbed wire under very tight security—there could be no forewarning of the airborne drops to come. In support of First Army, the American airborne divisions were prepared to capture the causeways leading inland from Utah Beach, seize the bridges over the Merderet and Douve Rivers to block enemy movement toward the invasion beaches, and seize and hold the key towns astride the roads leading to the port of Cherbourg—but they would have to wait one more day. Unfavorable weather postponed the invasion, and June 6 became the momentous date in history.

Generals Gavin and Ridgway visited the airfields and spoke to the troopers of the 82nd. Reminiscent of his talk just before the jump into Sicily, Gavin's exhortations evoked a deep response from the assembled paratroopers. A year later, Gavin received a letter from a trooper who vividly remembered the day Gavin spoke to Task Force A: "I was a sergeant then, and when you had finished, my buddy turned and said quietly, 'I'd follow that guy to hell.' I was one of the two sergeants in the briefing room the night before Normandy D-day when you and the commanders . . . went over the plans, and I came out . . . filled with the knowledge of the awesome plan and the sight of America's finest officers."[8]

★ ★ ★

June 5, 1944

Dear Barbara,

It is now evening, we take off tonight. As well as we can foresee our needs everything has been provided for. I thought that before going I would drop you a line and perhaps give you some idea of what makes Pappy tick at a time like this, or for that matter, what makes them all tick.

It does appear at this stage to be about the toughest thing we have tackled. Remembering the exhausted stage of most of us the first morning in Sicily, I have tried to get some sleep this afternoon but to no avail. Too many well-meaning well-wishers have come by to get in a last word. The boys all look fine, Zip's [the 507], Roy's [the 508] and the old crowd [the 505], they all are in tiptop shape.

This has been quite an experience working with them the past several months. I have never seen, heard, or known of soldiers like these combat-experienced parachutists. For us older professional officers it can be taken for granted that we will do whatever duty requires but for these young lads just from school, the farm, or home, it is quite an undertaking. With few exceptions they are highly idealistic, gallant, and courageous to a fault.

They will take losses to do anything. Needless to say, it has been a source of considerable gratification to have the privilege of working with them.

Someday you will no doubt wonder why in the world I got into this business when there are so many apparently safer ways to go to war. And I expect that by the time you are old enough to wonder, in an analytical way the reason will be evident throughout our service. Because you see, someday most of our Army will be either airborne or readily capable and trained to be airborne. Nowadays one reads in some newspapers that bombing will win the war without the aid of ground forces and in other papers that the ground forces can accomplish anything without the air corps. Manifestly someone is wrong, actually neither of them completely are because the answer lies in combining the air bombing with air transporting of troops.

During this present phase of our development, the participation of airborne troops in the form of parachutists offers particular hazards because of the newness of our technique. But in time, parachuting or what will take its place will be no more dangerous than riding a tank is today. Until then therefore if progress is to be made, risks must be taken and, of course, will be taken by those who believe in what they are endeavoring to accomplish. The presence of danger in present-day airborne operations isn't the bad thing that it is made out to be anyway. It is an essential in that it exacts out of the participants peculiar qualities of courage. These things all contribute to making a soldier what a soldier is reputedly supposed to be and what we especially need in an airborne soldier.

I will write you as soon as I am able. I am enclosing some invasion money. By the time you receive it the shooting will have started and so I am sure that I am not violating any security. It should be an excellent addition to your collection.

I hope that summer camp is everything that you want it to be, I am sure that it will be. When you return next fall and start school again, keep up the good work of this past year. I would like very much to know that you are applying yourself to the best of your ability in everything that you undertake.

Love to everyone,

Pappy

chapter six

OPERATION NEPTUNE —
NORMANDY

Encountering dense cloud banks and heavy enemy antiaircraft fire as they flew over the coast of Normandy in the predawn darkness of June 5–6, 1944, the transports carrying the paratroopers of Task Force A were unable to maintain their required formation, altitudes, and speed. In an unfortunate repeat of the flights over Sicily, the pilots scattered the paratroopers across the Cotentin Peninsula instead of onto the designated drop zones. Adding horror to the confusion, many of the paratroopers drowned, or nearly so; what had appeared in aerial reconnaissance photographs as flat grassy pastures along the rivers' banks were actually marshes and swamps — natural antiairborne obstacles that the Germans further exploited by purposely damming the rivers. With the best drop of the Division, the 505th Parachute Infantry Regiment was the only regiment able to function as a large cohesive force. Still, the scattered paratroopers formed into ad hoc groups of soldiers determined to accomplish the mission.

Landing on Omaha Beach in the face of heavy fire from the enemy's coastal defense guns, General Bradley's amphibious forces struggled to get off the beachhead. Those landing on Utah Beach faced less resistance and were able to move inland across the causeways cleared by the airborne troopers. Notwithstanding the enemy resistance and the resulting heavy casualties, the landings on all of the Allied beaches were ultimately a success.

General Ridgway, having jumped with the 505, was able to locate most of his staff and established the Division command post as planned just east of the town of Sainte-Mère-Église — a Division objective astride the highway to the port of Cherbourg. Elements of the 505 routed enemy forces within the town and secured it by 0600 hours, giving it the distinction of being the first French town liberated on D-Day.

Jumping with the 508, Gavin and his aide, Hugo Olson, landed on the edge of a marshy swamp on the western bank of the Merderet River approximately two miles north of their intended drop zone. Having also jumped from Gavin's plane, war correspondent Bill Walton was in a position to observe, and later cable to Time magazine, that Gavin "did a wonderful job of assembling men, forming patrols to guard [their] perimeter and feel out German strength." While reconnoitering, Olson discovered a raised railroad track across the swamp. Knowing that this track crossed the Merderet River and ran close to the eastern end of the La Fière bridge, a key Division objective, Gavin led his small group of paratroopers and Walton as they "plunged into the chest-deep swamp, holding guns overhead and wading" with "machine gun bullets pinging" around them to reach the track.[1]

Following the track and arriving at the bridge, Gavin found the First Battalion of the 505 (mixed with elements of the 507 and 508) fighting to get control. Taking men with him, Gavin continued to follow the track to where he hoped to be able to force another crossing of the river farther south to capture the bridge's western end. Finding the water too deep, and with no boats and the Germans dug in on the far bank, Gavin abandoned the attempt, instead moving to the bridge at Chef du Pont, another critical objective. There, a fight similar for the bridge at La Fière was taking place.

Arriving in Normandy, the Division's glider regiment (325) was thrown into the fight. The critical bridges assigned to the Division were seized and held, but it was not until D+3, with the heaviest fighting on that day, that the bridge-heads were secured and pushed westward. General Ridgway would later write in his memoir that the fight for control of the La Fière bridgehead was "as hot a single battle as any U.S. troops had, at any time, during the war in Europe."[2] Gavin, always leading from the front, would be awarded another Distinguished Service Cross.[3]

★ ★ ★

June 11, 1944

Dear Butch,

Just a short note to let you know that all is well with Pappy. A bit shot at but not shot. I am having a grand time. Everything is going fine. I am glad to have gotten the jump back of me. I was sweating it out a bit, it was rather rough.

Zip [Millett] is unfortunately in some trouble [captured] but generally all goes well. I'll write you again when circumstances permit.

Love to everyone,

Pappy

★ ★ ★

June 12, 1944

Dear Babe,

The war is improving as you can see since I now have a typewriter. Things in general are going along very well. There is little that I am permitted to tell you. Anyway, I presume that the newspapers are giving the entire situation adequate coverage. Mr. Walton of Time and Life who accompanied me wrote up some of his stuff and sent it out several days ago. You may run across it in those periodicals although I believe that he is forbidden to mention me by name. We had a rather rough time although by all past performances things went beautifully. One particular episode he named little Dunkirk, it so struck his fancy at the time. Later we came back and took the krauts to a fare-thee-well.

These parachutists have been nothing short of remarkable in their fighting. Admittedly I am very biased, but I believe that the violence and savagery of their combat technique is without parallel in our military history. The germans fear them now and give them lots of elbow room. We [remainder of line blacked out by censor].

This is a very beautiful country but seems surprisingly cold. I always thought that it was supposed to be a warm country. Later in the summer it should be lovely. I hope however that we have moved along by that time.

I feel that Providence has bestowed upon me more than my share of favor and that I am fortunate to still be here, and the more experience that I have, the more I realize how lucky I am to have survived three combat jumps so far. It is a rugged way of going to war but certainly most exciting and interesting.

Write me when you get a chance, and by the way, now that I am still in circulation how about sending me some of those salted nuts. The last that I tasted you sent me when I was on duty in London in December or January.

Love to everyone,

Pappy

Successfully completing their airborne mission by June 10, the 82nd should have been withdrawn. However, as had happened in Sicily and Italy, the general officers in charge of the conventional infantry units did not want to part with the aggressive paratroopers and continued to use them in the drive westward across the base of the Cotentin Peninsula.

★ ★ ★

June 21, 1944

Dear Babe,

Today for the first time in a week or more I have an opportunity to write you so I want to make the most of it. When you receive this you will be either on the way to summer camp or there. I am glad that you again have the opportunity of going there, be sure to let me know what you do and what goes on.

We have been kept rather busy. I noticed in this morning's Stars and Stripes an account of a fight that we had several days ago so I suppose that the papers have made some mention of the Division. If this is the case, you no doubt have some idea of where we are. The Division, especially my own first crowd [the 505], are doing especially well, remarkably well as a matter of fact. Their performance has been one of the amazing aspects of this scrap so far. Being paratroopers, plus plenty of combat experience, has made them very formidable fighters.

For the past several days it has been very cold. Fortunately I have managed to put the snatch on some blankets. I am still living out of my pockets with mostly what I came down with. A bath and a change of clothes would go a long way. I expect some new clothes soon. About the bath, well I don't know, maybe soon.

I do not know what news you receive back in the States, probably more than we are in a position to get here. Everyone is getting along fine. Zip probably likes cabbage soup and black bread [as a prisoner of the Germans].

As a matter of fact, I would like a piece of white bread myself, just this evening someone asked me where the field bakeries were that are so often shown in the newsreels back home. White bread must be something like cake. Actually we are doing well and the food is entirely satisfactory, better than satisfactory under the circumstances.

Anyway, if and whenever I feel that some little thing is not quite the way I would like it, I thank Providence that I am here at all. I have been very lucky. Love to everyone and as usual don't worry about me. I must be a poor target.

Love,

Pappy

★ ★ ★

June 26, 1944

Dear Butch,

What a fine report card, I am very pleased, that certainly is fine work. I would like to send you something for it but there is little obtainable in these parts. However in keeping with our past practice, I have obtained some money which I will send along as soon as I can as a reward for your good work. The coins consist of a few german coins and Italian and French coins. I don't remember where I got the French money. The german came from a kraut who made "the supreme sacrifice" as the newspaper boys say. After one of our most recent fracases, my striker [Walker Wood] turned up with a pocketful of german coins. I had wondered why he was giving each kraut such careful attention but being an avid souvenir hunter as well as coin collector, he missed no opportunity. The Italian coins came from a kraut who had evidently served the fatherland in Italy.

My striker, by the way, almost was winged a day or so ago. His helmet received quite a dent from a bullet that would have clipped him had it hit any other place. Yesterday while out on reconnaissance my aide [Hugo Olson] was hit by shrapnel. He has been evacuated and I miss him very much. He was a very good aide and exceptionally fine in combat and under fire.

For some reason a very kind Providence has so far looked after me. I have had some close calls but so far have not been scratched. I do not know how much information you have been able to receive of what goes on, probably much more than we receive here or know here. Today I saw for the first time a copy of Time of June 19th. There is an article on page 13 by Mr. Walton covering some of our escapades the opening day.

In answer to your question about being the only jumping general, I would imagine that by now there are other generals who jump when combat conditions require it. You may hear of them.

We are having cold rainy weather today, at the moment it is pouring. Fortunately I have an excellent tent of German manufacture that some of the boys captured a week or so ago. I have a very deep hole in it that is in the ground in the tent. A hole in the ground, of course, is part of every well-regulated home in combat. I can dive in the hole as quick as a flash given the proper impetus. It is at times remarkably comfortable and it is with reluctance that other duties necessitate my giving it up.

Actually we are all having an exciting time and some fun. Dangerous at times but never dull. Parachutists thrive on danger anyway and frequently they would sooner be scared than secure.

Hope that you enjoy your camp, please let me know how things go.

Love to everyone,

Pappy

★ ★ ★

June 29, 1944

Dear Babe,

Just a note to let you know that all is well and Pappy is still intact. Today I read a short note in the June 19th Time that you might enjoy, rather short, but it tells more than I am able to. Actually I read it several days ago but I am quite sure that that is the issue.

The other day I almost came across Frank Greer. I met his boss in the big city. The report was that he had hurt his ears the evening before when a demolition charge intended for the krauts backfired.

You probably are aware of our activities through the press. As you no doubt know, officers of the grade of colonel and above may not be mentioned by name so you should hear little directly of me. Time is doing an article on Matt [Ridgway] that is going to place him on the cover, it should be interesting; it is due out in the next several weeks, perhaps by the time you receive this letter.

Regarding ear troubles, I am having some of my own. Ever since Sicily I have not been getting much registration on my right ear, not that it was much good before Sicily but it was better. Anyway, as it works out it is a blessing because it enables me to sleep through rather heavy shelling without hearing it (the ground bounces a bit) provided I sleep with the poorer ear uppermost. After a bit, however, I become concerned because I might miss the warning whistle of a close one and not get into my hole in time so I remain awake just in case. It poses quite a problem, whether to sleep and hear little or keep awake and keep alive. The solution is to always sleep in a deep hole but I have come to dislike holes for sleeping. This must sound silly, it is, but it is what concerns people up here, how to keep alive.

Love to everyone,

Pappy

★ ★ ★

July 10, 1944

Dear Beautiful,

This is a gala day. [After thirty-three days of almost continuous fighting, and the accomplishment of every assigned mission, the 82nd was released.] I think that I will be able to get a bath this afternoon, and I have just been awarded a DSC. The bath, if I get it, will be my first since the invasion started, a bit overdue. This has been a very busy week. I haven't had my shoes off since a week ago yesterday, looks like I will be able to take them off tonight, and for the bath I hope. The DSC was pinned on by General [Bradley] (you knew his daughter at West Point) a few minutes ago. I am awfully lucky, both to get it and to be here to receive it. After the experiences of the past year, I am beginning to feel as though I am living on borrowed time. But by now I am getting a good idea of how to take care of myself. These parachute lads, especially those that I landed at Casablanca with over a year ago, have been marvelous. They devastate and destroy every German unit that they come in contact with. They are wonderful to be with, a rather exciting existence anyway.

Today is cold and rainy, it seems as though every day has been that way of late. It has been a much more uncomfortable campaign than the one in Sicily, much more hazardous too judging from the losses.

I hope to get more time to myself in the next few days, I'll drop you a line. I hope that you are having a good time in camp. I haven't had any mail for several weeks, some should come in any day now. I have some more money for you which I will send in a separate letter. Some German and some Russian. The german army [with its many Eastern Europeans] isn't all german by a long shot.[4] I have read this in the newspapers but never paid much attention to it.

I suppose that you get all of the news from the newspapers, there must be a great deal going on. We do not hear very much, occasionally a Stars and Stripes finds its way up.

Write me when you get the time. I will send the DSC to you for safekeeping when I get to a place where I can mail it.

Love to everyone,

Pappy

chapter seven

COMMAND OF THE 82ND
AIRBORNE DIVISION

Returning to their bivouac areas in England, the weary troopers were given short furloughs while fresh replacements were integrated into the Division's units. Though the 507th Parachute Infantry Regiment was released, the 508 would remain with the 82nd.[1] The 504, now refitted and rested after their return from Italy, rejoined their airborne comrades. Knowing that at any moment the 82nd Airborne Division could be called upon to mount an airborne operation, Gavin and the Division staff carefully followed the ongoing battle on the Continent.

★ ★ ★

July 13, 1944

Dear Babe,

Today I received your letter containing the snapshots taken at West Point, also the five-leaf clover and pictures. Thank you very much for them, I was particularly glad to get another snapshot of you, my you have grown. It must have been very nice to be at West Point again. I would like very much to go back for a visit. We will have to do that together.

I am enclosing some money that I accumulated during the past several days fighting before my return. I am sure that it will all make an interesting addition to your collection.

It is very nice to be back in the United Kingdom again. Last night I took a bath for the first time in five weeks. I have never worn my clothes that long before without taking them off. The bath was wonderful. Having spent the last combat period in and on the ground the bed did not seem comfortable. I had gotten so used to curling up in a hole or in a ditch that it was difficult to feel that the bed was safe. In about another night I will be right at home. It feels good to be back safe and sound.

I almost made it without a scratch. Almost, because the night before last I got scratched up a bit when a shell detonated overhead in a tree.

Some flying dirt and gravel scratched my forehead and face a bit and then I probably scratched my nose by burrowing deeper into the ground with it, but it all turned out well since that was the extent of my damage.

The old refrain "Old Soldiers Never Die" is beginning to have a new meaning. The saying is that old soldiers never die but replacements must be replaced and replaced. In about ten percent of the cases one either learns quickly or discontinues living and the remaining ninety percent is luck and you can't do much about it anyway.

By now you are at camp and I am glad that you are. Washington certainly is no place to spend a summer. I have your address and will write you there. I am sending this to [the apartment address on] Columbia Road because it contains the money. Have a good time and let me know how you are getting along.

Love to everyone,

Pappy

With the probability of future large-scale airborne operations on the Continent, an overarching command — First Allied Airborne Army (FAAA) — was activated to administer the airborne divisions, along with their aligned troop carrier wings, of the various Allied armies now fighting together in force. Commanded by an American (Lieutenant General Lewis H. Brereton) with a British deputy commander (Lieutenant General Frederick "Boy" Browning), the FAAA consisted of two corps — the American XVIII Airborne Corps and the British I Airborne Corps — and the U.S. IX Troop Carrier Command (supplemented with British troop carrier groups as needed).

Matthew Ridgway, now promoted and given command of XVIII Airborne Corps (comprised of the 17th, 82nd, and 101st Airborne Divisions), strongly recommended Gavin's promotion to commanding general of the 82nd.

* * *

July 21, 1944

Dear Babe,

I am glad that camp is going so well, your swimming has improved. Winning the 100-yard freestyle was quite a feat and one of which I am very proud. When is camp over?

Did I thank you for the snapshots at West Point; they were very, very nice to get. Everything looks the same and looks very nice. I hope that we can go up there again in the not too distant future. Maybe next year. Seems like a long war.

Provided you do not give it to [Walter] Winchell [a gossip columnist and radio broadcaster], I have some news for you. I have been recommended for promotion. It of course may or may not go through and it may take quite awhile but somewhere it is in the mill. This fighting and jumping and running around has been rather exciting and even in spots fun but it gets somewhat sobering in the next higher grade. I hope that I will be equal to the responsibilities that will be my lot. With you pulling for me, I figure I can't go wrong. We are all very busy.

I continue to receive very welcome letters from Rosie and Aunt Lil.

The other day I was in town [London] and I stopped by to inquire about your kilts. Next week, the Scotsman says. I have never seen such tailors. This one is evidently kept busy making kilts for the British army and they insist on priority, and I presume that if it is a case of going to war without, their insistence on priority is justified.

While I was in town a few doodle bombs [the V-1, a rocket-powered flying-bomb] dropped in. Very interesting but sort of devastating.

Hope that you continue to enjoy camp and do not be taken aback if Pappy is a Major General.

Love to everyone,

Pappy

★ ★ ★

July 31, 1944

Dear Barbara,

It has been about a week since I wrote you last. In the meantime I received a letter written from camp. I have not written to camp figuring that my letters would be of some interest to everyone in view of the big clambake that I was involved in in Normandy and so I had better just write to 2006 [Columbia Road]. Now your date of departure from camp is approaching rapidly and so I will continue to write to 2006, knowing that Mommie will send my letters to you.

We continue to be quite busy. I believe that I may have said something about a promotion in my last letter, that is something that might best be forgotten for a while anyway, lots of politics.

I just received Rosie's letter telling of the article in the paper re Chick [Charles] King [of VII Corps Headquarters staff, killed in action on June

22]. That was rather quick notification by the War Department. *[Mrs. King was a close friend of my mother's, and their daughter, Jan, a friend of mine. We were stationed together at West Point and Fort Benning. — BGF]*

It has proven to be extremely embarrassing to me to be aware of the death of a friend, like Art Gorham for example, and to be unable to answer the requests for information from their families until after the War Department has notified them. Yet it is the only system and it must be so. Frequently when people are obviously dead they are not, and when they are missing they are not, especially in the parachutists. We cannot have everyone whenever their fancy dictates writing and giving information that is probably erroneous to grief-stricken families. It could cause such needless pain. Consequently we must wait, perhaps for weeks or months, before we dare write. And some people never understand and think that we are indifferent and unconcerned when in fact the opposite is true.

I saw a great deal of Chick, had a lengthy conversation with him several days before he was clipped. People new to combat never learn apparently except by experience. They either do not believe what they are told or they don't pay attention. If they are lucky to live thru their apprenticeship from then on with a bit of luck they are OK. It is pretty difficult for a corps staff officer to get clipped by kraut small arms fire unless he is decidedly out of place in the scheme of things. They never believe that krauts are the mean vicious killers that they are. Well, our combat parachutists know and the krauts give them lots of elbow room.

There is a saying that the definition of a replacement is someone who replaces a replacement, which is well said. The old song about "Old Soldiers Never Die" has come to have a new significance, [Ed] Krause and [Ben] Vandervoort [commanders of the 505's Third and Second Battalions in Normandy] were talking to me about it the other day. I believe I told you that Ed Krause was clipped three times and Van broke his ankle in the landing. Neither of them were evacuated. Van commanded his battalion in heavy fighting wearing a walking cast. It is difficult for a young parachutist not to fight well with commanders like those two.

But enough of this. I'll write to Uncle George at his new address. I am glad that he is in a place more to his liking.

I have been hearing some good news from Rosie about your fine work in camp. I am sure you must be enjoying it.

Love to everyone,

Pappy

P.S. Please send some nuts.

★ ★ ★

August 2, 1944

Dear Butch,

Let's get something straight, I haven't been wounded. You embarrass me. There have been so many wounded who deserve sympathy and consideration but not Pappy. I just had my face scratched, just that, nothing more really. A day or two later I was talking to someone about it and I couldn't find the scratches. When it was over we talked and laughed about it the next morning. For some unexplainable reason when someone almost gets clipped but doesn't it is considered very humorous, especially if it's someone else. It is funny, I don't know why. Anyway, I wrote you shortly after it happened, mentioning it in the letter. Now Rosie and Aunt Lil inquire about my wounds. As I said, it's embarrassing.

I was so glad to get the report from Rosie on the state of affairs at camp and to know that you are enjoying it as much as you expected to.

I really have just time for a short note but I wanted you to know that my "wounds" are fine. The only time that I have ever had occasion to go near an aid station was in Sicily and at the moment I have never felt better.

Love to everyone,

Pappy

★ ★ ★

August 6, 1944

Dear Skipper,

Thought that you might like to have these photos for the family archives. I came across them the other day. The soldier with me is Wood who has accompanied me through Sicily and Italy, he is a gem. A fine cook, courageous to a fault and above all is a good soldier.

The other is of some friends that I am sure you will recognize. The occasion was the awarding of the DSC. In the other you will no doubt also recognize some of our friends. Col. [Robert] Wienecke is reading the citation.

It must seem egotistical of me to insist on sending so many pictures of myself but I thought that they would be of interest, especially in later years when you are older. They are taken by various agencies, news and otherwise, and usually I get a copy.

I hope that camp is going well, I am sure that it must be. We are very busy, at the moment perhaps busier than we have been since Casablanca. But much better to be busy than idle.

Remember me to everyone and love to the family. I wrote to Uncle George the other day.

Love,

Pappy

With Ridgway's recommendation accepted, Gavin was eager to take command and place his own mark on the 82nd, confident that he could "give the Division life blood and warmth and give it a personality."[2] Just sixteen months earlier, James Maurice Gavin had left for war as a colonel commanding a parachute infantry regiment — now, at the young age of thirty-seven, he was the commanding general of America's first airborne division.

★ ★ ★

August 13, 1944

Dear Babe,

This is Sunday morning and no different than any other day, a bit colder perhaps. It promises to be a busy day, like most of them really.

I have a grand staff, many of them you probably know. Al Ireland G-1, Walter Winton G-2, Jack Norton G-3, Albert Marin G-4. You probably do not know Marin, he started out in Rube Tucker's clan [504]. They are a fine bunch, very young for a division staff, extremely young by most peacetime standards but just what I need for this business. They are very bright, keen, good parachutists and know this airborne business like no one else in this world.

Our work continues to mount up but should clarify a bit after we get an opportunity to settle down, that is, if we get the opportunity. It certainly has been a full year.

By now you probably will be returning from camp. I do hope that you enjoyed it this year and that you profited by your weeks there. It must have been very nice.

Did you ever get the foreign money that I had sent you? There was quite a bit of odd types of rubles, marks, and kronins taken from our super-aryan friends. Amazing the composition of the local version of the Wehrmacht, a miasmic mass of discontented humanity. It is nice the way the lads are pushing them about now, rather nice for a change. It does, however, keep us busier than ever and every new headline is reflected in newer and bigger plans.

Where and when are you going to school, probably the same place?

Love to everyone,

Pappy

★ ★ ★

August 16, 1944

Dear Butch,

Today I received your letter telling me of Mommie's visit to camp. It is so nice that she could get to see you. Someday I would like to see the camp also.

In the meantime I find myself quite busy. Gen. Ridgway left [to assume command of XVIII Airborne Corps] this morning in the midst of a very nice ceremony. I find myself in an odd, and I really do not believe very enviable, spot. Having lost considerable staff, practically all of the staff [experienced in running the Division], and taking over a unit that has established itself as second to none in our service or any other for that matter, I find myself walking in and taking over. At least one of the old staff told me that he did not think that I could do as well as the old commanding general. On the other hand, the 505 feels that it made this organization. Well, there will be lots of "tsk-tsking" before we are through.

I have a thousand ideas and I am going to carry them through, in combat and out, with zeal and determination come what may. Either this Division will rise to heights of combat attainment unprecedented in our service or rush to oblivion, and in either case, I will be with it all of the way. To those of us who have had a lasting and firm faith in the efficacy of airborne troops as a means of waging war, there is of course no doubt about the future of this or any other parachute division, nor is there any doubt or concern really with what value posterity will place on what we do now. We are supremely confident of ourselves. I suppose we would not be in the hazardous business we are in if we, in the slightest degree, lacked this confidence.

Since the day I entered this airborne service there has never been a dull moment. Always a new challenge, always a new horizon. That is the way it should be. Despite the alleged hazards and apparent uncertainties of it as a way of service, we love it. With this abiding confidence in our professional creed and a determination to excel in combat unmatched in any army anywhere, all airborne soldiers look to the future, certain that they have a rendezvous with greatness.

Please let me know when school starts, what your plans are, etc. Did you ever get the money that I sent from Normandy?

Love to everyone,

Pappy

P.S. Thanks very much for the nuts, they just arrived.

Pappy

* * *

August 20, 1944

Dear Babe,

We are having a nice day today, sunshine for a change. The news is good too. My guardian angel may as well be in Garfinckle's bargain basement as around here for all of the need I have for her. It must be a wonderful big rat race that they are having on the Continent. I don't see why I have to miss it, it is very upsetting.

Now that Patton is again in the good graces of the public, I suppose that everything will be forgiven. [Patton had slapped a soldier suffering from combat fatigue in Sicily.] I have always liked him since D + 2 in Sicily when I came into his Command Post at Gela after a very trying two days and three nights. He took a big flask out of his hip pocket and gave me a drink. The situation seeming to call for something more than just "thank you," I made a speech about being honored to drink from the flask of such a fine soldier. Not to be outdone, he came right back with a much better one. I later came to know him rather well and learned to regard his combat effectiveness with great respect.

Now in retrospect the speeches seem melodramatic and perhaps out of place but at the time they were quite proper and in order. People seem to get stirred up emotionally in combat and sometimes do things that at a later time seem odd.

Well soon you will be back to Washington and back to books. You must be growing, I'll hardly know you. And incidentally, I believe I'm getting older in appearance too, you will hardly know Pappy when he staggers in on his walking cane. Gosh, I hope it isn't that long.

Love to everyone,

Pappy

P.S. The nuts were greatly enjoyed.

★ ★ ★

August 23, 1944

Dear Babe,

It seems fitting to me that I write you at least once on the official stationery of the Division since it isn't every day that one has a division commander in the family. It may look well in the family archives. It is most
interesting and at times trying enough to keep me rather busy. I hope
someday that you will be able to see the Division together. They are a
rugged, hearty lot, and superb in combat.

Love to everyone,

Pappy

*The First Allied Airborne Army remained on constant alert as the Allied war
machine pushed Hitler's armies through France and Belgium toward the German border. Numerous airborne missions in support of the Allied advance were
quickly planned and just as quickly cancelled when the rapid advance either
overran the selected drop zones or diverted the required aircraft to ferry supplies
to the front lines.*

★ ★ ★

September 1, 1944

Dear Babe,

Here it is September, time is really moving. I am enclosing some of the
invasion currency. I sent some just before the Normandy takeoff but you
have never acknowledged receiving it. I also sent you some German and
Russian money from Normandy, did you ever get it?

I want to remind you that all of my insurance policies are in good order,
including yours with Lincoln National Life and Mommie's with Travelers
of Atlanta. Also that I am paid up several months ahead with the Book-of-
the-Month Club and have several magazine subscriptions, TIME (thanks
to you and Santa Claus), NEW YORKER, and READERS DIGEST. My
income tax is way behind but the less said about that the better. Circumstances have made it impossible under these conditions to obtain the
proper forms, let alone fill them out. Let's hope that all is forgiven by
Uncle Sam when the shooting stops, if it ever does.

It seems to me this sort of thing just goes on and on, a never-ending
affair. I really do not mean that I need rotating but a look at things back
in the States just to be sure that it's all still there would help. Well, the job

is to be done and we have the lads who can do it. You will hear more and more of the 82nd before this affair is over, they are a grand crowd, superb in combat. Do not worry if you do not hear from me for a while, no matter what happens, I will probably be so carried along by the excitement and exaltation of the moment that in retrospect it will seem most pleasant, the job is to be done.

Love to everyone,

Pappy

★ ★ ★

September 5, 1944

Dear Beautiful,

I am afraid that my cautions re the insurance policies, etc. were a bit amiss. I have never seen such weather as we have had for the past few days. History is being made, time marches on, and we wallow in the mud. I don't know why I always have to miss the best clambakes.

I am very proud of your record in camp. An outstanding young lady. By now you must be home which will seem rather confining at first.

I had Dr. [Charles] Waring [from Airborne Command's research and development section] in to dinner with my staff several days ago upon his return from America. He brought some grand pictures of you which I was very pleased to get.

Things are going very well over here as you no doubt know from the newspapers. The kraut has been taking a good kicking around for a change.

Love to everyone,

Pappy

★ ★ ★

September 12, 1944

Dear Butch,

Received the pictures from camp today and enjoyed them very much. Gives me a much better idea of what it was like. Very nice looking and a nice appearing group of girls.

I am enclosing some belgas [Belgian franc notes] which you may like to add to your collection. I do not know what could have happened to the invasion money. It was mailed just before the takeoff. I have some about somewhere that I carried all through Normandy that I will send along as soon as I find it.

We are kept rather busy, so far this week I have been averaging about three or four hours sleep a night and the staff at times much less. Jack Norton is doing a nice job for me as G-3.

For some time now the filling that I had in a front tooth has been rather loose. Things have been moving too fast to take time out to have it cemented in and today I forgot how loose it was and swallowed it. So far no ill effects.

Summer here has been disappointing, little or no sunshine. I believe that I told you that they do not have corn on the cob, no corn will grow because of the lack of sun. That is one thing that we will have to wait until we get back to the States for. The days are getting wetter than usual and a bit colder. Another winter at war will seem like a long one.

I hope that all goes well in school. Let me know what your courses are and how things are going. I am still in the United Kingdom so feel very much as though the war is going off and leaving me. Not even buzz bombs [V-1s] anymore. They are even threatening to lift the blackout very soon. In a way, I rather wish that they wouldn't until the war was over for us.

Love to everyone,

Pappy

Rapidly driving east toward Germany along a broad front, the Allied armies were competing for the necessary stores of ammunition, fuel, and rations. If the broad advance continued, logistically depleting the Allied armies, a quick end to the war might not be realized. As a solution, British General Bernard Montgomery proposed concentrating the broad advance into one narrow thrust to be executed by the British Second Army crossing into Holland at the Belgian border in the south and traveling north to outflank Germany's border defenses (the Siegfried Line). Swinging past the Siegfried Line, Second Army would turn east and then drive south into the center of Germany's vital war industry region — starving Hitler's armies of their needed matériel and thereby shortening the war. To secure the crossings over Holland's numerous canals and rivers along the route in advance of the British armor and its supporting infantry, Montgomery further proposed that elements of the recently activated First Allied Airborne Army be the tip of the thrust, clearing the way.

chapter eight

OPERATION MARKET-
GARDEN — HOLLAND

Montgomery's proposition became a plan — code-named Operation MARKET-GARDEN. Advancing northward from the Belgian–Dutch border, the British Second Army would drive for the Lower Rhine at Arnhem where elements of the British I Airborne Corps were to secure a bridgehead — an assignment that would come to be known as "a bridge too far." Crossing the river, Second Army would then swing eastward above the Siegfried Line and attack down into the Ruhr, the seat of Germany's war industry. Expecting to reach Arnhem within forty-eight hours after its jump-off, Second Army would have to travel over sixty miles along a raised narrow road, thereby exposed to enemy attack, and would utilize a succession of river and canal crossings seized by the paratroopers and glider troops of the 82nd and 101st Airborne Divisions — beginning with the 101st just north of the Belgian border.

To the south of Arnhem and north of the area assigned to the 101st, the 82nd's objectives were to seize the rail and road bridges over the Waal River at Nijmegen, at least one of the smaller bridges over the Maas-Waal Canal, and the bridge over the Maas River near the small town of Grave. The Division also had to seize and hold the high ground within the objective area.

Though the bulk of the airborne forces were coming from Ridgway's American XVIII Airborne Corps, command of MARKET (the airborne phase of the operation) went to the commanding general of the British I Airborne Corps, who was also FAAA's deputy commander — General Frederick "Boy" Browning.

Operation MARKET-GARDEN was a gamble — the airborne troops would have to hold on behind enemy lines, without armor and without resupply, until linkup could be made with Second Army. Gavin quickly readied the Division for its difficult assignment. D-Day had been set for September 17; however, due to restrictions imposed by the troop carrier command and a shortage of allocated aircraft, the drops and glider landings would have to be spread over several days.

Responsible for an area with a perimeter that extended beyond twenty-five miles, Gavin worried that his forces would be stretched too thin. It looked "very rough," and if they got through it, Gavin and the Division would be "very lucky."[1]

On September 15, the troopers were moved to their assigned airfields and confined. As in the past, they readied their equipment and received final briefings. It would be the Division's fourth combat jump and the first executed in daylight — Gavin decided to jump with his "boys" of the 505.

   ★ ★ ★

September 16, 1944

Dear Barbara,

I don't believe that I have reminded you of the subscriptions, etc. lately. It's about time. We continue to be very busy.

It is getting quite cold, seems like fall except that it isn't exactly like it here because the change is not so marked. It rains all of the time generally. If I go into another operation, which of course I will because that is why we are in the war, I expect to wear all of the woolen underwear that I can get on underneath my jumpsuit. I may come down a bit speedily but I will be warm. I have never thought well of fighting in a cold climate but soldiers can't be choosers. Looks like the krauts are taking a good kicking around these days.

Get off to a good start in school and let me know how you are getting along. And don't worry about what is happening to me. No matter how things turn out, we are all doing a very necessary chore in our own way. A bit hazardous it may seem at times, and by now I must admit it is, but it is a completely satisfying way. One experiences the full satisfaction of engaging those people at close quarters and gaining a decision in his own backyard.

This is an odd war, as a general I am probably getting to be a most proficient private paratrooper and small-unit leader but the time comes to be a general too and run the works. As I say, it is an odd war. Take good care of yourself.

Love to everyone,

Pappy

Hiding his worry over their tough assignment, Gavin spoke to the men assembled at the airfields as he had always done. Listening, the 505's regimental surgeon turned to one of the chaplains and said, "I hope he doesn't ask us to jump without parachutes, because I'm sure no man would refuse to go."[2]

Jumping into Holland with unprecedented accuracy and assembly in the early afternoon of September 17, Gavin's paratroopers quickly captured the bridge over the Maas River at Grave, as well as one of the smaller canal bridges. Because the Germans were caught by surprise, initial enemy resistance was minimal. However, the Germans soon recovered and reacted quickly and decisively throughout the length of the MARKET-GARDEN corridor. Allied intelligence had either failed to discover or had discounted the enemy's armor and troop strength in the area. Control of the high ground in the Division's sector was not easily gained or held; Gavin's worries about being stretched too thin were not unfounded, especially since inclement weather in England would delay the takeoff (planned for D + 2) of the Division's glider infantry regiment until D + 6.

In the battle for the bridges at Nijmegen over the Waal River, Gavin's paratroopers faced a skilled and determined enemy. After a daring and costly simultaneous assault against both ends, the bridges were under Division control by late afternoon, September 20. Shortly before the assault launched, Gavin received word that the Germans had begun strong counterattacks at one of the critical canal bridges near Mook and also against the high ground near Beek. To know where, and if, he should commit the Division reserves, he had to evaluate the strength of the German counterattacks firsthand. Gavin quickly went first to Mook and then to Beek, where his leadership helped to repel the enemy counterattacks and regain control. For his actions, he would receive the Silver Star.[3]

With the crossings over the Waal River secured, Second Army's armor, having reached Nijmegen, could now continue north to Arnhem where the British airborne had been valiantly fighting for more than seventy-two hours—cut off behind enemy lines for too long. However, in accordance with their doctrine of not moving tanks at night along an uncontrolled road, the British decided to wait until the next morning's light. As a result, the Germans made good use of the time after their rout to reorganize in strength—the way to Arnhem was now blocked.

Unfortunately, the attempt to secure a bridgehead at Arnhem had failed, and the troopers there were awaiting rescue—Montgomery's plan had indeed included "a bridge too far."[4] Only about 20 percent of the forces at Arnhem were able to safely make their way to friendly lines. Though the 82nd and 101st Airborne Divisions accomplished all of their assigned missions, MARKET-GARDEN was termed an operational failure.

Once again, the 82nd was not withdrawn. Under the control of the British Second Army, the Division was deployed in a defensive posture along the Nijmegen salient, where it would remain for almost two months.

★ ★ ★

September 25, 1944

Dear Butch,

I understand that mail will get through today so I want to get this off. A week ago today we landed, the softest yet for me but also the hottest. But we really cleaned the place out and all is going very well. The boys are doing a grand job.

Holland is a grand country. The people are especially nice. The finest group of people that I have seen. Very clean and tidy and most kind to us. Things are going very well, most interesting and rather exciting.

I hope that your school got off to a good start.

Love to everyone,

Pappy

★ ★ ★

[Undated]

Dear Butch,

I thought that you would like this [Wehrmacht letterhead]. We captured a lot of it in a German headquarters the other day. I am also enclosing some Dutch money. I jumped with it and have since had no use for it. I am sure that it would go well in your collection.

Congratulations on the two firsts and a second at Gibson Island. *[A private club on the Chesapeake Bay, between Baltimore and Washington, where Uncle George was a member. — BGF]* It seems hard to believe that the little girl whom I would not allow to swim to the raft at Delafield unescorted is now winning swimming meets.

I am again most fortunate. Despite lots of flak and nasty krauts I am still very much in circulation but I rather feel that I know what a clay pigeon feels like now. It has been very exciting and rather hard fighting. The lads are doing beautifully. I am afraid that you'll hear little of me through the newspapers since I have not been "released" by the War Department. There really are some stories here to tell but I guess everyone thinks the same thing.

The Dutch are a wonderful people most deserving of everything that fortune can bring them. They hate the krauts, me too.

Hope this goes thru OK.

Love to everyone,

Pappy

★ ★ ★

October 4, 1944

Dear Babe,

A typewriter at last. I much prefer to type my letters to you and I would imagine that to you they are much more legible. We captured a number of german typewriters but they have keys with an odd script. In Italy the typewriters lacked some letters, this too was equally as inconvenient. We have learned by experience that typewriters are most essential in rendering casualty reports, supply requisitions, etc. as soon as ground troop contacts are made, and in order to do this we must capture enemy typewriters. They are high on the list, possibly next to blankets and mess gear.

This is quite a place. The Dutch are very nice people and have very clean tidy homes. They are sincere and courageous in their desire for freedom from the germans. They have without exception been very kind to us. The closer to the border they are, the more intensely anti-german they are.

The germans in their homeland are rather quiet and perhaps a bit sullen.[5] It is an odd feeling to sense the feeling of hostility after the enthusiasm of Sicily, Italy, and Normandy.

I am not looking forward to the winter war we have ahead of us. Even now it is uncomfortably cold most of the time. I wear everything that I can get on but I feel as though I will never be warm again. It is not the passing temperature as much as the continuous exposure to it. Well I imagine that we will all get used to it after a bit. The drop was rather exciting, a bit of flak and stuff, I drew my knees up under my chin. I was very lucky I guess. Made a fine landing, flat on my back. I was carrying so much stuff I had a hard time staggering to my feet. *[Years later, an x-ray revealed that he had actually fractured his back on the landing. — BGF]* Every time I take something additional that I am sure that I am going to need. By now, I look like a man leaving a pre-Xmas sale at Woodward-Lothrops [department store].

Everything is going fine, the boys are doing a wonderful job. I have been trying to spellbind a few newspapermen the past few days. You may run across some of the stuff. I believe, however, that I have not yet been "released." By the way, Mr. Walton of Time has a short article on our affair in Normandy in a new book that I would like to get my hands on. Pick it up for me if you can and save it. Walton is a very fine chap, he was in my Command Post a day or so ago, he is very intelligent and most interesting.

Love to everyone,

Pappy

Understandably, as head of the American XVIII Airborne Corps, General Ridgway did not like having his divisions pulled out of his control and put under the command of the British for the Corps's first assignment. Expecting them to revert to his command shortly after the operation launched, Ridgway arrived at the front (after an arduous and perilous journey up the corridor) on September 20—the most hectic day for Gavin and the 82nd. Entering the Division's command post just as Gavin was hurriedly leaving to evaluate the German counterattacks at Mook and Beek, the exhausted and frustrated corps commander felt ignored when Gavin did not stop to brief him. As a reprimand, Ridgway insisted on a written explanation for the seemingly flagrant breach of military courtesy toward a superior officer. Feeling that he could not "continue to serve in a strained critical atmosphere," Gavin responded, further asking to be "relieved of command of the [82nd] and assignment to [the] corps, the XVIII."[6]

★ ★ ★

October 7, 1944

Dear Barbara,

Just a note to let you know that three weeks after our arrival all still goes well in the Lowlands.

There is a matter that deserves some mentioning since it may come to you through the press or in a roundabout way and under circumstances difficult to understand. This operation, as an airborne operation, is well on the way to being wound up. We have contributed our bit, and if I may say, in an excellent manner. Having trained and led these units in this affair, the only one of its kind or magnitude in the history of the world, it would appear as though everything were beer and skittles and everyone was completely happy. Unfortunately this is not the case. In commands at this level involving several nationalities, all of the service's different nationalities, and many complex ambitious personalities, there are certain to be present many sources of friction. They occasionally manifest themselves to the discomfiture to some and to the furtherance of others. There is little that censorship will permit me to say. I have however this date requested my relief from command of this unit, involving as it probably would a reduction in grade.

The point has arrived when I must either have the complete full and sympathetic backing of some people or step out of the picture. In the interests of our cause, I am quite willing to do the latter if necessary. There is an even chance that my request will be granted. If it is, I wanted you to understand that my motives are impersonal and sincere. It is difficult to fight a war and politics too. This should be kept strictly in the family since the probability is that nothing will ever come of it. But if it did, I wanted you to understand that I have initiated my own request for reassignment.

The boys are doing remarkably well. They are certainly veterans now. Those who have been with me through Sicily, Italy, Normandy and here, and there are quite a number, are pretty rough customers for the krauts to deal with. Many however still fall by the wayside. This is the sad part and yet it seems unavoidable. If there must be fighting there must be killing, and if there must be killing there must be many young men cut down at the start of a promising life. It really shouldn't be. There should be no fighting, no wars. Above all else this is what we hope we are fighting for now.

Love,

Pappy

Regretting his hasty reprimand, Ridgway ignored Gavin's request to be relieved. With the Division put under control of British General Brian Horrocks's XXX Corps on October 8, Generals Gavin and Ridgway would have the opportunity to spend more time apart, perhaps allowing cooler heads to prevail.

★ ★ ★

October 15, 1944

Dear Babe,

Well the crisis in my political troubles is past and my last letter probably would be best forgotten. I shouldn't have mentioned it, and I wouldn't have except for the possibility of some misunderstanding if it hit the headlines.

An airborne division is a weapon of such international scope, and this one in particular is capable of dealing such a devastating blow, that it potentially can quickly become the plaything of internationalists. The command of it at times implies a great deal more than fighting, although that is certainly a first requirement. If it couldn't fight with imagination, daring, and effectiveness, no one would want it. If it can, everyone wants it. It's a great war. Very fascinating in some respects and it sometimes gets dangerous. I have been very lucky so far and it is difficult to predict how long this sort of thing can go on but while it lasts it's quite an education. I'm enjoying it.

Of the stouthearted gang that left Oujda with me to jump into Sicily there are few left. But those who have gone out the door for the last time with us have given this Division a combat determination and esprit that knows no obstacles and certainly finds no equal in the Wehrmacht. They have done a superb job here.

The king [George VI] stopped by the other day, as you probably know we are closely tied up with the British. He was very nice to talk to and most complimentary regarding our American paratroops. You may have heard of his visit, a number of newspapermen were present. However, the British press carefully handles our publicity in connection with our present association with them. Quite a war.

Hope that you are enjoying school.

Love to everyone,

Pappy

★ ★ ★

October 16, 1944

Dear Butch,

I just remembered today that Aunt Lil told me about your sinus trouble some time ago. I should have warned you that under rather identical circumstances in 1928 I had some sinus trouble also. I had been in a summer camp instructing in swimming. This necessitated me being in the water a great deal each day. At the end of the summer I had a touch of sinus that went away as soon as I stopped swimming so much. I have not had any difficulties since.

Things are going along as well as could be expected. Today Gen. [Miles] Dempsey [commander of the British Second Army] sent me a British caravan. Quite a job. It is a huge trailer complete with a desk, bed, running water, electric lights, etc. I am to use it as long as I am fighting on the Continent. Caravans are a British institution developed during the desert battles of the Eighth Army. Since I am now working with his army he thought it fitting that I have one. Evidently I am the only general without one. Well it was a rather embarrassing situation. As a parachutist I wouldn't be caught dead in one when a battle is going on or any other time for that matter. Certainly I'd be mortified if my boys knew that I had one. On the other hand I couldn't refuse to accept it. I finally took it and have it hid near my Command Post. No one is going to use it and I hope that it all works out all right.

At the moment, I have Field Marshal [Bernard] Montgomery for one of my current superiors also. I have talked to him several times and he is a grand person. Very sharp and quite nice.

You should soon be picking up some news of our whereabouts. I have talked to a lot of newspaper people lately; today, Mrs. Ernest Hemingway [Martha Gellhorn] of Colliers and Mr. [Mark] Watson of the Baltimore Sun. If they are permitted to publish half of the stuff I tell them, there should be some tall tales in the American press.[7] Most of these people are a pleasure to meet and talk to. There are so few people who can talk about anything but the war and in this sector there are mostly British about. They had a pretty tight rein on the publicity in this affair so I am not sure what the U.S. press got to read. Probably about the Arnhem lads.[8]

This war has lately taken a most unfortunate turn. It is getting so that an old soldier with the most discerning and discriminating ear gets caught flat-footed time and again. There was a time when after some service in combat, and a minimum amount of attention to sounds created by the enemy, a soldier never had to waste a second or ounce of energy making a mistaken dive for cover. When novices fell on their faces in their anxiety to find protection near good old mother earth, the experienced old soldier could with well-deserved disdain pay no attention to their antics, knowing full well exactly how close the shell was going to land. Probably even know the caliber and german arms factory in which it was made. As the war went along, however, this unerring judgment of his came in for trouble because the krauts began using very high-muzzle-velocity shells, like 88s, that seemed to get there before their whistle. Then they began using "screaming meemies" that announced their coming in no uncertain manner long before. Rather nerve-wracking and devastating upon impact but at least one knew that they were coming.

The "screaming meemie" was our old friend the Nebelwerfer [a German weapon firing a volley of six rockets]. Now the Nebelwerfer makes an odd "furniture moving" sound that is followed by a dead silence for about ten seconds. Then a terrific blast that lays everything low. Combined with the new and increasingly intriguing sound effects are those of the doodle-bugs, pickaback demolition loaded planes, jet planes, screwy types of mortars, etc. As I said, a self-respecting old soldier never knows anymore whether to continue acting like a recruit and dive for cover at every sound or just try to outguess fate and probably get winged in a dignified manner befitting his service. It's a hard war. But enough of this, I must get back to work.

Love to everyone,

Pappy

★ ★ ★

October 21, 1944

Dear Babe,

Well this is a fine state of affairs, a Major General. I feel as though my years must be slipping up on me. I just received a telegram this evening and some of the lads came in to help pin the extra stars on.

I am enclosing a snapshot herewith, my Corps Commander [General Brian Horrocks] sent it over to me today and I thought that you might like to have it. The British officer on the left is my Corps Commander, a fine man and a good soldier. I am just back of the King, immediately back of me is a lineup of my commanders. Most of them you know, a wonderful group. Starting on the left: Col. [Andy] March of the [Division] Field Artillery, [Roy] Lindquist of the 508, [Rube] Tucker of the 504, [Bill] Ekman of the 505, and [Chuck] Billingslea of the 325.[9] There are no finer regimental commanders in the Army, rough, tough, and all of them good paratroopers and ready for anything. I am most fortunate that they have all lived through this far.

It looks like a rough winter, Holland is getting a bit cold and it seems to stay eternally damp or it is raining.

Today's paper, The Stars and Stripes, carried the news of the invasion of the Philippines. It is nice that they are getting back there this soon but I am disappointed that we are not along. We had been looking forward to jumping in the rice paddies.

But these krauts seem to get tougher every day. The last day or so they have been shooting some very good propaganda leaflets at us. They figure that we are getting tired of the war and that we might be induced to surrender. Rather amusing, they think that we are about fed up with the war and are ready to surrender, or at least entertain a suggestion that we do surrender and the people back home figure that the war is about over and the battles are all won. Some very clever propaganda, it's a great war. The only thing that we can't figure out is why the krauts thought that paratroopers would surrender, sometimes they are awfully dumb that way.

Hope that school is going well.

Love to everyone,

Pappy

★ ★ ★

October 30, 1944

Dear Barbara,

Your cablegram [with congratulations on the promotion] came through yesterday and was quite a surprise, very nice to get.

Would you ask Mommie to get me a copy of the latest volume of "Lee's Lieutenants" by Douglas Southall Freeman, I believe that it is Vol. III and has just been published. It may be difficult to obtain. I'll send a check along when I can get to my checkbook if you will let me know the cost.

We are kept busy as usual. Temperature down to 28 degrees this morning. I never thought that from the siroccos of Africa we would move to the freezing mud of the Lowlands, which just goes to prove that you cannot tell about the Army.

I have slept on the ground every night and am getting to the point where I don't believe that I could sleep in a bed. My hole is about three feet away, I don't like to get into it unless I have to, so far I have had the inclination on a number of occasions but have compromised by flattening out a bit more and staying in my sleeping bag. I had a good sleeping bag that I bought in Portland that I kept all of the way to Normandy. It landed after me in a glider in Normandy. I had it stowed away in my jeep with some uniforms and things. About the time the glider touched down it was hit by kraut artillery and the whole darn thing went up in flames. Weber, my driver since Alabama, beat his way through the sides of the glider and came through nicely. I believe it made him a bit nervous after that though, finally had to get a new driver.

Anyway, I got one of those little GI jobs for Holland, it's like sleeping in a sock. Sometime after arriving by parachute (I believe the censor likes it this way), I was watching the landing of some of our gliders when in the sky appeared two red canopies carrying bundles. They had no reason for being there, I knew since I was responsible for everything that was coming in. Wood, who has been striking for me through Sicily, Italy, Normandy and here thought that it deserved looking into. Forthwith, he took off cross country. One of the bundles had in it what appeared to be a British-type sleeping bag so he promptly captured it for me. So that is what I have now. It must be for a little fellow though because it ends up somewhere between my navel and my chin. The remainder of me I cover with a blanket that usually stays on, for a few hours anyway.

I have not had a cold since leaving the States so although the conditions may appear to be rather rugged for living, they must be healthful. We must be getting used to the cold, at first we thought it was very uncomfortable, now no one seems to say much about it.

Of late, we have had a number of visitors from higher headquarters, some not more than a week away from Washington. Of course we always ply them with questions about conditions back home and ask them what makes the people think that the war is about over, over here, etc. They always seem to think that it is quite cold and uncomfortable and seem anxious to move rearward after a quick look around. An airborne unit is a bad one for visitors since all of us spend about as much time in the front lines as in the Command Posts and expect the visitors to share our curiosity for what goes on up there. But it is nice to have visitors. We ask them many more questions than they ask us. Mostly they like to have their pictures taken in a foxhole looking out towards the front, then they go home.

I am having some very interesting and most educational experiences. Being in Holland, I believe that everyone knows that we are in the British army so the censor will not object to me telling you this. Our rations are entirely British, including the rum ration, NAAFI [Navy, Army, and Air Force Institute] ration, etc. Too much tea and no coffee which our boys miss very much. I have managed to fly some over from the United Kingdom though. Everything, such as staff procedure, orders, etc., must be learned over again and so we are having a rather educational time to say the least. Very interesting and I am enjoying it very much. I have lots to learn.

The boys are doing a wonderful job although we continue to lose some of the best.

Happy Birthday, Babe! I will have to owe you a birthday present until I get somewhere where I can do something about it. Maybe Paris, hmmm.

Love to everyone,

Pappy

★ ★ ★

November 9, 1944

Dear Santa Clauses,

It is difficult to imagine, and more difficult to describe, what a pleasant surprise it is to receive packages from Santa Claus in the front line in early November. They were most welcome. Well-prepared with the descriptions of the fruitcake packages, I did not open them yet but I did open the others. The contents were most welcome. I cannot imagine them being more welcome at any other time, including Xmas. I particularly needed the tie. Thank everyone very much for having Santa Claus come so very early, their receipt at this time had all of the pleasantries of the Yuletide season as well as the surprise of a birthday party.

We are all getting alone fine. My fellow associate in the other outfit, Max Taylor [101st Airborne Division commander], was clipped a bit yesterday, shrapnel in the leg, should be out OK in ten days. I have certainly been lucky. I was swanning about the front a day or so ago with Matt [Ridgway]. We stopped to ask a few questions. When we started out again, a shell burst a few yards ahead of us, hitting no one. We decided that we were lucky to have stopped. We started to backtrack when one burst again just ahead of us. Looked like Jerry had the finger on us. But we all slipped out OK. Keeps you on your toes sort of, very interesting. I am getting to where I know his artillery habits and patterns as well as he does, that plus the luck of the Irish keeps us in circulation.

Had our first good snow yesterday, mixed with a bit of sleet and rain. You would think that we would be extremely uncomfortable but actually we are not. We have all become quite accustomed to the cold and while it may be harmful to us in the long run, right now we just take it for granted. We have all noticed that the visitors from the rear shiver and complain of the cold so I guess it is cold, and it is snowing, but except for icy wet feet all goes well with us.

Everyone was interested in the outcome of the [presidential] election and rather gratified that Mr. Dewey turned in such a good show. Change in the governmental head is an essential ingredient in our type of democracy, and I guess we all like to feel that no one man is indispensable and can perpetuate himself in office. Mr. Roosevelt can probably do more for us in the post-war world than any citizen we have so it is perhaps as well that his hand will be at the helm for a while longer. The soldier voting was a difficult problem. It is fortunate that the election was not a close one.[10]

Love to everyone and thank them for being such early Santa Clauses,

Pappy

Relieved by elements of the Canadian Army, the 82nd was released from the Nijmegen salient on November 11. A large portion of Holland would remain occupied and oppressed by the Germans until spring; however, the enemy never retook the areas that had been liberated by the two American airborne divisions during Operation MARKET-GARDEN. Returning to the control of XVIII Airborne Corps, now headquartered in France, the troopers of the 82nd were billeted at old military barracks in the small French towns of Suippes and Sissonne.

★ ★ ★

November 14, 1944

Somewhere in France

Dear Babe,

That "somewhere in France" is what the censor says I may now say just in case you didn't notice it. It is nice for a change to be away from the immediate range of the krauts. I now have a bed, a room with electric lights, and a bath. The bath is a rather primitive French affair. I guess from what I hear that all French baths are primitive but it is nice to have. The hot water is furnished by a coil in which a fire is built. The water must be kept running thru the coils or they will blow up, consequently all during the bath hot water runs into one end of the tub. In order therefore to keep from being boiled alive, it is necessary to keep cold water running into the tub at the same time. That means that the bath must be started when the water is quite low in the tub and must be finished in a rush or the tub will flow over.

Holland was lovely. Clean, nice homes, and the people all sturdy characters. Hard-working, well-behaved, and any of them apparently ready to die if necessary for that liberty from the german that they were striving for and we were trying to bring them. All in all, a pretty good people.

I hope that you had a nice birthday. I tried to arrange a cablegram and I hope that it got through. I had it flown out of Holland to the United Kingdom and there it was sent. I haven't had a letter for some time, probably been traveling around too much. It is nice to get under a roof again.

Love to everyone,

Pappy

★ *chapter nine* ★

THE BATTLE OF THE

BULGE — BELGIUM

Unable to outflank the Siegfried Line in northern Holland, the Allies elsewhere continued their drive toward Germany, all the while incurring heavy losses in fighting a Wehrmacht ordered by its Führer not to give an inch. Without refitting the depleted forces, further Allied advances along the entire front would be difficult, especially with the onset of harsh winter conditions. Believing that the German military was no longer capable of mounting any significant counteroffensive and would continue in a defensive posture only, the U.S. Army allowed part of its force to become static along a portion of the front — the dense forest of the Ardennes in southeastern Belgium. During the expected winter stalemate, this static element would be able to recoup, refit, and absorb new divisions, while to its north and south the push against the German defense would continue as weather and logistics allowed. The winter weather would also prohibit any further airborne operations.

Hitler, however, had other plans — a daring and desperate counteroffensive that would strike westward through the Ardennes to capture Allied fuel reserves. Hitler believed that with enough fuel, German armor could drive across the Meuse River to recapture the port of Antwerp in Belgium and split the Anglo-American forces in the process. He also believed that a successful surprise attack would then lead to a disintegration of the Allied coalition in the west, allowing him to negotiate a separate peace, after which Germany could divert all its resources to defeating the Russians. In France, unaware of what Hitler had in store, Gavin anticipated having at least three months to refit the Division and absorb replacements.

★ ★ ★

November 19, 1944

Dear Butch,

It was a year ago today that I landed by plane in England from Africa. I didn't think at that time that I would be sitting in France slugging it out a year from then. My aide then, he was my first aide and a very nice boy, was lost in Normandy. An odd thing, when he was wounded he was very proud of his wound, feeling I suppose that he had done his full share for the common cause. He was shot in the chest and it looked bad. He talked to me about it. We looked it over and he thought that he was very lucky that it hadn't hit his heart. A few hours later shock set in and he died. It was all very sad. I felt very bad about it.

The next aide, Capt. Olson, recovered from his Normandy wound and is now back on the job. He has since been promoted and is doing a grand job. I have a junior aide now, Lt. [Rufus] Broadaway from Mississippi. He is a very good young officer and so far has come through in fine shape.

It is getting much colder now as I am sure it must be in the States. We are busy getting reorganized a bit. There is an awful lot to do. I have some more people attached to me now so the command stretches over a lot of territory. There seem to be a thousand things like fuel, gasoline, food, clothing, electricity, water, civil relations, that all need attention for 24 hours a day.

The winter is going to be a hard one for lots of people besides the germans. I always felt very sorry for the Dutch people, the way their homes were destroyed and their personal property lost. It is difficult to imagine how hard it is for people in these countries until you see them homeless and without food and warmth. The French, Belgians, and Dutch will all have a trying winter and I wouldn't be surprised if civil flare-ups were inevitable. Not the least of those affected will be our own troops. Winter fighting is not much fun and although rather nasty it must be carried through until the job is wound up.

I am enclosing an Xmas Club check for your Xmas shopping. It has to come from me instead of the bank this year. Thank everyone for my grand Xmas packages, they certainly were nice to get. Especially so early, never had Xmas in October before.

Love to everyone,

Pappy

★ ★ ★

December 3, 1944

Dear Barbara,

I am enclosing herewith some stamps that I am sure will be a welcome addition to your collection. They were captured by the Division on that memorable day, September 17th. The post office [in Nijmegen, Holland] was held by the germans and particularly heavy fighting took place there because they had the power switches in the post office controlling the demolitions in a nearby bridge [over the Waal River]. We wanted to get them under our control and we finally did, thus saving the bridge for our own use. Quite a sizeable affair it was too, about half again as big as the Arlington [Memorial] Bridge [over the Potomac River].

As a matter of fact it should remain one of the classic battles of all time, to us it represented the results of a year and a half of fighting and learning the hardest way, by trial and error and experience. Anyway, the boys snatched the bridge right out from under their noses intact.

The stamps in the envelope marked with the yellow cross were kraut stamps that the germans made the Dutchmen use after they took over the country, that is what the Dutchmen say. The men of the Division have assembled a number of these stamps, about the same as your group, and they have asked me to present them to Mr. Roosevelt. I have written to Gen. [Edwin] Watson [presidential assistant] and in time we should be able to get it done, if the War Department does not interfere.[1]

We are kept about as busy as usual. It rains most of the time. Last night I listened to the first half of the Navy game being broadcast direct from Baltimore. It was very good. I wanted to listen to the second half but had too much to do. It was a wonderful season that Army has had. [Army won. — BGF]

I am glad to hear that you are doing so well in school.

Love to everyone,

Pappy

★ ★ ★

December 5, 1944

Dear Barbara,

The enclosed Xmas cards are not much but will have to do, really this is the best that we have been able to do, and if it were not for Dutch friends we would not have these. As a Santa Claus I have got to give up, I can't find a thing suitable as an Xmas gift. I am enclosing a check therefore for fifty dollars with which I wish you would get something from me for you and Mommie, also Rosie and Aunt Lil, also Aunt Jane. I had better make that a bigger check. I do hope that you have a nice Xmas, have all of the turkey that you want and that Santa brings you some nice things. The enclosed Xmas cards are going to have to do for everyone so will you please circulate them.

Love to everyone and a Merry Xmas,

Pappy

★ ★ ★

December 8, 1944

Dear Babe,

Last night I received the package brought back by Gen. [Harold] Bull [of General Eisenhower's staff]. It was a most pleasant surprise.

Seems as though you must have had quite a time over the promotion. I am glad to know that you went to the Army-Navy game, it must have been quite an experience for you.

Let me know about your recital. I had not realized that your musical training had progressed to that stage.

Thank you and Mommie for the picture. *[This was a photo of my mother and me taken for a Washington newspaper when the news appeared that my dad had just become the youngest major general since the Civil War. — BGF]* I hope that you continue to get along with the press. I have some good friends among the correspondents, it helps a great deal. About people who make inquiries re the Division, tell them to write me.

At present we are terribly busy, at least I am. I have an awful lot of responsibility with little or insufficient trained help. But it has always been that way in war. I am sorry that I have been kept too busy to write more. I'll make up for it when I can.

Thanks for the clippings, don't forget I'm still a captain and really not a very high ranking one at that. *[Wartime necessitated quick promotions. After World War I, many officers reverted to their prewar rank and my father antici-pated that happening to him. It did not. — BGF]*

Love and a Merry Xmas to everyone,

Pappy

P.S. Max Taylor should be along shortly.[2]

★ ★ ★

December 13, 1944

Dear Babe,

I am afraid that it has been awhile since I last had an opportunity to write. I do not know where all of the time goes. Each day is filled to over-flowing and they are never long enough. It is now 9:45 which is early for me to be finishing for an evening so I am going to make the most of it and get in a letter.

I have just returned from a war bond sale that wound up our two-week campaign. We are all quite proud of our record, the Division bought one and a quarter million dollars worth of bonds. It was the largest amount per capita ever bought by any unit overseas, so our finance people told us tonight, so we think it is all right. I bought one for you and it should be along shortly.

I appreciated the clippings and picture brought over by Gen. Bull. I am enclosing two snapshots taken during the Holland affair. You should have something on hand in case one is asked for, for release, just in case. The one of my Headquarters Commandant [William H. Johnson] taken shortly after landing has been the cause of much jesting. When it was taken he had just come up to me all excited to report that he had just gotten two of them. There were about 100 germans about 400 yards away at the time. I am in the act of telling him that killing germans is not the thing to be doing when there is other and more important work to be done. He is a grand chap, graduate engineer of the University of Colorado. He has been in each of the four parachute battles with me, in fact, he jumped from my plane in this one. He really had other work to do in this affair but apparently couldn't resist the temptation to get a couple. Oddly, the sequel to this is that about fifteen minutes later one of the germans shot at me across a road about twenty feet and missed. It was a very interesting place but I thought that you may have some use for the pictures.

I am so glad that you had the chance to go to the Navy game. By the way, I sent you some French books the other day. Obtaining them reminded me of getting the books for you in Naples last year.

I hope that you have a nice Xmas. I am sure that you will. I am sorry that I could not do something about an Xmas present for you. It really has been impossible. Everyone seems to get some time to shop or do things like that but me, I don't know where my time goes. The days are never long enough. Well, perhaps next year I will have an opportunity to deliver it in person, then I can make up for this year.

Merry Xmas and love to everyone,

Pappy

In the early morning hours of December 16, Hitler struck. German armor, rapidly rolling through positions of understrength or inexperienced American divisions throughout the Ardennes, created a "bulge" in the thinly-held American line. As a designated SHAEF (Supreme Headquarters Allied Expeditionary Force) reserve, XVIII Airborne Corps was soon ordered to move its available forces into the battle to regain control. Since General Ridgway and the 101st Airborne Division commander (Maxwell Taylor) were away when the call came, Major General Gavin was made acting Corps commander and responsible for its deployment at the outset of the "Battle of the Bulge."[3]

Boarding trucks in France on the morning of December 18, the 82nd arrived at its positions on the northern flank in Belgium just before dark. The Division's noteworthy actions in successfully helping to repel the German counteroffensive are best described in Gavin's own words in a letter distributed to the Division, dated January 10, 1945:

> This date brings to an end a period of arduous and intensive combat unparalleled, I believe, in American History. . . . You advanced into German positions with the mission of extricating what was present of three U.S. divisions then engaged. . . . Your advance enabled you to cut off the armored spearheads. . . . The spearhead of this [German] division in your sector you destroyed. All efforts of the Germans . . . to relieve this spearhead were also dealt with severely and driven back. On the south flank of the division's advance, the Germans [were] beaten off in repeated, determined, and costly attacks. [Other infantry] divisions were wholly, or in part, withdrawn . . . into the area of our division. Covering positions were held, and these divisions were again withdrawn farther to the rear. From this covering position, upon receipt of orders . . . you withdrew in excellent order to a defensive position. . . . Here you met and repulsed the powerful and costly attacks of the Germans . . . who were attempting to continue the northern advance. When finally permitted by higher headquarters to resume the offensive . . . you inflicted upon the Germans a great loss of men and equipment, and you captured over 2,500 prisoners. In the offensive, you attained the objective assigned . . . thus placing the First U.S. Army in an excellent position to resume the offensive. These accomplishments, gained under most trying conditions of winter warfare, are a vital contribution to the ultimate decisive defeat of the Wehrmacht. I have received numerous commendations for your combat behavior in the past few weeks and these I have transmitted to you. I would like to add my own to you for a splendid soldierly job superbly done.[4]

★ ★ ★

December 27, 1944
Somewhere in Belgium
Dear Babe,

Well this has been a most hectic ten days. Everything seems to be pretty much in hand now however. It is very cold, somewhere around zero, snowed quite a bit when we first arrived. Awful hard on the boys in the foxholes. Christmas day was one of the busiest although they have all been full. Don't think I have ever had less sleep in a week. But as I said, everything is looking up now. For our boys this was all quite an experience. They have done marvelously well.

Pinned a Silver Star on young J.C.H. Lee [of the Division's engineer battalion, the 307] this morning. Quite recently he spent most of an evening in an icy swamp blowing up a bridge right under a kraut column. The sum total of those individual deeds wins the war and he has been doing a nice job.[5]

I hope that my lack of letters has not been disturbing. I'll write more often when I get the chance. Hope that the holidays were nice. Did you have turkey for Xmas?

Well, being a Major General is OK I guess but in a war like this one a division commander certainly earns his chips. It's *some* job. When the war is over I am going to spend my life just sitting and whittling with absolutely no responsibilities or worries in any shape or form. Paratroopers are fun but commanding many thousands of them in this razzle dazzle type of warfare has its anxious moments.

I just learned yesterday that the British government has given me the British Distinguished Service Order for the Nijmegen show, I like that.

Happy New Year and love,

Pappy

★ ★ ★

December 31, 1944
Dear Babe,

This is New Year's Eve and if stray shots ringing thru the cold winter air traditionally signals the arrival of the new year, then I am in the right place. Looking back on the papers of this date, you will notice that I probably had time to write a letter for a change since to some extent the pressure is a mite off, off from what it was a week ago anyway.

This afternoon I attended a short ceremony at which I was awarded the Silver Star.[6]

I am sending it to you tomorrow for safekeeping. I am very glad to get it. It was a warm occasion, sometimes I was afraid that I wouldn't duck fast enough. We have been kept rather busy broadening our military education, it has been a new experience for me and one that I would much rather not repeat. The krauts do well when they are winning.

It is very cold here and has been snowing for the past two days. The mountains are lovely, really didn't know that there were mountains like these around here. It is surprising how the older soldiers, and I suppose they are all veterans now, take care of themselves. They build substantial dugouts with few tools and somehow manage to keep warm. It is surprising how accustomed to living out in the cold one gets after awhile. They would die of exposure if they had to live as they do now when they first left the States but somehow they become accustomed to everything.

The krauts have been making a confident, desperate, and well-planned and executed bid for supremacy that appears at the moment to be coming to an end. Their bid if it fails should in the long run shorten the war. So beating them, as I am sure we will, will materially shorten the days of fighting ahead. It may appear at times to be a costly, perhaps too costly, venture this war. Well, costly or not, we are in it and win we must. Everyone must realize this and winning the war consists in part of supporting it fully, both in work and speech. It is too late really to question the merit of being in the war, we *are* in it. And those of us who have come into active, close, and intimate contact with the subjugated peoples, the Italians, French, Dutch, Belgians, all know what losing would mean to our people. It is hard to realize until one sees conditions how frightful they can be. Amen.

Love and Happy New Year,
Pappy

* * *

January 10, 1945
Dear Butch,

Well another chance to write a letter. Thought that I might as well make the most of it since these opportunities are few and far between. First, thank Rosie for me for a wonderful fruitcake and very nice box of candy. They came in the midst of fighting and I shared them with the staff one cold winter evening. They could not have arrived at a more opportune time.

These days have been rather rugged but things are improving daily. My aide, Capt. Olson, was hit again, this time shrapnel in the legs. *[Hugo Olson told me that my dad wouldn't leave him when he was hit, both in Normandy and Belgium, until the medics had arrived. — BGF]* To make matters worse my striker who has been with me for ages, Wood, was hit a day or so before that. His wasn't very serious though, mortar fragment and just a small bit. Both are doing nicely, thank you. Trouble with it all is that it looks as though I bring people bad luck, perhaps they don't dodge fast enough.[7]

My greatest loss however was Ben Vandervoort who has been one of my most dependable people since the early days in Alabama. You probably remember that he fought through 33 days in Normandy with a broken leg wearing a walking cast. The day before yesterday he was hit in the head by some shrapnel and may lose the sight of one eye. It is all very sad.[8]

I don't know how much you are told of what goes on but the Division has done splendidly. I am enclosing a clipping from this morning's Stars and Stripes which I believe should be the picture of the war [a lone soldier, no helmet, crouched and running over an open field toward a barbed-wire enemy machine gun position with gun in hand], typifying as it does their gallantry and determination and zest to close with and destroy the german wherever they can find him.[9] Quite a crowd of boys. If there were enough of them the war would be over tomorrow.

This is what I suppose passes for a lovely locality at any time except during war. The mountains are as beautiful as they are unexpected. We didn't expect to find them here. The evergreens are a bit remindful of our Northwest. And the snow also reminds me of Mount Hood. I haven't seen so much snow since West Point. Very rugged living in a foxhole, one wonders really how humans can keep alive let alone healthy. Yet somehow they do. They are confident that given the opportunity they can destroy their share of the Wehrmacht.

I hope that all goes well in school and that Xmas was nice, thanks for the Time [magazine subscription] for another year. I certainly will enjoy it.

Love to everyone,

Pappy

With the "bulge" pushed back, the Division was taken off the line and moved to a reserve area. There the exhausted troopers were billeted among homes in

several small Belgian villages, giving them much needed rest, hot food, and clean
clothes. During that time, Gavin visited each of the battalions and allowed the
troopers to ask questions — most of them wanted to know when they were going
home.

★ ★ ★

January 12, 1945

Dear Babe,

I have received your letter written after Xmas and am glad to know that Santa Claus was so good to you. He must have had quite a struggle getting down the chimney with all of that stuff.

The report card sounds wonderful, what would you like for your reward?

The Xmas tree must have been a sizeable affair, something like those that I have here.

We have lovely big evergreens in a real winter setting. Too much so really, the snow is rather deep and for one who never wanted to fight in winter conditions it is quite a lesson in what to expect in the Army, anything but what you guess you will get.

I suppose that the newspapers have published the news on the present affair, I believe that the 82nd was taken off the secret list for a bit. Generally we are kept in wraps, probably to keep the krauts worrying of our whereabouts in case they would.

Is it still possible to get liquid Vaseline in the States; if so, will you please send me a bottle, any size. Also some nuts and some candy if obtainable.

I had a nice letter from Harry Collins, he is with the 42nd [Infantry Division] at Camp Gruber, Oklahoma. Also a nice letter from Gen. [George] Grunert at Governor's Island.

I am sorry to hear from Uncle George's letter that he is homesick. I suppose that every soldier is really at some time or another. It is the longest war that we have ever fought so far away from our homeland. There is so little that can be done about it, everyone gets awfully tired of some things at times. And one gets tired of going without. But it is all part and parcel of winning the war which is what we are here for.

It seems to me at times that I have been in it forever, and during hard fighting when I get extremely tired and sometimes rather worked up emotionally and good friends are being killed and maimed, and I just seem to be a jump away from death itself, I get very angered over it all. But the war is to be fought and finished well, our people expect this of us individually and collectively and they are entitled to this expectation. We are certainly no smaller men than our forefathers, many of whom died to give us our country.

Love to everyone,

Pappy

★ ★ ★

January 13, 1945

Dear Butch,

Thought that you might like to have the enclosed. Barney Oldfield, PRO [Public Relations Officer] of the Ninth Army sent it to me today. Apparently was in the London Daily Sketch. I am afraid that I look a bit grim, must have been a bad day or my dyspepsia was bad.

Today was a good day, and at its best I am glad that no picture was being taken since I was taking a bath. The first in over a month so it was very much appreciated. We are presumably resting a bit at the moment, hence the bath.

Had a nice letter from John Copeland, he has the 65th [Infantry Division] at Camp Shelby [Mississippi].

The news around here looks a bit better right now, I guess you know that. The Philippine show appears to be going great guns, sure hate to miss it. I was hoping to get this finished in time to get over there. Every time that I mentioned this to the Division, the reaction was pronounced and opposed to the idea. But we are missing a real show. Always had a vision of the big splash that I could make with all of the equipment that I jump with now landing flat on my back in a rice paddy. Maybe they have rice paddies in Japan, that *would* be something.

Love,

Pappy

★ ★ ★

January 16, 1945

Dear Babe,

Still "resting," not bad. Did you ever receive the Xmas package with the French storybook and pictures? Do not misunderstand the pictures, I am not being carried narcissus-like with the edification of my own countenance. I really wanted you to have something on hand just in case the press ask, and they will.

I have tried in the interests of the Division to have a good press and I have as a matter of fact some very good friends among the press. It is a fine thing for the troops to receive from home press clippings extolling their accomplishments. They feel then that the folks back home are being made aware and are appreciative of all that they are doing. It all adds up. The Division gets a character and personality of its own. But in order to do this in a practical sense it is necessary for the press to exploit the old man, the Commanding General, if and how it can.

I do not know what you read about the Division in the home papers but it is obviously smart business to be as courteous to the press and as considerate of their requirements as we can be, and we try. Some of the finest people that I have met in the war so far have been newspaper men. Our American foreign war correspondents are almost without exception brilliant men and usually all around pretty good Joes. Bill Boni, of the International News Service I believe, has just returned and he said that he would call, perhaps he has.

Will you please send me some phone numbers. Just in case someday I find myself in a position to call, not that I might, but just in case.

It is quite cold and getting colder. This time last year I was living in London. Quite a deal, we were working up the summer's events [planning for the invasion of Normandy]. I really liked it there very much. I enjoyed my stay in England, those people are OK, and I believe that every soldier who has served there will share these sentiments. They are very deserving of a victorious peace. They have given about everything to winning the war despite what the U.S. press frequently says to the contrary. Their homes, their fortunes, their markets, their lives, without stint. They like Americans, even if their form of expressing it gives one a chill now and then. It is their own way, odd as it seems to us at times and even exasperating, they are sincere, hospitable, reticent, and love an understatement, both in expression and behavior.

Enough of this, I must get back to work, don't forget your phone number.

Love to everyone,

Pappy

★ ★ ★

January 17, 1945

Dear Babe,

Thought that I might as well write you a letter since I have the time. Rather unusual to have this much time but it will not be for long. Time has really flown during the past few weeks. It has hardly seemed like the Xmas holidays. In fact, probably few people noticed that it was Xmas.

I remember early Xmas morning at daylight being with some of Billingslea's boys [of the 325]. They were to take a town that we rather thought was saturated with krauts. I felt like I wanted to be with them, being Xmas etc. As we neared the town the shooting started. A boy dove in a roadside ditch, remarking as he went, "Hell, this is more like the 4th of July." That was the only acknowledgement of it being Xmas that I heard all day.

The weather however has left little doubt but that winter is here. Although we are becoming accustomed to lots of snow and cold, we nevertheless miss the balmy breezes of Sicily and Italy. Africa was too hot but Sicily was ideal. I had the pleasure of capturing Trapani with some 6,000 Italians. A rather nice city. Filthy dirty and very smelly as all Sicilian towns are but in the outskirts there were some lovely homes. The germans had just run out the back door of one villa as we came in the front. They had been using it for a headquarters for some years. A lovely place. Swimming pool, citrus and fruit gardens, and just a little bombed. We took it over complete and spent several happy weeks there. I had the rather edifying job of being in charge of about a thousand square miles of the western part of the island. Not too exacting a task and quite a relief from the trials and tribulations of Africa. Spent most of the time trying to flush out hidden krauts.

Well, what we are looking forward to now is being in Berlin, and goodness knows how far away that is and who is going to get there [the Americans and the British approaching from the west or the Russians approaching from the east]. There is a lot of fighting to be done between now and then and a lot of dying and many sacrifices to be made but with the help of God we will get there.

Love to everyone,

Pappy

★ ★ ★

January 24, 1945

Dear Babe,

Wafted on the chill winter breezes, the perfume of your last letter preceded it to my Command Post, penetrating every nook and cranny and causing no little consternation among the orderlies and staff. It was a harbinger of something extra special and almost before its arrival everyone was aware of my getting perfumed mail. Being most appreciative of a letter, I certainly am not of a state of mind to criticize its odor, and I am not really. But it was a surprise, and surprises of that sort are a welcome relief on this front.

The snow seems to get deeper and the krauts meaner, both to be expected under the circumstances. Our own mental attitude would never interest Dale Carnegie [as the troopers were not trying to "win friends," but rather to kill Germans], but it does suit our present environment and way of life rather well. Everyone is getting along fine. I have yet to have my first cold since leaving the States and I hardly know why. Although conditions are rugged the boys are adapting themselves remarkably well. We are now looking forward to spring very, very much. I suppose there will be an Easter this year.

I have gathered the impression that some of our lads who have been granted thirty days at home [on furlough] have had a few minutes on the radio, that with bits of news from the press probably will give you some idea of where we are. Perhaps the War Department releases complete information. The other day I had a long talk with a Mrs. [Helena] Pringle of the Woman's Home Companion. She seemed interested in doing an article on the Division. Her home is in Washington, Columbia Road and 16th St., near there anyway. If I have a chance to see her again before she returns, I'll give her a letter to take back to you.

The other night I had a short talk with Jack Thompson whom I haven't seen for some time. He and his beard are both doing nicely. He is doing a book I believe.

I will be awfully glad when we get out of the snow and mud, we all will be really. In the meantime the job is to be done and the boys are doing quite well. This is almost beginning to seem like a long war. The current catchphrase "Golden Gate in 48" may be more fact than fancy.[10] It seems to me that I said that once before, perhaps it's on my mind.

Love to everyone,

Pappy

Hitler's desperate effort had succeeded only in depleting what reserves and strength his armies still possessed. On January 12, the Russians had begun a fierce drive into Germany; having to fight the Russians in the east, the Germans would be unable to strongly defend their western border against the advancing Anglo-American armies. It was time to crack Germany's Siegfried Line.

★ *chapter ten* ★

CRACKING THE SIEGFRIED
LINE — GERMANY

Having once again proven themselves as aggressive and highly successful ground troops during the Battle of the Bulge, the 82nd Airborne Division was thrown into the Allied assault against Germany's western border defenses. The attack jumped off early on January 28, and though progress was slow due to waist-deep snow, below-freezing temperatures, and German resistance, the Division penetrated into Germany on the morning of February 2.

★ ★ ★

February 3, 1945

Dear Babe,

Back in Germany again, this time the hard way. Difficult to say really which is the harder way but this did not seem very easy, certainly not to those that we have left by the wayside.

I am very glad to have had several letters from you lately. There has been some mix-up and some recent letters were in transit over two months. Xmas must have been a lot of fun.

We have been very busy lately, far too much so I guess. Consequently I have not had the usual opportunities to write. This I intended to be just a note to let you know that all goes well and I am afraid that it will have to do as that.

Love to everyone,

Pappy

On February 10, the 82nd reached the western bank of the Roer River. It had been anticipated that the Division would be ordered to force a crossing of the river — instead they remained in a static position, much to the chagrin of Gavin who understood that his airborne troopers got "furious, impatient and finally disgusted with the vacillation and delay in getting going in a ground fight with ground units."[1]

★ ★ ★

February 11, 1945

Dear Babe,

Just received your Valentine, very nice and most thoughtful. I haven't written as often lately as I normally like to but things have been pressing. I will be glad to get a breather, I hope next week or the week after to get a chance to get a bath and maybe take some time out.

All is going well and the boys are fighting marvelously but it takes lots of work and I suppose worries. The german civilians are a stoical group, reserved, quiet, and well-behaved. It is perhaps as well since few of us now are in a frame of mind to show much patience with any misbehavior.

A great deal of our snow of last month has melted leaving everything covered with mud. I wear an old jumpsuit and shoepacs [insulated rubber boots] day in and day out, presenting not a very good appearance at higher headquarters. I don't know how some of these generals that I meet keep so clean. Only way that I can figure it is that they do not spend much time in the front lines. I still like to spend a lot of time where the fighting is close just to keep my hand in. It's a good idea because I usually end up as a squad leader with more krauts than my own around for the first few hours in an airborne operation.[2] Besides, after a while one finds that a bit of excitement is a necessary daily ingredient of one's sustenance or something. But it all makes the time go by and brings the war nearer to its certain conclusion.

I had a short visit from Fulton Lewis [a radio broadcaster and news commentator] yesterday. He promised to call when he returned to Washington. He is a very nice man to talk to, very intelligent and a pleasing personality.

I am pleased to learn from your last letter that you are moving to the Wyoming [an apartment building]. Be sure to send me your correct address. Also your phone number.

Love to everyone,

Pappy

P.S. Please be *my* Valentine

★ ★ ★

February 14, 1945

Dear Butch,

The enclosed [newspaper article] reminded me of a letter that I wrote you on the same subject during my stay in Italy. Quite a hazardous business, that of negotiating the narrow byways of the Italian villages.

I have received several letters from you in the past few days which is commendable. I will have to think up something as a reward. I have inquired of the tailor in London who is making your kilts but evidently the British army still has a priority. Next time I get over I'll look them up. The miniature medals I have not ordered for lack of an address. I will get this done however as soon as possible.

I thought that it would be a good idea to write you tonight because tomorrow I move my Command Post up a bit and in a cellar. Hardly a place pleasant to contemplate but secure from not only the effect but the sound as well of our current nemesis, the "screaming meemies."

For the past few days I have been covered with mud, it seems anyway, from head to foot. A far cry from the good old days when all a general had to do was manage to stay topside a horse despite the un-stabilizing influence of what must have then passed for the [British] NAAFI [rum] ration, all the while uttering incomprehensible nonentities for the benefit of posterity like "Turn boys, we are going back," etc. Oh me oh my, some war. I am quite ashamed sometimes when I visit other headquarters. I must at times be the sloppiest general in the war. I have a lot of fun though and get shot at often which tends to relieve the tedium that begins to become apparent after two years of this stuff.

Looks like the krauts are rocking on their heels at the moment. Interesting analysis that, that the krauts are about beaten. Some deep thinking Pentagon commando [far removed from battle] always comes up with such an idea and perhaps in the larger sense he is right, but to the boy facing a machine gun the war is yet an eternity away from its end. And there are many of those, I can hear the shooting from here. Let's hope though for the many fine lads yet surviving that the end is not too far off. They deserve respite and rest, those who have been over here two years.

Love to everyone,

Pappy

★ ★ ★

February 17, 1945

Dear Babe,

Thank you for the Valentine, also Mommie. I liked hearing of your first date. I am looking forward to the time when I can take you to the movies too.

I thought it would be nice to write you a short note before leaving my cellar. It is rather a nice cellar as cellars go. Not having lived in one before, I am not an authority on them but this one has many admirable character-istics, not the least of which is a thick ceiling. The walls are chewed up a bit and the ceiling scarred from shelling but it still beats a tent, especially when it snows. It is deep enough that when I am in it I can't tell whether or not the artillery is going out or coming in. There is just a deep rumbling and everything shakes. This means it is pretty deep because by now I can just about not only tell whether or not it is coming or going but tell who is on the kraut gun crew today. Maybe it is Herman, maybe it's Wolfgang.

But I don't spend much time in the cellar anyway. At night when there is planning to be done and reports gotten out or letters written. I have always written to the family of every boy who has been a fatality so by now I have an awful heap of [condolence] letters to write.[3] It is a very deep tragedy, and no doubt a lasting one, to an American family to lose a son or brother. Their letters wring one's heart and unfortunately there is so little that one can say. Anything that I would say would be woefully inade-quate and the censorship regulations do not allow the transmission of anything having to do with geographical locations, etc.

Butch, there is a man at the door knocking. Business is pressing. I'll write you later. I hope to be in a better locale shortly.

Love to everyone,

Pappy

chapter eleven

A BRIEF RESPITE — FRANCE

Anticipating that an airborne operation, most significantly a drop on Berlin, might have to be mounted, the Division was pulled off the line in Germany and returned to its camps in France. Gavin would be able to re-equip and refit the Division after the losses sustained, as well as continue the training that had been interrupted in December.

★ ★ ★

February 24, 1945

Dear Babe,

It has been some time since I wrote you last. We have been on the move and now are at the moment under a bit better circumstances since I last wrote. I had a bath the other day and it was wonderful. I heard some music over a radio and it too was wonderful.

I am very pleased to hear the fine reports on your report card. That is really fine work. I'll send you, or have sent to you, the miniature medals as soon as I can get them. Next week I am going to look into the kilts. I'll probably run over to where they are being made, I have some other business over there anyway. I have a couple of grand pilots and a good ship. A C-47. Tried a jump out of it just before the Ardennes affair.

My Chief of Staff [Colonel Robert Wienecke] brought in a clipping from the New York Times this afternoon, that picture taken in the snow in Belgium. I remember the occasion very well. The picture is fine except the caption. It said that I was talking to the troops. A fine thing, all that I had to do to talk to the troops was say, "Hey, Joe." They were all around. That is why I had the rifle, I was among them at the front. The phone was being used to talk to the Command Post which was some distance back. To be accused of using a telephone to talk to the troops is embarrassing.

The Ardennes was some place to spend the winter, wow. Sure glad to be out of there. I never knew that man could adapt himself so well to unbelievable discomforts, especially cold. After awhile it just didn't seem to make much difference. I always worried about the wounded more than anything else. The cold was bad for them, their survival rate was not too high. But the boys did wonderfully, from the siroccos of Africa to the winter storms of the Ardennes is a big span.

Thank you for the phone numbers. Some time ago one of my higher commanders suggested that I make a quick trip back to Washington for a couple of weeks. I must have looked tired. It was in the midst of the Bulge business. It seemed like a good idea at the time. Since then however my work has increased so and my command has reached a size that I had better stick close by to it, for a while anyway. Besides, I would sure hate to miss any of this and especially have any shooting start with me away. The boys wouldn't like it.

How about some candy or nuts if they are available and not rationed? Congratulations again on the fine report card. Thanks for the Valentine. Aunt Lil asked about her Xmas package. I'm sure I asked you to thank her for me, or did I? I intended to.

Love to everyone,

Pappy

★ ★ ★

February 28, 1945

Dear Barbara,

Dr. Waring came in last night. He had dinner with me and stayed over-night. Thank you for the candy and cute Valentine. It was very nice to get. I also received Rosie's package with the ties which were most welcome. About the picture in the New York Times and no gloves, I had gloves which I had in my pocket, just put them there so that I could use the telephone more easily.

We are doing nicely now, getting fat and catching up with a few things. We have lots of work ahead of us, really the days are just simply not long enough. It seems to be getting warmer. It can hardly be soon enough to suit us. After last winter I don't think we will ever be warm again.

I was especially well pleased to hear of your good work in school. I am sorry that you expected me to get a trip back. I could, if I wanted to ask for it as a real medical necessity, get a short stay in the U.S. but that would hardly be fair to all of the boys who cannot get back. Besides, I'm always afraid I'll miss something. Keep up the good work in school.

Love to everyone,

Pappy

★ ★ ★

March 10, 1945

Dear Babe,

I am sorry that it has been so long since my last letter. We have been quite busy. Right now I am in my C-47 on the way to Normandy to award two gold watches to a couple of Frenchmen who were of assistance last June. You may hear about it although I have done everything to avoid the formation because I am really too busy to take the time. I just couldn't get out of it. There will be considerable press coverage. I left my present home at eight this morning and expect to arrive in Normandy at ten. The day is to be filled with speeches etc. The itinerary goes something like this: speech of welcome by the mayor, presentation of flowers by schoolchildren, lunch, speech by prefect, depositing of flowers at Monument de Morts, schoolchildren recite poetry (hail to the liberators, etc.), presentation of awards, speech by Butch (me), schoolchildren sing national anthems, good-byes. I should be home by seven this evening and then get going on what will undoubtedly be a mass of administrative stuff. Night before last I got to bed by three and last night by eleven and so it goes. The reason I mention all this is so that you will understand why I have not been writing more often. I hope to catch up soon however.

I was over to the United Kingdom the other day and inquired about your kilts. Not ready yet, promised for next week. I explained about how you undoubtedly have grown some since I gave him the measurements, and he said I probably didn't realize it but that there was a war on. I am not sure what that has to do with it but sometimes they appear odd, the British. But they are fine people, almost without exception I have found all of the English to be tops.

I will let you know how today's formation turns out, it will be something. When the French start making speeches, it's time to take cover.

Love,

Pappy

★ ★ ★

March 12, 1945

Dear Babe,

The enclosed I thought would be of interest to you since we are always writing of our hardships. They were taken at a recent prop blast. Prop blasts being what they are, are still conducted with the traditional fanfare and ceremony. The impressive sized goblet [a champagne cooler] in front is marked with a plate "Jim's Jug" and it comes from the scene of its captivity, Berg en Dal in Germany, where it fell to our lot in the Nijmegen operation.[1]

By the way, I sent you a picture of the Nijmegen bridge site and a book of autographs that the people of Nijmegen sent to me several days ago. I do hope that they get through OK. The picture is allegedly of considerable intrinsic value, but whether or not it is of great sentimental value to me. That was quite a hot corner once upon a time.

The other day I made a trip to Picauville where I presented two gold watches to two very deserving Français. It was quite an affair. It was most impressive and I have never been in anything quite like it. We made lots of speeches, including one of mine, and I hardly know if we understood each other but certainly we were all carried away by it all. Lots of arm waving, salutes, and vivas. I am sending along a paper making me an honorary citizen of Picauville which you might like to have. Also a paper that was read with great ceremony and excellent diction by a little girl, aged eleven, all dressed up in red, white and blue. She reminded me very much of you and I told her so, although I am afraid that she did not understand me.

I had a chance to jump test a C-46 [with exit doors on both sides of the rear fuselage] yesterday. Going out the door on the wrong side was a bit of an experience for an old fire horse like me but I made it intact.

Love to everyone,

Pappy

★ ★ ★

March 14, 1945

Dear Babe,

Munro Leaf, author of "Ferdinand the Bull" and the "Watchbird" has been visiting with me for the past two days. He sends you the enclosed [drawing].[2]

Love to everyone,

Pappy

★ ★ ★

March 18, 1945

Dear Babe,

I thought that you might like to give the enclosed to Mrs. Ridgway.

They were taken by Ed Krause. He gave me the prints the other day. The locale is the delightful setting of our past winter mess in Germany. The village scenes were taken in a town where I had my Command Post in a cellar for a while. A lovely spot comparatively, the rats objected at first to my usurpation of their domain but any such objections could only be but short-lived. We outlasted the rats. They finally gave up and moved down the street three cellars.

It is getting very nice here now, sun is shining and the temperature is mounting. I am sending a scarf that I managed to get in London. I think that you will like it. It is for the last report card. The rations coupons were provided by an English family. This is quite a sacrifice and she would probably appreciate a note of thanks. Mrs. Valerie Came-Porter, 82 Portland Place, London, W-1.

We have been kept rather busy [training] lately, especially the last week. Had an affair take place like the one in the Carolinas a couple of years ago [when a transport plane lost power, slicing through a stick of 505 paratroopers, killing three], only this one [with the 508] was about twice as costly [killing seven]. Ship got into a pattern.

We went up immediately and jumped with the same pilots and had a very uneventful time. It made three jumps however for me in three days. Almost too many for what is to be done.

Things in general look much brighter than they have for some time. I'd certainly like to see the States again. Has Uncle George shown up yet, that should be quite a day. Happy Easter.

Love to everyone,

Pappy

★ ★ ★

March 20, 1945

Dear Butch,

I thought that you might get a kick out of this [French newspaper, *La Presse de la Manche*]. It covers that [award ceremony in Picauville] affair of several days ago. Can you read any of it? Col. Winton returned from a short trip to Paris. He brought back several French books which I am also forwarding to you.

Love to everyone,

Pappy

★ ★ ★

March 21, 1945

Dear Butch,

I hope that you have noticed that I have had no occasion to call to your attention lately my magazine subscriptions, etc. All is well and too quiet.

Had a letter from Rosie today in which she expressed some uncharitable observations on the 101st publicity [for their stand while surrounded at Bastogne during the Battle of the Bulge], they were attributable to you I suspect.

Never be disturbed by what you read in the newspapers about units. You see war correspondents, and I know many of them intimately by now, write with two objects in view. First, making more money. Second, what does the public want to read. The second is a corollary to the first really. Public relations are fascinating and in this war have been extremely interesting. There have been brilliant examples of selling the public a view for a purpose, notably Arnhem and Bastogne. They were splendidly handled from a public relations viewpoint.

Never feel any animosity towards the 101st, they are grand people. As a matter of fact, I was in Bastogne with them their first night and gave them their order [as acting XVIII Airborne Corps commander] to stay while I joined my own crowd farther north. The 101st did a grand job and deserve all of the credit that the public can be persuaded to lavish upon them [for responding "Nuts!" to the German surrender demand].

In a public relations viewpoint each division has a character of its own. If it doesn't have it soon develops one. We have carefully cultivated a long-range plan of making ours a steady, courageous, dependable unit that can, and does, do the impossible in combat as a matter of course. By now the press in general knows us for this, we have a very good press.

Glamorizing and spectacular exploitation of insignificant things are sooner or later a "kiss of death" in the public relations field, and the press is inclined to tear one down as quickly as it builds one up. Besides, it frequently has its own reasons for publishing a certain story that has little to do with what actually happened. The easiest thing in the business is to get personally publicized and this must be avoided; it's poor long-range policy, although at times unavoidable.

So do not judge our accomplishments too much by the newspaper lineage. The author of the article and the quality and publisher means more than anything, almost more really than what actually happened. This is a lot of writing about public relations but it is a subject that interests me very much. Mrs. Hemingway (Martha Gellhorn) who writes for Colliers spent the past weekend with the Division and she may do some stuff on the boys. She struck me as being a rather brilliant person. Bob Capa of Life is due in a day or so. He has been talking about jumping with me but I am not sure if he will make it. They all talk great jumping in the Hotel Scribe bar in Paris but it is not too easy to get them in the ships and for that I can hardly blame them.

Well, by the time you receive this things should look rather good. Remember that I have had no occasion to remind you of my subscriptions etc.

I sent the [British] DSO yesterday. Today I received notice that the De-Gaulle government has been kind enough to make me an Officer of the Legion of Honor for the Normandy affair. More fruit salad [decorations].

Love to everyone,

Pappy

Having crossed the Rhine River and established bridgeheads by the end of March, Anglo-American forces continued to move east through Germany while, moving west, the Russians quickly closed in on the capital of Hitler's Third Reich — Berlin. Nazi Germany's total collapse was imminent. With airborne operations uncertain, Gavin received orders to return the 82nd to Germany as conventional infantry.

★ ★ ★

March 31, 1945

Dear Babe,

I was just clearing my desk and I came across this insignia and copy of La Presse. I do not remember whether or not you have seen it, it should go well with your French classes. Tomorrow is Easter and it will be a *very* busy day for me [as the Division will close its camps in France]. Next Easter let's have an Easter egg hunt.

Happy Easter and love to everyone,

Pappy

chapter twelve

BACK ON THE LINE —
THE FINAL FIGHT

*Returned to Germany, the 82nd Airborne Division was deployed along the west-
ern bank of the Rhine River near Cologne. Gavin's orders were to aggressively
patrol the city and its perimeter, while sending patrols across the river to engage
and identify enemy formations.*

★ ★ ★

April 3, 1945

Dear Babe,

It is nice to be back in Germany again although our mode of travel this
time was not nearly as interesting as the usual way. The place in spring
looks rather nice. A lovely country really. Not quite as nice as England
but nevertheless quite attractive. Things are getting green and trees are
blossoming. The homes are well cared for and except for the bombed local-
ities things look much better than in any of the other countries. The germans have apparently lived well except for the interference of bombing.

I am enclosing a sample invasion mark. I may have sent you some of
these from germany during the Nijmegen show, we were in for the first
time then.

Thanks for the Easter message.

Love to everyone,

Pappy

★ ★ ★

April 9, 1945

Dear Babe,

Thank you for the nice Easter card which I received today, also two very
nice letters. I take it that you had a good visit from Uncle George. I know
that he was very glad to be back for a while. Could use some of it myself.
Perhaps the way things are going it is not too far away.

We are sort of busy fighting and taking care of krauts as well as their past slaves. To be more specific as far as the censor will permit, we have quite a bit of fighting on our hands, but it is not too arduous, especially compared to Normandy or the Ardennes or Holland.

The new thing however is some 650 square miles of germany full of krauts that I am charged with the supervision of the military government of, some sentence. In addition, I have several camps of Displaced Persons. And what could be said about that even the censor should not be exposed to. I remember reading some years ago of the germans moving thousands of people of other countries that they had conquered to germany to be slave labor. At the time my impression was that it was rather effective propaganda and that slaves couldn't have meant just like the Egyptians capturing the Jews, as it says in the Bible for example. I realize very much now that it was much more than propaganda. I suppose that there are many more than a million but I have seen many thousands and they are a pitiful lot. All kinds, especially Russians and Poles, big, little and all sexes, just liberated by the advancing armies.

For the past four years they have been held as slaves and used in homes on menial tasks, on farms, in factories, and in heavy industries. In fact, anywhere that a human could function. Their only wage was their daily keep and that was cut to a minimum. Consequently they are all thin and hungry and most of them dirty and lousy [lice-ridden] and many quite ill.

It could not be believed if one did not see it. Upon their release, of course, the first thing that a Russian wants to do is find a German that he can delight in beating to his personal satisfaction; if not that, he would like to burn or loot his home. All of which may not seem like too bad an idea but it is conducive to rioting and disorder, all of which could seriously hamper our own war efforts. So all in all, it poses quite a problem.

I have had a couple of visitors for the past three days, Bob Capa of Life and Martha Gellhorn of Colliers. They are grand people and it is nice to have them around the Command Post for a while. Bob had qualified [as a parachutist] with us in the United Kingdom and has been with us on and off for the past two years. He made his first combat jump with the 17th [Airborne Division in their jump across the Rhine, Operation VARSITY, on March 24, 1945] and evidently covered it quite thoroughly for a recent issue of Life. He must have had a lot of fun besides making a lot of money. We have been trying to get together for an airborne show for some time.

He was to go into Rome with us and that was called off, Normandy something else happened, and about the time of Holland he was in Spain. Miss Gellhorn does fine work and thinks very well of the Division.

Met Happy Brooks yesterday. He reported in for duty much to my surprise. Just left the States in February. Asked him a lot of questions about what it was like now. If things continue to go as well as they are now I may see it this year. But the Japanese war beckons and we don't want to miss it.

All my love to everyone,

Pappy

★ ★ ★

April 11, 1945

Dear Babe,

Thought that you might like to have the enclosed [stamps], they came from the local post office. Which reminds me, I have not been able to get the miniature medals. I will though. Be patient.

All goes well. Dr. Goebbels [the Nazi propaganda minister] and Berlin Bess gave us a few minutes on the radio yesterday. Claim they kicked us around. Very likely some eager beaver in the sack bucking for oak leaf clusters and diamonds for his Iron Cross made the claim. It is such a rare opportunity for them to ever be able to claim any, even temporary, advantage over these lads that when they can they can be heard all of the way back to the Unter den Linden [Berlin's main boulevard].[1]

Actually we have been giving them a good shellacking. They have just found out that we are around again, and they spend most of their days watching and shooting and all of their nights shooting flares. These lads give them the jitters, they pack an awful lot of strength in front of them [with artillery barrages] and the krauts get out entirely when they show up.

Gosh the weather is nice. It is so much better than the Ardennes.

Love to all,

Pappy

★ ★ ★

April 13, 1945

Dear Babe,

I am sending along the enclosed official copy of the French award of the Croix de Guerre Order of the Legion of Honor. I have not received the medal yet, and since circumstances could well make this impossible in the future, I thought it best to save the order. I would rather not lose it.

This morning we received the news of the death of our President and needless to say it came as quite a shock. I had just received a letter signed by him a day or two ago congratulating the Division on its affair at Nijmegen. Regardless of his political shortcomings, the armed services looked to him as their supreme leader and consequently held him in high esteem. We will miss his leadership in world affairs in the next three or four years.

I believe that every veteran who has seen war at close quarters and the death and devastation that follows in its wake sincerely hopes that our people will take the leadership in world affairs and insist on the establishment and maintenance of peace, by the use of force if necessary. As Mr. Wilkie said, it is "One World." It is one large community and as such it needs a police force as well as the smallest community. We cannot depend on the existence of peace by nations just getting along well together, no more than a community can depend on people just getting along well together. There will always be gangster nations as there always are people who take advantage of others at every opportunity.[2] Dumbarton Oaks [conference] was a good start and the San Francisco meeting is a sound step in the right direction [toward establishing the charter of the United Nations], regardless of who participates or what commitments our presence necessitates. But enough of this.

Love to everyone,

Pappy

★ ★ ★

April 15, 1945

Dear Babe,

Sunday in Germany. Today promises to be a quiet one, most of the shooting in my area has quieted down. I have my Command Post in the nicest place that we have ever had. Quite a contrast to the cellars and holes in the ground that we were in, in the Hürtgen [Forest near the Roer River]. This place was the home of a nazi and it is rather modern. The main living room is a lovely long affair with a fireplace at one end, beautiful overstuffed furniture, and a very nice grand piano. It can be played with rolls. Shortly after taking over, a visiting war correspondent felt sorry for us and went looking for piano rolls, finally returning with a jeep load. So we do not lack for music. The dining room is very lovely, crystal chandeliers, linen, etc. Our House of Savoy silver goes well with it all. It is surrounded by extensive grounds that include a swimming pool (it is too cold to use, very dirty too since it was used to put out incendiary bombs), a tennis court (that has been converted into a victory garden), a large hothouse containing tropical flora and fauna (all of the glass has been broken by artillery and mortar fire), beautiful flower beds (chewed up a bit by trenches), and very extensive walks and large trees. Really a very nice place. I am sure that he must have been very, very nazi. That is always the case if they own any property otherwise the krauts take it away from them and send them to the salt mines. Either that or make fertilizer out of them in Poland.

For the past few days I have had a lot of headaches with my Displaced Persons, the Russians especially. They are most interesting. We sent the band around the other evening. It played polkas and anything they wanted. They went wild, jumped up and down, danced singly and in crowds, and generally had a wonderful time. They said that it was the first music that they have had in five years.

You can't imagine what things like this are like. It makes quite an impression on one and makes you appreciate what you do have. All of us long ago learned that Americans take their liberties and luxuries too much for granted. But when one has civilians gladly offer their lives for what they believe in, unheard of, unsung, unknown, yet they will gladly go forward to certain death because they believe in a principle. Our histories teach us that our forefathers were like that, and I have no doubt but that they were, but one almost has to return to Europe to really see it actually exist. I guess the war has taught all of us much about values and the need for sacrifice. Trouble with me probably is that I have been away from America too long. I am sure that at home Americans are sacrificing as much as anyone.

But the war is going nicely now. With luck I may get an opportunity to get back this summer. This would be very nice and that's an understatement.

Love to everyone,

Pappy

★ ★ ★

April 20, 1945

Dear Babe,

Mail service seems to be rather good these days, your letter written the 9th arrived yesterday. I am glad that you like the DSO. I am still trying to get the miniatures, seems to be difficult from this distance. The French decorations that you asked about are two: the Legion of Honor, which is comparable to the British Distinguished Service Order, both being group-ings of people so designated by those governments because of demon-strated heroism in combat or something like that. The other is the Croix de Guerre with Palm, which is another combat award for services of an exemplary nature for the French government. The ceremony for the awards has not been held yet because evidently everyone is too busy fight-ing. We have however been given the ribbons, copies of which I will send you as soon as I can get my hands on them. They are very pretty. Red, and red and green.

I am so glad that Uncle George had a nice leave with the family. I am sure that he enjoyed it. I would have liked very much to have seen him.

Since things are getting a bit more quiet here daily, there may be a chance for some of us to go to the Pacific. As a matter of fact, the War Department has announced that many of the troops here would. You prob-ably read that in the newspapers. Things are getting far too quiet here, I feel like a fire horse with no fires to go to. What does a fire horse do when there are no more fires to go to? I love fires.

[I understood my dad's dedication to West Point's "Duty, Honor and Coun-try," but I thought that he and his boys had done their share and more. Some-how he had survived. I didn't want to miss my dad any longer. I wanted him to come home safely, and soon! I hated to hear him talking about going to the Pacific because I knew that he was preparing me for the possibility that the 82nd would be sent there. — BGF]

There are all sorts of rumors of course, most of which one should not listen to. Some units are evidently going to be sent to the U.S. for refitting, etc. and then promptly shipped to the Pacific. That would be nice. I am afraid however that if that happened I would be so very busy during the few weeks or months that we would be in the States that I would not have much time for time off. There would be a tremendous amount of work to be accomplished in a short space of time. All of the chewed-up veterans would have to be discharged and the new replacements taken in. Re-equip-ping and then very intensive training for a new theatre would take more time than one could possibly have. It looks like a lot of work. Even if I managed to get to Washington for a visit to the War Department, I am afraid that I would be too involved for any extensive entertaining. I am afraid too that I share the feeling of most returning soldiers of not wanting to be entertained or wanting to talk about the war and stuff. Enough is enough. Or vice versa.

But right now we have our hands full. I hardly believe that there is a good fight left on the Continent but there must be a million of hungry Russians, Poles, and assorted nationals, plus more krauts no less hungry but some of them still with some fight left. Which all reminds me, I had better get back to work.

Love to everyone,

Pappy

★ ★ ★

April 20, 1945

Dear Babe,

Herewith are the two ribbons — The red is the Legion d'Honneur and the red and green is the Croix de Guerre with Palm.

Love,

Pappy

★ ★ ★

April 24, 1945

Dear Butch,

All seems to be going well. My staff has a pool, each member having contributed a pound (we charged the Corps Commander $5.00), on the meeting place of the first Russian and American patrols. It makes the news a bit more interesting, otherwise it is very difficult at times to be interested in anything except what goes on in one's front yard. This to each one is always the most important war.

The local Stars and Stripes headlines seem to say a lot about the kraut concentration camp policies. We should know now that when the Romans plowed under Carthage with salt they set a precedent of under-perform-ance. The current scorched-earth program seems to include all of this as well as the methodical annihilation of the populace. Either that or convert-ing them into fertilizer as I believe I mentioned in a recent letter. This quaint practice at least will enable espousers of reincarnation to prove that one of their apostles turned up as a turnip so this creed will need no further factual proof. I don't know how I got started on this.

There are many wild rumors flying about on the subject of redeploy-ment, all of which are about totally groundless. Many of the heroes would like to go home and many of them would like to go fight japs. Of the former, many will be unhappy and want to change their minds soon after arriving home and of the latter, many will be unhappy and want to change their minds soon after arriving in the Pacific. Which doesn't prove much I guess except that you can't outguess a guesser. I would personally like to do both so you can see the dilemma I'm in.

Love to everyone,

Pappy

On April 16, the Russians attacked Berlin. Ten months earlier, the landings on the French coast had signaled the beginning of the end of Nazi oppression in Europe — now, with the Germans caught between Russia and her allies, the end was here.

Ordered to advance toward the Baltic Sea, the British Second Army was to prevent any attempts by Germany's defeated forces to flee across into Nazi-occupied Denmark and be prepared to quickly squelch any "last-stand" resistance by the occupation force. Second Army's position would also block the Russians from a possible preemptive communist takeover of Denmark.

Assigned to Second Army, Matthew Ridgway's XVIII Airborne Corps also moved northeast and was ordered to force a crossing over the Elbe River just south of Hamburg at the small town of Bleckede. Ridgway chose the 82nd to establish the last bridgehead of the war in Europe, and in the early morning hours of April 30, the 505th Parachute Infantry Regiment successfully led the Division's assault across the river.

That same morning, Hitler committed suicide in his Berlin bunker. Nazi forces, and civilians pleading for protection from the advancing merciless Russians, began surrendering en masse and continued to do so as the Division pushed farther east.

On May 2, the 82nd arrived in the small town of Ludwigslust, and shortly thereafter, a scout unit assigned to the Division made contact with Russian soldiers at Grabow. Meeting with their commanders, Gavin established the boundaries of their respective front lines with a "no-man's-land" buffer between them.

★ ★ ★

May 5, 1945

Dear Butch,

This has been a week to top all weeks. It has been impossible to write because of the topsy-turvy state of affairs existing hereabouts. I am uncertain of what the censor will permit me to write, but I know that you know from the radio that we have cleaned out this corner of Germany. A complete german army [21st Army Group] surrendered to me yesterday. The troops were moving rather fast and had been for about a week, and to make a long story short as well as suitable for the censor, before either side were fully appreciative of the extent of our penetrations, we were completely into the german rear areas. The commanding general decided to surrender rather quickly. He had little choice.

We lost too, the fighting in places was heavy. Anyway, the troopers of the Division were wonderful and more than anyone they appreciated what they have done. It has been two years of hardship and sacrifice and they have left in their wake hundreds of their dead from Africa to Germany and thousands of wounded.

I am enclosing one of the two copies actually in existence of the German surrender. I am sending it so that you can put it in a place of safekeeping for me. The other, the original, will remain in the Division records.

By now spring has come and you must be getting ready for summer camp. Camps are a lot of fun and I am glad that you like yours so much.

At the moment we are very comfortable. We captured the palace of the Archduke of Mecklenburg which we are using for a home and a Command Post. He actually has three in different parts of germany. This one is in excellent state. We captured the place complete with staff and put them all to work. It is a beautiful place, rather beyond my descriptive abilities.

Had an interesting meeting with the Russians, a wild affair, that's *some* army. I like them very much. The germans fear them beyond belief. They leave complete and utter destruction in their wake, *nothing* is left undone. And they are probably just getting started.

Love to everyone,

Pappy

P.S. I sent the Croix de Guerre and Legion d'Honneur medal to you yesterday, also a Silver Star from the Ardennes fighting.

Pappy

★ *chapter thirteen* ★

VICTORY, RUSSIAN
CAMARADERIE, AND A
VISIT HOME

On May 7, 1945, the Germans signed an unconditional surrender with all hostilities ordered to cease by midnight, May 8. Twenty-five months earlier, Gavin had written his first wartime letter to Barbara, happy to hear that she was going to use her allowance to buy a war bond, thereby helping to end the war and hopefully bring the soldiers home soon. His daughter had done her part on the home front while he had done his part fighting overseas. Though happy, with the difficulty of giving "full expression to one's feelings while in uniform in command," Gavin didn't know whether he should "cry or cheer or just simply get drunk" in celebration.[1] One thing was certain: Gavin had repaid West Point — his "Spartan mother." He had accepted and met the Academy's "challenge 'to move toward the sound of the guns,' to go where danger was greatest, for there is where issues would be resolved and decisions made."[2]

Though the fighting was over, the full horror of the war came to bear on the Division's troopers when shortly after their arrival in Ludwigslust they discovered a concentration camp nearby. Recently built to hold political prisoners moved west away from the advancing Russians, it held "4,000 men . . . forced to live like animals." Rather than share the town's food reserves, the mayor and the town's citizens had allowed the victims of Nazi oppression to starve, "deprived even of the food you would give to your dogs." Those who perished were left in the camp, unburied. Gavin declared Ludwigslust's town square their cemetery — ordering the town's most prominent citizens to dig the graves, remove the bodies from the camp and bury them. The Division's Protestant, Catholic, and Jewish chaplains jointly conducted the burial service, committing the dead "into the hands of our Heavenly Father in the hope that the world will not again be faced with such barbarity."[3] Ordered to file past the graves, with their

markers of wooden crosses or Stars of David, many of the town's citizens wept,
insisting that they had been unaware of the nearby horror.

* * *

May 7, 1945

Dear Babe,

These have been busy days. Today is V/E [Victory in Europe] Day in the States I guess. Yesterday I received word of the unconditional surrender of the remaining germans. It had been expected daily. Well, I hope that everyone celebrates to their heart's content, there could hardly be a better occasion.

Our days have been rather filled. Two days ago we discovered that we had a concentration camp of our own. By now you have probably heard about it through the press. It is about four miles from my Command Post. Probably the less said about it the better. The enclosed [burial address by Division Chaplain George B. Wood] covers it all rather well.

Our continued exchange of visits with the Russians proves to be our most exacting occupation. The day before yesterday I had a delightful meeting with the commanding general of the 5th Guards Cossack Division. He presented me with a lovely silver plaque inscribed with the date and place of the meeting as well as the name of his division. That called for another toast to the spirit of "the Cossack cavalry." That called for another from them to the spirit of "the American paratrooper." Two essentials are always to our President and Marshal Stalin and to our continued association in combat and out. By the time we get around to toasting "The Jeep" (they think that the jeep is a wonderful thing), it is time to take down the shutters and take the guests home. Our toasts are straight scotch whiskey in sizeable glasses, theirs are the same in vodka. Very rugged affairs. But I believe that we think that they are fine people, and by now we fully appreciate why they do to the germans what they do.

At the moment we are up to our ears in german prisoners and slaves (more euphemistically, displaced persons). Goodness knows when anyone will get to go home. We've got lots of work to do yet. The Division fought wonderfully well in the final two weeks, they got in some very good and effective licks.

I'll be seeing you.

Love to everyone,

Pappy

* * *

May 8, 1945

Dear Butch,

That above [letterhead] represents the house of Mecklenburg-Schwerin. I have been getting along on captured stationery for two years and see no reason to change now. This is something that my aide liberated in our present dwelling.

We continue to survive the ardors of Russian hospitality in barely passing fashion. Yesterday my neighbor from across the way had myself and part of the staff over for tea at three, and by the time we had run the gamut to vodka toasts it was midnight. One of my most stalwart staff officers got "combat fatigue" and had to be evacuated, otherwise things went off rather uneventfully. "Uneventfully" at one of these affairs means that no one was shot or run over that anyone knows of.

They presented me with a Cossack saber and a Russian tommy-gun, both suitably marked with a silver engraved plate. I fortunately was able to present them with a big blow-up photo of one of our drops and a couple of engraved pistols. I had a ride in one of their tanks and generally we had a quiet evening. But my scotch is running out and I am scouring the continent, I hope that I can find some. They rather look with disdain upon wine as being a bourgeois affectation hardly becoming Cossacks and defenders of the red banner.

Love to everyone,

Pappy

* * *

May 13, 1945

Dear Skipper,

I thought that you might like the enclosed. We have had a great time with the Russians. We start returning our obligations tomorrow night. The pictures were taken at one of the division headquarters opposite us. After dinner which really was supposed to be a tea, it started at 3:00 p.m., they gathered in a circle, clapped for each other and danced. Finally moved the dance out in the street. That seems with them to be the normal thing to do. There was another reason, earlier in the evening when I started to dance I bumped my head rather slightly on a very low hanging chandelier. With that, a Russian staff officer steps up and rips it down completely with one good yank and a couple of tugs. Consequently we had no light later but no one seemed to be concerned about it. The officers stand around in a circle and one at a time they take the center and go into their dance, the accompaniment is usually an accordion and a violin. They call their national dance something that sounds like a mazurka but I don't believe that that is what it is. Anyway, everyone takes a turn including guests and by now I am getting to where I can squat and kick my heels out with the best of them.

The current pastime is figuring one's points, I have 162 I believe; as you probably know, 85 gets one home and perhaps out. *Perhaps.* This doesn't apply to officers anyway, but our troopers have some rather high scores [determined by months spent overseas, time in service, battle campaigns and decorations, number of dependent children, etc.].

I think that it would be a good idea, however, if people at home took a completely realistic view of the situation and realized that many of us will not return for some long time. I would like to be in the States by Xmas but I will probably be fortunate if I am. Above all else, I would like to go to the Pacific but everyone looks upon us as though we were all combat neurosis cases.

I mailed your kilts yesterday. I had my aide run over to London to get me a footlocker and do some other shopping and the kilts were ready so he brought them back. I am certain that you have outgrown them since they were ordered but they are worn short and you may be able to do something about them. I hope that you like them. *[I loved it, and the fit was just right; then my Aunt Lil let it down as I grew taller. My daughter wore the kilt after I had long outgrown it. We have no girls in the next generation, but I'm hoping that perhaps in my great-grandchildren's generation there will be a little girl to wear the kilt which is carefully packed away for her. — BGF]*

It seems awfully strange that there is no more shooting anywhere.

Love to everyone,

Pappy

★ ★ ★

May 16, 1945

Dear Butch,

Well all seems to be going well. We have finished up our worst unpleasantry, cleaning up our concentration camp.

The Russians continue to be a hazard and a source of considerable pleasure. The other evening Chuck Billingslea [commander of the 325], in the best parachute tradition, made a perfect exit from a second-story window only to misjudge his drop zone and land on a cobblestone road. He broke his ankle. The Russians were hilarious. It is in a cast now but should be well in a few weeks. I am having him attend another formal exchange of visits tomorrow. *[The story goes that, unknown to Chuck, the land dropped off sharply behind the two-storey house. Chuck thought that he would be making a two-storey jump, but it turned out to be four stories with a cobblestone drop zone to land on. — BGF]*

I was just interrupted by a soldier [a "high-point" man] who goes home tomorrow. He landed at Casablanca with me, jumped with me in Sicily and Salerno, was with me when I captured Naples with the 505, jumped with me in Normandy and Holland, and fought all through the Ardennes, Belgium, and into Germany until we met the Russians. He feels bad about going but it is the thing for a man to do who is to be released. I am going to talk to a large group of them in the morning, our oldest most decorated veterans, it will be a tearjerker and I would almost as soon skip it.

As for me, I never knew that there was so much to be done; millions of prisoners, we have prisoners like some people have mice, Displaced persons, and many square miles of territory to be occupied. I still would like to make Xmas if that were possible.

Did I tell you that I finally sent the kilts? I believe that I did in the last letter.

Going to bed early tonight to get in training for meeting the Russkis tomorrow night.

Butch, could you send me a copy of J. Frank Dobie's "A Texan in England," I'll send you a check.

Love to everyone,

Pappy

★ ★ ★

May 22, 1945
Ludwigslust, Germany
Dear Babe,

For the first time in two years, I can dateline my letters with my location. This is a nice town, the seat of the reigning family of Mecklenburg. I am using their castle for my Command Post and home of the staff. A very lovely place, we will probably give it up in a few days. It has been nice, we captured it on May 3rd and it was here that I accepted the surrender of the 21st German Army. That was quite a day for all of us, really our V/E Day. We knew for certain then that the German could never get off the flat of his back again.

To many of us, all of us present who have survived since Casablanca, it was a fitting climax and we were deeply moved by the entire business.

Even our hatred for the German, deep-seated and intense as it was, was to be added to when we found the concentration camp a few miles from here. The first burgomeister [town mayor] committed suicide with his family the night that I arrived, we couldn't understand why until we found the camp. Those things must never be forgotten. It is frequently maddening to us the way that boys just from the States are nice to Germans, even complete units. This has been something like nothing else in the history of the world that we have been dealing with. It may well have been our own people in these concentration camps, in fact, it would have been had we not finally gained the upper hand. We must never forget this nor must we fail to keep the peace.

One senses from the news clippings from the States that there is a general distrust of the Russians. Why the Russians have trusted no one and have been so selfish in their inexorable and persistent effort to destroy everything German can readily be understood when one sees both peoples. The german propaganda works on the theme of us being against them [the Russians]; even now, prisoners tell our soldiers that we should fight the Russians with them. It is hardly believable that they yet occasionally find a receptive ear.

I have spent a great deal of time with the Russians lately, not with politicians nor people with an axe to grind but soldiers who have fought the German for five years and who have lost everything in the war but the final victory. They want to get along with us, they are most anxious to but of course they distrust us. If we were Russians, we wouldn't trust anyone after what they have been through. We must and will get along with them and no one is more anxious to leave us alone and still get along with us than the Russians. This is an awful lot of heavy politics for a little girl, far too much.

The Vaseline and the nuts have arrived. Thank you very, very much.

I doubt most seriously that I will return during the summer while you are in camp. No one knows when we will return, you see it took two years to get all of these people over here so they can't all be sent back next week. I would like to make it by Xmas. I've got points, wow, I've got points like some people have mice but they don't get me home.

I've been getting a very cold reception to my requests to go to the Pacific so that probably can't be accomplished until we get back to the States.

Love to everyone,

Pappy

★ ★ ★

May 24, 1945

Dear Babe,

This morning I received a bill from Ridabock & Co. in New York for some miniature medals that I had ordered. Unless the bill is incorrect, they must have sent you a Distinguished Flying Cross instead of a Distinguished Service Cross. Will you please let me know right away if this is so and I will so inform them. In the meantime, you can return them for correction of their error if they made one.

All goes well on this front. There is no chance of me returning during the time that you are in summer camp. Too much to do around here and too few boats [to transport soldiers to the States], etc. etc.

Let me know about the medals as soon as you can. *[The medals were perfect and beautiful. In those patriotic days, any relative of a serviceman who had earned medals wore the miniatures or ribbons with pride. — BGF]*

Love to everyone,

Pappy

With the war over in Europe, Gavin expected to receive orders to return the Division to the United States for possible deployment to the Pacific Theater of Operations; instead, the Division was to remain in Europe as part of the Allied occupation force.

Gavin, however, would personally have an opportunity for a brief visit home. The War Department was flying him to the States, as a representative of America's victorious forces in the European Theater, to tour in a war bond drive in support of the continuing war in the Pacific.

★ ★ ★

May 24, 1945

Dear Butch,

Hold everything. I'm going to sell war bonds. Wow! *[This was the best news I had ever had in my young life. I couldn't wait! — BGF]*

Pappy

★ ★ ★

May 26, 1945

Dear Babe,

The enclosed came with a medal [Order of Alexander Nevsky, awarded to outstanding Red Army commanders displaying personal courage, boldness, and bravery] that the Russians were nice enough to give me yesterday. It isn't exactly a medal, there is no ribbon to it, it is a cluster that is worn on the right chest pocket. So I'll look funnier than [Hermann] Goering [who wore extravagant and exaggerated military regalia — sash, medals, ribbons — and often carried an ornate marshal's baton as Hitler's deputy]. I sent you my Bronze Star from the fighting around Cologne, you probably have it by now.

My staff is giving me lessons in how to sell war bonds, they are also drafting a memorandum on the subject of "How to Behave in The United States." I have been told that I do my stint in San Antonio, you can probably find out more about it in Washington than I can over here. I am ashamed to leave the boys but I believe that they understand, anyway it is just for a couple of weeks. It is going to seem awfully strange to be back in America.

I have a very nice grand piano here in the castle that I would like to take back for you, but I am limited to one piece of hand baggage and it of limited weight.

Don't know what I'll do for summer uniforms, haven't worn anything like that since Africa. This going to America is much worse to prepare for than going into combat, or perhaps it is that we are much more accustomed to the latter. Anyway, it is going to be fun and that is an understatement.

Love to everyone,

Pappy

[During the few days he was home in Washington on the war bond selling tour, my dad and I walked for miles down Connecticut Avenue to Dupont Circle or up Connecticut Avenue, and across the Calvert Street bridge back to Columbia Road, just talking. He asked about my school, my friends, my camp, and I responded with questions of my own. One day we stopped at a drug store for a Coca-Cola. My dad was in uniform, including paratrooper boots, because he had no civilian clothes fit to wear. He was a very handsome and impressive sight. When the pretty, young blonde behind the counter offered to trade him our cokes for the Alexander Nevsky medallion, he laughed and declined. I had to learn that he wasn't just "my daddy," but was someone now whom strangers would recognize and approach for a conversation. I was proud to be his daughter. — BGF]

★ ★ ★

May 29, 1945

Dear Babe,

General Ridgway should be back by now so I presume that you have heard of what is to happen to me. I apparently am to participate in a war bond drive in Texas. I believe that I am to go directly there although I may find out more about this later. I am not sure of my schedule and I am making a guess but I estimate that I should be in San Antonio by June 14th, perhaps the 13th. If I do have to go direct, I will give you a call from there when I arrive. I'll call sooner if I can. When the bond business is over, I apparently will have some time in Washington. I may go to Fort Benning or New York. I probably won't be able to tell until I know more about my itinerary.

At all events, late in June I should be able to be with you all in Washington for a short visit. Please don't plan anything for me to do or accept anything for me contingent upon my being there. Everything is too indefinite and there is a lot that I want to get done.

It is grand to be able to look forward to seeing you again after so long a time. As my schedule takes more definite shape or as I get more information, I will let you know how things are going. In the meantime, I will be very busy here, there is lots doing. By the way, ask Mommie to get out some civilian clothing if I have any. I'll be seeing you.

Love to everyone,

Pappy

The 82nd returned to France, where an exchange was made of the Division's high-point personnel for low-point personnel from the other divisions slated to return to America. After the end of the war bond tour, Gavin would rejoin the Division.

★ ★ ★

June 2, 1945

Sissonne, France

Dear Butch,

This place was our home for some weeks last winter, specifically for the time between Holland and the Ardennes which really wasn't for very long, about three weeks. I am glad to see the troopers come back this time. Germany and non-fraternization was rather unpleasant.

About my bond selling campaign, it appears now as though I will be sent directly to San Antonio. I had hoped for a while that we might stop by Washington but I am afraid not.

Sometime after mid-June you may receive mail for me at 2006 Columbia Road, just hold onto it. I have quite a bit of mail now from former veterans of the Division, families of casualties, etc., all of it must be answered carefully. I am having it forwarded to your address.

Today I flew by Piper Cub down to Epernay to see [Ralph] "Doc" Eaton [XVIII Airborne Corps chief of staff]. He is at the moment hospitalized with some sort of foot trouble. Yesterday I flew in here from Ludwigslust by C-47, took about three hours. Tomorrow should not be too busy. Monday, I intend to fly over to London for about two or three days of partly business and partly shopping. I am having trouble getting summer uniforms since they are never worn in Europe. It is quite cool here.

Tommie [Captain John S. Thompson], my aide, went into Paris today to try to get something as well as arrange our schedule to get under way to the States later. Tommie is a fine trooper. A professional baseball player in civilian life, played for Boston. He has been wounded twice, Sicily and Italy, and has been decorated several times. A very fine young man and a good soldier. He returns with me.[4]

It will be good to see you again Butch.

Love to everyone,

Pappy

[Tommie was a young, blonde paratrooper with the looks of a movie star. It seemed to me that he and my dad were in concert in a different world, more serious than the one I lived in. They had fought together, and both were heroes. Tommie went on to his home while my dad stayed with us for a few days. — BGF]

★ ★ ★

June 5, 1945

London

Dear Butch,

I am trying to get some summer uniforms and not having much luck. I by chance have exactly the same room in the same hotel in which I stayed when I first arrived in London from Naples on November 18, 1943. It seems like a long time ago. We flew from Naples to Palermo, Sicily, then to Algiers, then to Marrakech in West Africa, then way out over the Atlantic towards America, coming in at dawn over Northern Ireland and landing in Scotland. The final loop brought us to London where I was stationed with SHAEF for several months.

Bill Oakley accompanied me as my aide. He was killed in Normandy. Which reminds me, the first anniversary is about due, June 6th at 5:00 a.m. I will have to celebrate a different day since we jumped about six hours before the amphibious landings. I do not expect our lads to get excited about the anniversary. They have had so many firsts, particularly Sicily and Salerno, that Normandy was just one more.

My plane is set up for next Monday and I hope everything moves on schedule. I'll call you in any case whenever I can get to a phone long enough. Certainly I should be able to from San Antonio.

London hasn't changed much, no V [rocket] bombs so it's a bit more quiet. As a city, I like it as much as any that I have been in in Europe. I have a few friends here now and I belong to at least one club so that helps.

I am looking forward very much though to seeing America again and seeing you, Babe, and all of the family. Take it easy, I'll call.

Love to everyone,

Pappy

★ ★ ★

June 7, 1945

Sissonne, France

Dear Babe,

Things are a bit topsy-turvy at the moment. There is so much to be done. We [the Division] are all here now and getting settled down for a bit. Yesterday I returned from a short trip to London, I wrote you a letter while over there. During my absence things piled up a bit.

In a few days I will be under way and I have no idea what my itinerary is except that I am to go to San Antonio. I am very anxious to see General Ridgway and take care of some things in the War Department.

Incidentally, you will be receiving some mail of mine forwarded from here probably before I arrive. I get the darndest mail, yesterday I received a piece of wedding cake from a trooper's family. His parents had celebrated their 50th wedding anniversary and sent me a piece of their cake. I have an awful lot of letters to be answered concerning casualties and their place of burial, missing effects, etc. But anyway, hold everything.

Love to everyone,

Pappy

[My mother and I drove to the MATS (Military Air Transport Service) terminal, next to Washington National Airport. We had waited so long for my dad's return that it was hard to believe that it was really about to happen. It was a sultry summer day in the capital, and air-conditioning was still a thing of the future. We sat perspiring, waiting for my dad's plane to arrive. Suddenly it had landed and passengers were coming into the terminal. I was afraid that he might not be on this plane. Then I saw him and ran to my dad, wanting to never let go of him again.

My dad had never seen our apartment. He liked the large world map that we had used to paper one whole wall in the entrance hall and the small American flags that we had used to keep track of troop movements from country to country. My mother fixed my dad's favorite food for dinner, steak (we had been saving our meat ration coupons), corn-on-the-cob, and fresh tomatoes.

The next day my dad went to the White House with Lt. Gen. Alexander Patch Jr., Seventh Army Commander, and Lt. Gen. Lucian Truscott, Fifth Army Commander, to present Hermann Goering's diamond-studded baton to President Truman. The days after that took my mother and dad to his hometown of Mt. Carmel, Pennsylvania, for a parade in his honor, then to Staunton Military Academy in Virginia, where he gave the graduation address. His days at home passed much too quickly and he was off again on a plane for the war bond drive in San Antonio, Texas, and from there, back to Berlin. But I knew that no one would be shooting at him this time. He would be home soon for good, maybe in time for Christmas. — BGF]

chapter fourteen

OCCUPATION DUTY — BERLIN

Germany's entire infrastructure was damaged or nonexistent, with no civil au-
thority in place and millions homeless and hungry. Though no longer a military
threat, the "soldats" of Germany's Wehrmacht also had to be processed and
interrogated — Nazis held accountable for their war crimes.

Germany had to be controlled. To do so, the Allies divided the country into
four zones, each overseen separately by military governments of Great Britain,
America, Russia, and France. Located within the Russian zone, the city of
Berlin was further divided into sectors administered individually by the four
Allies, with the four powers forming a joint governing command. First Allied
Airborne Army — now renamed First Airborne Army — was given responsibil-
ity, under the command of General Floyd Parks, for Berlin's American sector.
Parks passed the responsibility to the 82nd. Back from the United States, Gavin
flew to Berlin to organize the Division's move.

★ ★ ★

July 24, 1945

Dear Babe,

We have just passed over Frankfurt, Germany, on the way back from
Berlin to Epinal [France]. Had a busy day, Berlin is appearing better every
day now, streets getting cleaned up, etc.

I received two very nice letters from you just before leaving Epinal, both
told of the fun that you were having in camp. I am so glad that they have
such nice horses this year. You have always liked horses. Sometime you
must have Mommie get out the pictures taken at Fort Sill when you were
quite a tiny girl and I used to take you riding with me. I would hold you
on the pommel of the saddle in front of me and we would gallop about the
stable area. Every Sunday afternoon we would go by the stables and feed
the horses sugar. You had one favorite named "Sunshine." He learned to
recognize your voice when you called him, and what was more important

to him, he learned that when he came you gave him a lump of sugar. You liked to go by the stables and call him and have him come up for his lump.

Although it is quite warm on the ground today, there is frost on the wings of the airplane because we are flying above 9,000 feet. It is very cold. We are flying up here in order to take advantage of a tailwind. Normally it takes about three hours from Berlin to Epinal. Today I hope to make it in two and a half.

Someday you will have to visit this part of the world with me, you would enjoy it very much.

Love to everyone,

Pappy

Arriving in force by early August, the 82nd occupied the sector between the British and Russian zones. Finding adequate billets for so many troopers, and offices for the Division staff, was difficult — most of Berlin's buildings had been destroyed or severely damaged. Food needed to be found and rationed to feed Berlin's citizens, coal was in scarce supply, trees needed to be cut down for fuel, and the thousands of corpses throughout the city needed to be buried.

★ ★ ★

August 14, 1945

Dear Babe,

A very nice letter from you yesterday telling me of your Red Cross life-saving tests. I am very glad that you were able to bring up Miss Libby, otherwise I can well imagine the ill fate that would befall her. *[Miss Libby was the swimming instructor at camp, the one I had to "rescue" to pass the Red Cross tests. — BGF]* You were very lucky to find that many shark's teeth. I didn't realize that there were any sharks up around Maryland.

I knew that Mommy was coming out to see you, and I should soon hear from her telling me of her visit. I know that she had a nice time. It is too bad that she could not have spent more time with you but I realize that the gas shortage makes that impossible. Now with the end of the jap war in sight there should be more gas for everyone, more food too.

Last night I saw the Ernie Pyle film [based on the war correspondent's dispatches from North Africa and Italy], "GI Joe." It was very good. Most of those pictures are not very realistic and are overdone in parts. "GI Joe" is much more like what happens [to a rifle company in combat] than any picture that we have seen.

We are rapidly settling down and making a home for ourselves in Berlin. We will have shelters this winter but not a great deal more. But nothing could be worse than last winter. The Ardennes was rather cold.

Soon school will start and another year will be under way. I hope that you do well in school this year. Your music should improve. Continue to study and work hard.

Love,

Pappy

World War II came to an end on August 14, 1945, when Japan also agreed to an unconditional surrender after atomic bombs were dropped on the cities of Hiroshima and Nagasaki. Learning of America's use of atomic weapons, Gavin found it "frightening and unbelievable in its implications."[1]

★ ★ ★

August 21, 1945

Dear Babe,

No letter from you for some time. You must be very busy in camp. As I remember, just before the close of camp everyone is kept very busy there is so much to do at that time. I was so glad to hear that Mommie had an opportunity to get down to see you. Now that the gasoline restrictions are lifted it will be much easier to travel about in the car.

We have been busy trying to get settled in our new homes. Sunday I had my first jump in Berlin. It was a very nice day, little wind, so everything went well. I am enclosing a clipping from The Stars and Stripes which explains things as well as anything.

Now that camp is about over you must be thinking about school. I sent a check to Mommie to use in getting some things for you for the next school year. It is from the Infantry Journal for a short article that they were nice enough to accept for publication. I'll send you a copy of the article after it is published.

Now that the war with Japan is over most of the soldiers here are thinking of going home. Many of them have not been home for several years so I can hardly blame them. I do not know when I will have another opportunity to get back to the States, there is an awful lot of work to be done here.

Love to everyone,

Pappy

As they arrived at Berlin's airport, the many government officials, dignitaries, and celebrities drawn to visit the former seat of Hitler's Nazi Germany were greeted by a special honor guard. Formed by Gavin from the ranks of the Division, its members were all highly decorated — rows of ribbons on their uniform jackets were very impressive — and they were also all six feet or more in height. General Patton was so impressed by the tall, decorated paratroopers with white gloves on their hands, white scarves cut from silk parachutes at their necks, white bootlaces in their jump boots, and special chromium-plated bayonets on their rifles that during his visit he pronounced it "the finest honor guard I have ever seen."[2] Picked up by the wire services and sent around the world, Patton's statement gave the All-American Division the distinction of becoming known as "America's Guard of Honor."

★ ★ ★

August 30, 1945

Dear Babe,

I certainly have a hard time writing letters the past three weeks. I have never been so busy before, and even now I do not see how I can get everything done that must be done.

This morning in about another hour, I am having Gen. Dwight Eisenhower and the Senate Foreign Relations Committee as our guests for an airborne division review. It is a very interesting affair that we have worked up. The troops walk by in review as they would land, with the artillery of the parachute battalions hand-drawn, etc. As the last man passes the reviewing stand, the first gliders pass overhead, they cut loose and land to the left of the reviewing party, they open and armed jeeps and motorcycles emerge together and pass in review. As the last vehicle passes in review, the first parachute transports appear in formation overhead and to the front. They jump in front of the reviewing party. As the last paratroopers land, the troop carrier pilots fly by "on the deck," passing in review before the reviewing party.

Quite a deal but very difficult to coordinate properly. We have tried it once and it worked OK. I'm sweating out this morning. Friday I have the same thing for about fifteen Russian generals, I'm sweating out the toasts that follow that one.

Gen. [Andy] March [Division Artillery] goes home to Washington for three weeks about September 26th. I'll ask him to call. My assistant commander, Gen. [Ira] Swift, goes to the War Department for duty in the next few weeks. I'll ask him to call also. I guess you have heard from Dr. Waring.

The enclosed money is Polish, just brought from Warsaw by a war correspondent who shouldn't have been there in the first place [because of the fighting between communist and anticommunist factions for control of the country]. Thought that you would like to have it.

I'm awfully busy and must continue to work if I expect to stay out of jail. This is dynamite and I'm responsible for an awful lot.

Love to everyone,

Pappy

★ ★ ★

September 3, 1945

Dear Butch,

Well camp must be over and you are back home again. I know that you have had a lot of fun and you must miss the girls that you spent the summer with.

I have not written as much as I would like to have this past summer. Principally, and solely really, because I have been terribly busy. Yesterday I took over the command of the Berlin District and the First Airborne Army [FAA]. It is a wonderful opportunity. I never thought that I would get to command an army. It will be quite an experience and I should learn a lot.

Gen. Swift left for Washington this morning. He said that he would call you so you should hear from him. Dr. Waring leaves shortly and he will call also. Gen. Parks, who I relieved of the command of the FAA, may also call.

I have never worked as hard as I have the past few weeks and there is so little to show for it. Now that I have the command of both the Division and the FAA, as well as the Berlin District, as well as being a member of the Kommandantura [the joint governing command], it doesn't look like I will have much time for play nor for letter writing.

The Kommandantura as you probably know consists of four generals, one Russian, French, British, and U.S. They govern the city of Berlin. I am the U.S. one and have 887,000 germans in my U.S. sector of the city. They are a source of a great deal of worry. I am afraid that many of them are going to starve to death this winter despite all that I can do for them. We are bringing in tons and tons of food daily but a million people eat an awful lot. I believe we have a million or better but the burgomeister's official count shows only 887,000.

Fuel will also be a bad situation. I am at present trying to get coal from the Ruhr. I can get 6,500 tons from there this month if I can get transportation to haul it with. This will barely handle my military requirements so what the civilians will do goodness knows. They have been told to cut down all the trees that they need now so that the wood will be dried out and burn, otherwise they are all going to freeze to death this winter because there will be no coal for civilian use. Many of them are on the verge of starvation now. The Russians are, of course, comparatively unconcerned. They say that 300,000 civilians starved to death in Leningrad last winter while the city was under siege by the Germans and they are expecting to even up the score this winter.

The troopers of the Division have been doing a wonderful job. They are working very hard for me and really trying to do the job well. Thursday we had a review for Gen. Eisenhower and a group of Congressmen. He was very complimentary. Friday we had another for Marshal Zhukov [the head of the Russian zone] and his staff. It turned out to be for about forty Russian generals who had heard about it and all came along. After the review I had about thirty of them to my house for lunch. It was a nice affair with the usual number of toasts. Marshal Zhukov is very nice. *[Many years later, my father told me that several of the Russian generals arrived, saw Marshal Zhukov, turned on their heels and left. He said that they were obviously terrified of him. — BGF]*

Bob Capa of Life moved into my house today, he will probably stay a week. I like him very much, a fine chap. Senator [Claude] Pepper is due tomorrow. I plan on having him for dinner, guess I'll have to find some troopers from Florida for him. Gen. [J. C. H.] Lee was in the other day, said that he was on the way back to Washington and that he would call you.

I have searched high and low and I can't find that address that Aunt Lil gave me to look up for someone. *[Johanna Henzman, a friend of my great-aunt, had asked if my father could find information on her friends and relatives in Berlin. — BGF]* Will you ask her to send it to me again. Now that I am mayor of the city it is a simple problem.

Please understand if I don't write too often. If I can stay out of jail I will be doing well. What a job.

Love to everyone,

Pappy

★ ★ ★

September 12, 1945

Dear Babe,

I received your letter written, or started rather, at Gibson Island. Glad to know that you are back home again and all ready to start school.

Do you have any idea when Uncle George will return? My own future is a bit indefinite, it does appear pretty certain that I will remain here in Berlin through the winter.

In addition to the above [letterhead of U.S. Headquarters, Berlin District and Headquarters, First Airborne Army] I still command the 82nd. The Berlin District and the Kommandantura, however, take all of the time. I have never been so busy. I'm spending most of my time learning and a little doing.

My opposite number in the Russian sector of Berlin has just been replaced by Lt. Gen. [Ivan] Smirnov who I had the good fortune to meet in Mecklenburg before V/E Day. That helps. Last evening he and his staff came over to dinner and we had quite a reunion. My British opposite number has been Gen. [Lewis] Lyne whom I have served with in Italy and Holland and know quite well. That helps too. My French partner [Geoffrey de Beauchesne] I have not known before. We had him and his staff in for dinner the night before last and had a very nice affair.

My staff seems to get along well with everyone and that helps tremendously. If I can manage to stay out of jail for the next month, I will be doing well. But it sure is a lot of fun and quite an education.

Love to everyone,

Pappy

p.s. If you could find a copy of Tolstoy's "Peter I" would you please send it to me?

Love,

Pappy

chapter fifteen

THE CALL HOME

Gavin received good news — the 82nd Airborne Division was to be returned to the United States, but with that came bad news — the Division would be demobilized upon its return, ceasing to exist in the U.S. Army. With the war over, Army headquarters in Washington recommended that only two airborne divisions be retained in the Regular Army: the 11th Airborne Division (currently on occupation duty in Japan) and the 101st Airborne Division (still in Europe).

★ ★ ★

September 19, 1945

Dear Babe,

Glad that the check has arrived. Since I hadn't heard from you for some time I was getting a bit concerned about it.

I was not a bit surprised to hear about your sinus troubles again. If you recall, I wrote to you about it exactly this time last year. I too had sinus trouble at the end of each summer camp. I am quite sure that it comes from too much continuous time in the water. So I hope this will save you from the fate of a pincushion.

About the stamps, I have already dispatched the low man on the totem pole, Lt. Lowder the junior aide, to find some in Berlin. He can get lots of them. Tomorrow I'll send them to you.

I have not been able to do any riding over here although there are many beautiful horses. I rode some in Mecklenburg when we were at Ludwigslust. All over continental Europe there are many horses, people do not have cars like in America, everyone rides a great deal. In Mecklenburg we captured a regiment of cavalry, Hungarian cavalry that had been fighting with the Germans. They had exceptionally fine horses and good equipment. I gave most of the horses to the Russian Cossack division that we had met. They used the horses to match with those that they already had. When they were through they had two regiments of cavalry, one gray and one bay.

You have probably heard through someone in the War Department that the Division leaves Berlin in the latter part of October. It goes directly to the Assembly Area Command where it readies itself for the return trip home. It should, according to present plans, arrive in the States in mid-December. This is all tentative and subject to change. I believe that it will be closely carried out so you should expect me in time for Xmas.

But the heartbreaking thing and saddest thing about it all to us is that the Division is to be broken up and demobilized. The only airborne division that fought as a [conventional infantry] division in the last war, the oldest airborne division in this war and by far the most experienced. But that is the way it goes. It will be very hard on all of us, not the loss of our jobs of course but the end of this fine spirit that has taken us through so much. It has done a wonderful job in Berlin and is very highly thought of by all of the nations represented here.

Yesterday I returned from an overnight visit to Nijmegen [for observances of the one-year anniversary of Operation MARKET-GARDEN]. The Dutch were wonderful. Everyone turned out. It was the largest crowd that I have ever talked to, somewhere around 50,000. I enjoyed it very much. Afterwards I had to have the guests for lunch and it too was my biggest luncheon check to date, $200.00. They were very nice. Included was Gen. Dikehorn, Chief of Staff of the Netherlands army, Gen. Matthews, Commanding General of the Canadian 2nd Division, First Secretary of the US Embassy at the Hague, Burgomeister Hustinx of Nijmegen, etc. Quite a wingding.

Last evening I went over to Gen. Beauchesne's for dinner, he has the French sector. He had wonderful crepe suzettes, brought in flaming. I am enclosing his invitation, you may find it interesting if you must still study French.

Love to all,

Pappy

★ ★ ★

September 26, 1945

Dear Butch,

I am up at about 6,000 feet about halfway between Frankfurt and Berlin. I have just talked to Gen. [Walter] Bedell Smith, Gen. Eisenhower's Chief of Staff [at Eisenhower's headquarters in Frankfurt], and the decision seems to be final that we will return to the States in early December. (This typing isn't too easy because when we go in and out of clouds the ship bounces.) I will know more about the exact date later.

I am glad for the troops' sake that they are getting to go home but they would have anyway. Practically all of our veterans have left. I will have about 3,000 to 5,000 of 82nd men and the remaining 10,000 will be from other outfits. The heartbreaking thing to all of us is that the Division is to be demobilized. There will be some airborne divisions left in the post-war Army but not the 82nd. Our trouble has been that we have too many high-point men and the simplest staff procedure has been to demobilize the Division. For the veterans it is very hard to take. Gen. Eisenhower is all for us and has recommended that we remain but the War Department says no. We are not licked yet. But the issue of our return appears settled, early December.

Life in Berlin continues to go on in a comparatively unexciting way. I believe that the city is well in hand. I have come to like the work and I have become very interested in the people and their rehabilitation. Yesterday I received about a half-dozen letters from people who had read the article [about the Division's demobilization] in the Zeitung [Berlin's newspaper]. They were in German and were just translated before I left this morning.

I would like to be able to do more for the people who really want a democratic form of government. It is quite apparent that our definition of "democracy" and that of our Russian ally are as far apart as the poles. Nevertheless, they are not irreconcilable. We have a lot in common.

Did I ask you to forward to me again the address that Aunt Lil wanted me to look up? I intended to, I cannot find the note that she gave me in June anywhere. I cannot transmit a letter for her but I can look up the people and find out how they are getting along.

I will be glad to get back this winter. I have no idea what will happen to me. Anything that I can think of would be very anticlimactic. If I had anything to do about it, I would like to go to school for a while, like the War College or the Army-Navy War College. Somewhere where I could shed all responsibilities for a while and read and study and attempt to digest the many things that have happened in the past two years. Undoubtedly, I will be reduced in grade [to prewar rank] and that I expect. But it is going to be very difficult to get interested in commanding a company again. This foreign relations field has proven fascinating, I'd like to know a lot more about it.

I hope that you are again studying at school and settled down for the winter. This winter I should be more aware of what you are doing. I regret very much that you will not get that opportunity for a trip to Berlin. I think that will have to remain one of the things to do when you are older, you will appreciate Europe much more then. Besides, traveling is impossible here now for everyone and will be for some time.

Love to everyone,

Pappy

★ ★ ★

September 28, 1945

Dear Babe,

Our football season opens tomorrow so I am enclosing a ticket to the first game. It is the first game in the Division's history. We have been too busy fighting up to now so it is difficult to guess how they will come out.

We still leave October 15th for another area. There we prepare for shipment. We should be in the States by early December.

All continues well here, the city and all of the people are in good shape for the winter. I believe that it is in better shape than any other occupied city in Germany. Gen. Parks is due back next week. He will take over running the city, and I will concentrate on getting the Division moved.

By now I am sure your sinus is over, if you do not swim too much it will stay away. Continue writing me at the same APO. If Mommy has not sent the ice skates tell her not to do so.

Love to everyone,

Pappy

★ ★ ★

October 2, 1945

Dear Babe,

These stamps are from the postal system of the city of Berlin. They are currently in use in the city. I thought that they might add something to your collection.

Love to all,

Pappy

★ ★ ★

October 3, 1945

Dear Babe,

Yesterday afternoon I found Aunt Lil's letter regarding the relatives and friends of Johanna Henzman in some papers that I had filed away after returning from the States last June. I immediately had my aide who speaks German fluently, not Capt. Thompson, go and call on them. This is his report:

Hans Orphal and his wife are safe and well.

Johanna Henzman's brother was bombed-out and lost everything but he is in good health and lives with Hans Orphal.

Marie Felgentreff is also safe and well.

Mrs. Gertrude Lamprecht is in Lubeck. She was very ill but is all right now.

Mr. & Mrs. Willi Kofalk are safe and getting along fine.

All of those people who are safe and well, except Johanna Henzman's brother, still have their homes. That is, they were not bombed or burnt-out. This is remarkably good. All of them are now able to obtain plenty of food, not by American standards but it is adequate. They seemed quite contented and considered themselves fortunate to have survived the war so well. I hope that this will give Aunt Lil the information for Johanna Henzman that she wanted.

Love to everyone,

Pappy

★ ★ ★

October 6, 1945

Dear Babe,

The Dutch shoes were obtained for me to send to you by a captain [Arie "Harry" Bestebreurtje] in the Dutch army [who had been liaison officer to the 82nd during Operation MARKET-GARDEN]. Like shoes in America, they are rationed and are difficult to obtain. They are the regular-type shoe worn by the Dutch people and are to be worn. The smaller pair, of course, is a souvenir pair.

Love to all,

Pappy

Assigned as a public relations officer to First Airborne Army, Barney Oldfield (former officer in the 505) was with Gavin in Berlin when he received the Division's demobilization orders. Oldfield quickly arranged a transfer to the 82nd and immediately launched a "blitz" of letters, phone calls, and interviews to his press contacts. Soon, Washington's decision to deactivate such a highly decorated division with its glorious history and lineage was being strongly protested on radio broadcasts and in newspaper and magazine columns throughout the United States and Europe.

★ ★ ★

October 11, 1945

Dear Babe,

It seems to me that it is about time that I wrote you and brought you up-to-date on what is happening. We have been very busy. Some of our activities should be hitting the newspapers so you may have an idea of what has been going on.

Gen. J. C. H. Lee called the other day to say that he had called when in Washington and that all was well. By now Gen. March should be back. Gen. Parks returned several days ago and yesterday I turned the city over to him. He is being replaced by Gen. [Ray] Barker.

The Division leaves Berlin October 21st. We should sail about the 26th or 27th of November. From Berlin we go to Reims [in France] and from there go to Le Havre [the port of embarkation]. We know the Reims area well, having lived there for several weeks after Holland.

About a week ago the Belgian Minister of National Defense came to the Division and awarded the Division the Belgian Fourragère. It is very nice looking. He and his party were on my hands for several days and we were kept quite busy.

Yesterday the Minister of War for the Netherlands and Ambassador Hornbeck came to the Division with a large party to award the Division the Order of Willem Nassau. It is the same as our Congressional Medal of Honor and the British Victoria Cross. The medal was pinned on the Division's colors. The Dutch have never made a similar award to an entire unit before. By special ministerial decree, Queen Wilhelmina granted the Division the privilege of wearing the Orange Lanyard on the left shoulder. It is a rare award, only made once before in the history of the Netherlands and then in 1850 in their colonial wars. It is a very attractive thing and the Division is very proud of it. In addition, the Dutch government made 72 awards to the members of the Division for leadership, gallantry, etc., in Holland during the Nijmegen fight last year.

I was given a very lovely affair [Dutch Order of Orange-Nassau, Degree of Grand-Officer], too valuable to ship in the mails. It has only been given to kings before; of course, kings are getting scarce around these parts nowadays and they must have had a few extra of these on hand. But it is very nice.

It appears to be definite that we are slated for demobilization and fini. This is very hard for the troopers of the Division to take. I talked to Gen. Eisenhower the other day and he has recommended against it but the War Department appears adamant. We have some wonderful friends in the press in the European Theater of Operations and they are getting all excited about it. They have formed what they call a crusade, and at their own expense they have wired their papers and press friends in the States protesting our demobilization. You will hear more about this.

I am trying to stay out of it as much as I can. But we do have some fine friends. The Division is exceptionally well liked by every newspaperman in the business over here, and they insist that they will not sit around and see the War Department end the 82nd Airborne when other divisions are permitted to remain in the post-war Army.

The Division is unquestionably the most decorated division in the Army. At present we are also being considered for the French Fourragère, which may or may not materialize. It would seem a shame to throw all of this away. The fur will be flying pretty soon. The Division will probably end up by being kept alive but I will end up in jail. But it is a lot of fun, and as for the merits of our case, there is no argument.

Nothing should be said to anyone about all of this now that I think of it, I just wanted you to understand some of the things that you may read about it in the immediate future.

Glad Uncle George is returning.

Love to everyone,

Pappy

★ ★ ★

October 13, 1945

Dear Babe,

The enclosed Polish banknote was given me yesterday by a newspaperman who just returned from Warsaw. The ticket is for a Russian moving picture that I attended the other night. It was remarkably good.

We plan on leaving Berlin October 21st now. However, if the present strikes [of dockworkers] in the States are continued, there is no telling when everyone will get home. It is too bad and very difficult for a soldier who has been fighting for over two years to understand. Our troops cannot understand it. I'll let you know what changes take place in my schedule.

Love,

Pappy

★ ★ ★

October 18, 1945

Dear Babe,

I have been rather busy the past three or four days or I would have written sooner. Monday I flew to Reims to look at the camp that we are to occupy upon our relief from Berlin. It is "Oklahoma City" camp about 25 miles from Reims. A rather dismal looking place but it will do for a few weeks.

Right now the entire shipping schedule is falling so far behind that we are not going to leave until sometime after the first of November. If you recall, we at first planned on leaving Berlin on October 15th, but with strikes, etc. and the loss of some of the ships it has been difficult to keep the schedule moving as planned.

If our latest plan is carried out, we should sail about mid-December, getting us into New York about Xmas. I am making a very strong effort to fly back to Washington when the Division is on boats and thus be able to say a few words to the right people about our contemplated demobilization. I may or may not be able to do this, I can't tell yet.

From Reims I flew to Paris where I stayed overnight. Monday I had a long talk with our attaché there and later with some French officials regarding our possibly receiving the French Fourragère. It was recommended for us by the Mayor [Alexandre Renaud] of Ste. Mère-Église, the first town in continental Europe liberated. The 82nd took it over from the Germans about three hours before H-hour [the hour designated for the amphibious forces to land on the beaches on D-Day] the night of June 5–6, 1944. I rather believe it will come through and we will receive it before leaving Berlin. All in all, it will be a remarkable state of affairs. Any division would be very grateful to receive one fourragère [a braided cord worn looped over the shoulder], the 82nd will have the good fortune to have three. I am not sure how they will look wearing them all.

I am of course very glad. Needless to say, I have left nothing undone to see that the Division's efforts were rewarded by other foreign governments, and I have the good luck of having a number of friends in the higher headquarters of the European governments.

From Paris I flew to Frankfurt, arriving Tuesday evening. There I talked to [Brigadier General] Art Nevins about our relief and then flew into Berlin, arriving about 9:30 Tuesday night. In Paris I talked to Dave Rumbough whom I hadn't seen for years. He was looking very well. Apparently he is on duty in Paris. *[Dave Rumbough was a friend of the family since our days in the Philippines. — BGF]*

Things around here have been going along at their usual giddy pace. Jack Thompson flew back from Paris with me. He intends to do an article on the Division.

If you have the time and dough, please pick up for me a copy of "The White Deer" by Thurber. Also pick up the new Decca record with "Lili Marlene" on one side and "Symphony" on the other, sung by Marlene Dietrich. Hold them for me until I return I guess.

I mailed back my long overcoat this morning. Glad to hear that Uncle George is OK and is on the way home. It will be good to have him there for Xmas. I hope that I can be there too.

Love to all,

Pappy

★ ★ ★

October 26, 1945

Dear Babe,

It is 6:00 a.m. which is a strange time to be letter writing but I woke up about 3:30 this morning and got to thinking of a lot of things that I want to get done and before I realized it, I was wide awake and unable to get back to sleep.

Gen. Barker, who is taking over Berlin and the Kommandantura, went away for several days so I have found myself again under a mountain of work. Yesterday I had a three-hour debate on the trade union issue at the Kommandantura, only to find it impossible to bring together the views of our British and Russian colleagues. I am nevertheless as confident as ever that our opposite views can be reconciled and they will, given time and patience. But I am learning a lot and have a great deal more to learn.

I was very pleasantly surprised to learn from Rosie's letter that I have apparently been awarded the Distinguished Service Medal [for exceptionally meritorious service in a noncombat position]. I hope that is right, I like that. I have never received an award like that, one earned outside of combat.

I am enclosing some stamped envelopes that may have some value for your collection.

We continue to prepare to leave for the U.S., still hoping that someway, somehow, the War Department will reconsider our demobilization. For one who has not been through what we have together, it is difficult to explain how we feel about this thing that the 82nd has. Elusive, indefinable, and abstract as it is, it is nonetheless a powerful and great thing to us. And we of course feel that it is a great thing for the American people to preserve.

Just last evening I received a letter from a lieutenant [later identified as John McNally of Division Artillery] which I am enclosing [reproduced in full below]. It describes the feelings of most of us on this subject as well as I have seen it done. It is eloquence of a rare kind.

Love to all,

Pappy

> Berlin
>
> 19 October 1945
>
> Major General James M. Gavin
>
> Sir:
>
> I know this letter violates military protocol, but perhaps you will overlook my temerity, as I know of no other way to let you know how I and many other men who serve under you, feel about the Division's status as Class IV [demobilized].
>
> In these days, when men and officers seem to have turned their thoughts exclusively to getting home, I want you to know that there are a great number of us who realize that the past few years have been climactic in our lives. Nothing we, personally, can ever do can recreate the atmosphere of the great airborne D-days. Once we had hoped to go on — to the Pacific, to Tokio itself; to go so far we could never get back, or want to. Now the exaltation which was once part of our daily lives as skyborne soldiers has subsided and we walk silently into the future remembering that once our comrades lent fire and a touch of greatness to the American cause.
>
> As a rookie, I stumbled from a troop train in Fort Bragg under a barracks bag crammed with unworn clothing, to face for the first time a line of paratroop officers in leather jackets and jump boots and a band playing the "All American." I guess I sort of lost my heart to the 82nd then and there. I remember close-order drill in the darkness of a Carolina morning, and the smell of pine-covered hills on hikes, and all the other places, Casablanca, Sicily, Italy, Normandy, in fact all the long road to Berlin. There was the night in a dimly-lit packing shed in Africa,

when I got my jump school certificate and realized I could have anything I wanted, if I wanted it badly enough. And the day you spoke to Task Force A in a hangar in England. I was a sergeant then, and when you had finished, my buddy turned and said quietly "I'd follow that guy to hell." I was one of the two sergeants in the briefing room the night before Normandy D-day when you and the commanders of Task Force A went over the plans and I came out after an unforgettable hour, filled with the knowledge of the awesome plan and the sight of America's finest officers.

The impact of your will has, through some process of osmosis, penetrated all the layers of the Division hierarchy down to the newest private, and I think I understand now how commanders like Marlborough and Sheridan and Lawrence were able to seize the imaginations of men and suspend them from it as if from a cord.

And so, for myself as well as those others in the Division who remember the roar of planes at night; the white-hot instant when the warning light flashes on; and the magnificence of night skies full of swaying chutes, I want to say this:

"We hope, with all our hearts, that your wish will be fulfilled, and that somewhere, somehow, there will always be an 82nd. If we can know that somewhere young men will dare the challenge to 'stand up and hook up,' and know the moment of pride and strength which is its reward, then a little part of us will always be alive, free and inviolate."

There aren't any words at all which can convey what I'm trying to say, except: "Thanks, General Jim." You've got to win this next fight and we're staying to do anything we can as long as you need or want us.

A Lieutenant of the
82nd Airborne Division

★ ★ ★

November 1, 1945

Dear Babe,

Mail is again a scarce article around here, because of redeployment I guess, haven't had a letter in a week. It has been a busy week. Monday took a few hours out to go up to Karin Hall, Herman Goering's old estate, to hunt deer. Tommie got one, I got shots. A nice place, what is left of it.

No buildings left, just the grounds and lots of Russian hunters. Seemed doubtful at times whether or not we would get a deer or a Russian.

Tuesday night had dinner at Gen. Koenig's [the current head of the French occupation zone] home which was very nice. Wednesday we had some of the French officers in for dinner and we had the venison.

Thursday was Kommandantura day and a very busy day. Finally wound up with a press conference at about seven. Today, Friday, I spent some time with the State Department and Group Control discussing the results of the press conference and the possible public and national reaction to what was released. I am quite sure that my position is OK; I know that it is, of course, but whether or not it is in a national sense time will tell.

A very touchy thing, this business of the press, public opinion, and the U.S.-Soviet-British-French relationship. Particularly the U.S.-Soviet position. Fortunately I get along very well in a personal way with all of them. William Shirer [a journalist and radio broadcaster who later wrote *The Rise and Fall of the Third Reich*] was present at the Kommandantura meeting and I guess covered it in his broadcast, so you may have heard something of it.

Sunday I am due to fly to Leicester and Nottingham, England. Monday and Tuesday in London and Wednesday back here. I thought that I had better write now so that you would know that I am still in circulation despite not hearing from me during my absence. We leave Berlin November 14th.

I have had some packages sent home so watch out for them. Please let me know what you receive, this is important. Some of these things have great sentimental value for us so I do not want to lose them.

You may sometime in the future receive mail for me or mail addressed to the 82nd Airborne Division Association, 2006 Columbia Road. Hold on to it all until I return. We will get a better address for our association later on.

Love to everyone,

Pappy

[We shortly began receiving personal goods that my dad had shipped to us from Germany in anticipation of his return home. That was a good sign. I hoped that it meant that he would soon follow the boxes.

I was often alone in our apartment and had explored every drawer and shelf in every room. The box that arrived by mail in the middle of December was made of wood, painted khaki and wired shut. In a former incarnation it had been an ammunition box. My dad's return address was stenciled on the top. For a curious twelve year old, opening it was a very small challenge. Inside, on the top layer was a tube container with papers rolled up in it. I unrolled the papers and found blown-up photographs of Wobelein concentration camp in Ludwigslust, Germany, liberated by the 82nd Airborne just a few months earlier. I was surprised, and as I saw the photos of bodies stacked like cordwood and the barely alive internees clinging to the barbed wire fence, I was horrified. I had heard stories of these camps, but never expected the shock of seeing the clear evidence of their existence. I quickly rolled up the photos, put them back in the box and never mentioned them to anyone until my dad arrived home. — BGF]

★ ★ ★

November 12, 1945

Dear Babe,

Since I wrote you last I have been back to Leicester for a short visit, went up to Nottingham and then down to London. In London had lunch with Charles Collingwood and Ed Murrow of the Columbia Broadcasting System. Charles is about to return to America to do a lecture tour and he may call you. He is a wonderful chap, rather young for his job and responsibilities but unquestionably one of the best broadcasters in the business.

Stayed at Claridges in London and had the press in for a drink. The final check came to 25 pounds so it was a bit costly but, nevertheless, very much a good venture in public relations for the Division.

Returning, we got all of the way up to Berlin after five hours flying only to find that we couldn't land on account of fog. We finally landed in Austria after seven and a half hours in a C-47 which is some kind of a record for that type ship. I checked in by phone with my headquarters in Berlin, and they told me that the Division had just been notified that it had been changed to Category II, which means that it will not be disbanded but will remain in the post-war Army. It is wonderful. Few people will ever know how it was accomplished and I am not going to tell what I know. Needless to say, it was the biggest press and pressure crusade that has been attempted in some time. But it was done and it is unbelievable to many.

Unfortunately, we now have our shipping date deferred until January so I will not get home for Xmas. I am sorry as can be about this but it is just one of those things. There will be a half-million other soldiers in the

ETO who would like to be home for Xmas so I am not alone. I'll know a lot more about my plans in another week, things are a bit upset right now.

Love to everyone,

Pappy

Briefing his staff officers shortly after the 505th Parachute Infantry Regiment's activation at Fort Benning in 1942, Colonel Gavin told Barney Oldfield that he would have no use for his civilian expertise as a publicist because his paratroopers were "going to fight" and wouldn't need "any publicity." Oldfield prophetically retorted that Gavin would need a public relations man someday because with that attitude he "might be the one to lead [America's] victory parade."[1]

Three years later in Berlin, Major General Gavin received a telegram from Washington informing him that the 82nd Airborne Division, representing all of America's World War II soldiers, had been selected to march at the head of the Victory Parade in New York City.

★ ★ ★

[Undated]

Camp Oklahoma City

Reims, France

Dear Babe,

Finally gathered together again in one place, the last of the troopers came in from Berlin today. I had planned on leaving Monday exactly a week ago today but weather prevented us from getting off. That gave me one more day to get in some more farewell calls.

Tuesday I went over to see Gen. Smirnov, the Russian commandant of the Soviet Berlin sector. Well with characteristic generosity and enthusiasm, he stuffed me with fish and caviar and vodka for a couple of hours, during which time the usual number of toasts were made by all present. It happens that I like Smirnov personally very much, having met him in Mecklenburg in combat under circumstances somewhat different than here in Berlin. After several hours of drinking toasts and farewells, he asked me what I was bringing back to you for a present; he first heard about you in Mecklenburg. Since there is nothing really suitable for a present in Berlin, I had to tell him "nothing." One of the staff suggested an accordion, another a shotgun, these being their idea of a present for you. I explained again that you were still a little girl, having grown little since Mecklenburg and that a shotgun or accordion would be a bit unwieldy. The idea was dropped and several toasts later one of the staff appeared with a wristwatch. It is from General Smirnov to you. I'll send it to you by separate mail.

He wrote a short note for me to give to you which I am enclosing herewith. You should take the note and go down to the Russian ambassador and ask him to translate it. Either the Ambassador or his First Secretary, no one else. The Ambassador would be extremely pleased, this is the sort of thing that he should know about. Go in to talk to him yourself.

[Translation: "Respected child, Barbara, from Russian generals, I send you with your father a small souvenir. Please take it and remember vision of pretty Russian children with American small people, such as you. With hello, respecting you, Lieutenant General Smirnov." I still have the watch, although it has never worked. My dad said that when he received it, "it was still warm," meaning that the staff member who had procured the watch may have removed it from someone on the street. The sentiment in the note is beautiful. — BGF]

Well we are under canvas [in tents] again and it is very cold. Perhaps we are no longer used to it. I use five blankets and a sleeping bag and then am not entirely warm. We should stay until January, wow, I hate to think of how cold it is going to be in a tent then. In any case it will be better than last winter in the Ardennes.

I am certainly sorry to miss that Xmas dinner. Incidentally, I have done no Xmas shopping because I expected to be back by then so everyone will have to understand. The DSM [Distinguished Service Medal] came and Gen. [Lucius] Clay [Deputy, American Military Government of Germany] pinned it on. I sent it to you the same day. Everyone who has been with me contributed to that one, the Division earned it for me. I'm very lucky.

Love to everyone,

Pappy

★ ★ ★

November 22, 1945

Dear Butch,

I have just returned from Paris. Drove down yesterday to talk to TSFET [Theater Services Forces European Theater] Headquarters about our personnel readjustment in connection with our return. I arrived just in time to learn of the latest change. The latest: we sail December 21st and 22nd, arriving at New York in late December or January 1st or 2nd. Sometime between the arrival date and the 15th we are to parade in New York, then we are I believe to go to Fort Bragg.

We start moving to the port about mid-December, and the work confronting us between now and then is overwhelming to contemplate. Somehow we must make it. Everyone expects a lot of the 82nd and we are going to try to give it to them, although most of our veterans have gone home already.

Somewhere I must get 8,000 white parachute silk scarves, orange lanyards, fourragères, plus several thousand pairs of jump boots, trousers, etc. I am sending staff officers all over Europe to get a few caps and things made. I had all of those things for our occupational role in Berlin but since leaving there many thousands of our veterans have left for home taking their belongings along with them.

Too bad that again I am going to miss Xmas, looks like we will have it on the high seas. We are all very pleased about the parade in New York, quite an honor for the troopers to be selected.

Today is Thanksgiving. We had turkey. I just got back from Paris in time for it. About two and one-half hours drive to Paris. A good city and I like it, although I do not know it as well as London but my French is improving.

Love to everyone,

Pappy

★ ★ ★

November 25, 1945

Dear Babe,

Seems like a good idea to keep you abreast of the latest changes, so here goes. Our sailing date from Le Havre is still about December 22nd. The Division ships across the Channel to Southampton where it boards the Queen Mary. It sails from Southampton on December 29th, arriving in New York January 4th. Formerly, it was scheduled to sail in three or four smaller boats. We are all very pleased to get the entire Queen for the whole Division. It is going to be a great day when it comes into New York Harbor.

In order to arrange the details for the parade, I am planning on having my Chief of Staff Col. Wienecke, my G-3 Jack Norton, my Public Relations Officer Barney Oldfield, and my G-4 Maj. Walter Caughran fly back as soon as possible. With luck, they should arrive in Washington about November 30th, just about the time this letter arrives. Jack or the Chief will give you a ring.

If everything else goes according to plan, I should fly back about December 26th, getting in Washington about December 28th. I will bring with me seven of the staff to complete the arrangements for the parade.

Tomorrow, Sunday, I plan on going to Paris for an early conference Monday. Monday afternoon I will call the War Department and wind up some of the details. If there are any late changes, I will let you know.

Bill Gillmore was assigned to the Division today, to be Commanding General, Division Artillery. Mommy probably knows him.

I am sorry as can be about Xmas [presents]. I have done nothing and it is too late now, and if it weren't, I don't know what I could do.

Love to everyone,

Pappy

★ ★ ★

November 29, 1945

Dear Babe,

Down to Paris again day before yesterday and about all that I got out of the trip was a bad cold. I did attend a very interesting teletype conference with the War Department having to do with our return. We exchanged messages back and forth as easily as though we were in the same room, very interesting. I had never done it before.

Anyway, the latest situation: the Division arrives in New York about January 4th, having sailed from Southampton about December 29th. Now, circumstances permitting, I should return about a day or so before Xmas by air.

I am returning a group of nine as an advance party to arrange for the parade, leaving here about December 15th by air. That should get them in the States about the 16th and in time for a week at home, including Xmas. They must all be in New York by December 26th or 27th.

I should include myself in that advance party, in fact I have been ordered to by the War Department but I have too much work to do here to get the Division ready so I am not leaving until my work is finished. This should be near the 20th or 21st. Therefore if the weather for flying is good, I should arrive in Washington about the 22nd or 23rd. I'll cable or something. I must be in New York the 26th or 27th and get to work on the accommodations for the Division and the arrangements for the parade. After the parade, I believe that the Division goes to Fort Bragg, although I am not certain.

This isn't a bad place although it is rather cold. I feel like the middle layer in a Dagwood sandwich, I have two blankets underneath and five on top. In bed of course.

Hope to see you soon.

Love,

Pappy

* * *

December 1, 1945

Dear Babe,

Heard the good news about your report card. I am glad that you want to go to Vassar, I hope that it can be arranged.

Also glad to know that you have been getting the stamps. The enclosed are the new French Republic stamps. They are the first that I have seen of this type. I have not sent the Russian watch yet. I had been hoping to get some suitable wrapping, etc., which is very scarce, but now I think that I will be in Washington before the package would if I mailed it. Yesterday I received a First Day of Issue letter from Rosie which I am returning herewith.

Monday December 3rd, I plan on flying up to Le Havre to check the arrangements for the Division there, Tuesday to Southampton for the same purpose, and Wednesday return. Thursday, a parade of what is now practically a new division, and Saturday a review here for Gen. J.C.H. Lee.

Monday the 10th, the Division leaves, and the 13th I plan on closing my Command Post here and living out of handbags and an airplane. I should be in Southampton on the 14th, London the 15th, 16th and 17th, and Paris from the 18th until I return. I am making a reservation for the 20th which would get me in Washington late the 21st, providing the weather is perfect which it never is. Probably fly back by way of the Azores and Newfoundland and will let you know by cable what is happening.

Love,

Pappy

★ ★ ★

December 5, 1945

Dear Babe,

I am enclosing a check for your Xmas shopping. I am sorry that it is not larger this Xmas but I am almost broke.

All things are moving according to schedule. I spent Monday in Le Havre, last night in London, and this morning in Southampton.

Everything appears set for the move of the Division. Hope to see you about the 21st or 22nd depending upon weather.

Love,

Pappy

Barbara Gavin Fauntleroy

It was December 21. We had received a telegram saying that my dad would arrive in Washington that afternoon. After so many delays and changes, I was afraid to believe it. My mother and I had put up our Christmas tree and were keeping ourselves busy putting the ornaments on it. Finally, the doorbell rang. There he was, at last home from the war to stay!

Standing beside him in the doorway was a tall, handsome man whom he introduced as Charles Collingwood, a war correspondent for CBS. Charles was a broadcaster with Edward R. Murrow in London. They had flown home together. He had become a close friend of my dad's in London. Charles's family also lived in Washington. On the floor of the hall behind the two men were several suitcases and a case of French champagne. After lots of hugs and bringing in the suitcases, my dad said that it was time to decorate the tree and open a bottle of champagne. Decorating alternated with drinking champagne and a number of ornaments hit the floor. My mother, who always warned me not to break the heirloom ornaments, didn't seem to notice. One ornament that didn't break was a small paratrooper doll, my favorite. I was sent to bed way past my bedtime, and Charles went home, and the long-awaited homecoming evening ended.

The next day, my dad told us that arrangements had been made for us to take the train to New York on New Year's Day to see the troopers of the 82nd arrive from England on the *Queen Mary* on January 3. He also had to attend meetings and make plans for the Victory Parade scheduled for January 12. We rode the train to New York and took a taxi to the Waldorf-Astoria, where a lovely suite had been reserved for us.

The boy in my father was beginning to show. We walked to FAO Schwarz to buy a bag of balloons, returned to the hotel, and blew them all up amid lots of laughter. We filled one end of the living room with them, from floor to ceiling. He was also learning that he could build up quite a large electrical charge with his thick-soled jump boots as we walked down the hotel's plushly carpeted hallways.

On January 3, my dad left the hotel early to travel to the docks where a tugboat would take him out to the *Queen Mary* in the harbor. He wanted to return home with his boys and be on board the ship when she docked. Later in the morning, my mother and I took a taxi to the pier to wait for the *Queen Mary*'s arrival. We waited for a long time in the cold weather as the dock grew crowded with friends and families arriving to welcome the troops home. Martha Tilton, a USO entertainer who had sung for the troops during the war, was there with her accompanist. Finally, we saw the ship coming in and watched as she was tied to the pier. The gangplank was lowered, and the first soldier ran down into the welcoming arms of a young woman. The same scene was repeated over and over as soldiers were reunited with their loved ones for the first time in almost three years. I saw my dad and jumped up and down, waving to him until he worked his way through the crowd to us.

We took the train back to Washington that afternoon, leaving the Waldorf with the living room of one suite filled with balloons. My dad spent the next week in meetings at the Pentagon and traveling between Washington and New York. Preparations had to be made to move the Division to Fort Bragg from Camp Shanks, where they were billeted for the parade. And then there were the hundreds of details to be worked out for the Victory Parade.

We returned to New York the day before the parade. This time, our suite at the Waldorf contained a beautiful, large arrangement of flowers, but no balloons. In an interview that morning, my dad said that he had received a large number of letters "from fathers and mothers of the Eighty-Second Airborne boys who lie buried in Europe. Some of them told me they will be 'watching' the parade because they feel their sons will be marching with us up Fifth Avenue, if only in spirit."[1] This would be a parade to celebrate their victory and to remember the boys who were lost along the way.

The day of the parade, my dad left the hotel very early to be sure that the Division was ready to go. The parade was scheduled to start at 1:45 P.M. from Washington Square. After breakfast, my mother and I took a taxi as far as we could up Madison Avenue toward 82nd Street and the Metropolitan Museum, where the reviewing stand was located. Leaving the taxi, we found a policeman who helped us push our way through the crowds lining Fifth Avenue and find our way into the stands. Rosie and Aunt Lil had come from Washington and were waiting for us there. The newspapers on Monday said that four million people had lined the curbs. The day was cold and it had rained a bit in the morning, but now the streets were dry. Just as the parade began the sun broke through the clouds.

Seeing my father marching at the head of the parade will always be one of the proudest moments of my life. Official accounts of the Victory Parade said that he led 13,000 men in that march up Fifth Avenue. An article in the newspaper the next day reported: "If you were there you saw at the head of this mighty column the youthful, slim, gallant figure of the youngest division commander in the United States Army, 38-year-old Brooklyn born Major General James M. Gavin." When asked if he would ride or walk, my father said that he had walked all over Europe with the Division and he wasn't going to ride now.[2]

There were forty C-47s flying overhead, each towing a glider, and above them were fighter planes weaving back and forth. Following the marching soldiers were tanks, jeeps, towed howitzers and antitank guns, and armored cars. It took more than two and a half hours for the parade to pass. When my dad arrived at the reviewing stand at 82nd Street, he joined the dignitaries there as the parade continued. General Wainright, just released from a Japanese prisoner of war camp, Governor Dewey, Mayor O'Dwyer, and former Mayor LaGuardia were all in the reviewing stand with my dad. But he left them and came up the stairs of the grandstand to give me a hug and greet his small family before returning to his official duties. I was so proud of him. I felt ten feet tall.

That evening I had dinner in our suite while my mother and dad attended a dinner hosted by Mayor O'Dwyer in the ballroom of the hotel. The invitation read, "In Honour of Major General James M. Gavin, Commanding General of the 82nd Airborne Division, His Officers and Men." On behalf of the City of New York, Mayor O'Dwyer presented my father with a beautiful gold medal made by Tiffany.

The excitement of the day was too much for my mother. She came in from the banquet and went directly to bed. My dad told me to bundle up because we were going out for a walk. It had been a big day for his boys, and he wanted to be sure that they and this American city were getting along all right. We walked for more than an hour, enjoying the honking horns and noises of Times Square and seeing the usual crowds, bright lights, and colorful neon signs. All was well in the big city. It was a very special ending to one of the most exciting days of my life and his.

The 82nd Airborne has remained a large and important part of my life. I enjoy attending their reunions and All American Week at Fort Bragg. I have returned to England, Normandy, Holland, and Belgium with my family to see the places where my father and his boys made history and to honor those who were lost along the way, never returning to their homes and families. I am so grateful that my father was able to come home to me.

★ NOTES ★

CHAPTER I: THE CALL TO WAR

1. Unable to repel the German invasion of May 1940, the government of France, then under Marshal Philippe Pétain, agreed to an armistice with Germany (and its ally, Italy). Seated in the town of Vichy (lending its name), Pétain's government was more than a puppet of the Nazis — it was one of collaboration, with its support of Germany's anti-Semitism and anti-communism. France's colonies in Morocco followed the dictates of the Vichy government and resisted, with force, the Allied invasion of French North Africa in 1942 (Operation TORCH), surrendering after two days of fighting.

2. In *War and Peace in the Space Age*, Gavin wrote of West Point: "From the day I entered until I left, each minute there seemed to give me something. I left determined to repay her, my Spartan mother, for what she had given to me. I went forth to seek the challenge, to 'move toward the sound of the guns,' to go where danger was greatest, for there is where issues would be resolved and decisions made." James M. Gavin, *War and Peace in the Space Age* (New York: Harper & Brothers, 1958), 35.

3. Paratroop officers were unofficially inducted into their unit with a "prop blast" ceremony. Part of the festivities included drinking from a ceremonial cup filled with a potent alcoholic punch (mimicking the strong blast of wind from the plane's propellers as a paratrooper jumped out the door). Max, a boxer belonging to one of the 505's officers, deserved his own special induction ceremony — with a big bowl of milk — because the dog, rigged with a special harness, actually made eight parachute jumps with the men.

4. While deployed, military personnel were encouraged to allot a portion of their pay for the support of their families. Automatically withdrawn and matched by a government allowance based on the number of dependents, the allotment, by arrangement with the recipient's bank, was directly deposited to a family member's bank account.

1. African flies hunted both the Allied and Axis troops; the quotes are from a German soldier, writing after the war about the North African campaign. Charles E. Pfannes and Victor A. Salamone, *The Great Commanders of World War II*, Volume I: *The Germans* (New York: Zebra Books, 1980), 114–15.

2. V-mail was originated to conserve valuable cargo space and was purported to be faster than conventional mail. The small sheet, once mailed, was reduced to minute size onto microfilm within the military postal system and then enlarged to one-quarter of its original size (making the letter very difficult to read) at the recipient's station prior to delivery. However, with V-mail opened and handled by everyone within the postal system, the contents of the letters were exposed to everyone and nothing could be enclosed with them. All packaged items, of course, had to be sent through the conventional mail system.

3. As the 505's personnel officer, Al Ireland was tasked with assigning key regimental officers code names, and it was he who gave Gavin (and history) what would become Gavin's well-known name of "Slim Jim," naming him after a popular pretzel of the time — "Slim Jim Pretzels." Patrick K. O'Donnell, *Beyond Valor: World War II's Ranger and Airborne Veterans Reveal the Heart of Combat* (New York: Free Press, 2001), 43.

4. In his autobiography, *On to Berlin*, Gavin recalled Patton's visit: "But the event that all of us remembered best was the send-off talk given us by General Patton. His talks on such occasions were usually quite good, earthy, and I was impressed. One thing he said always stuck with me, for it was contrary to what I had believed up to that moment, but when I had been in combat only a short while, I knew he was right. Speaking to all of us late one afternoon as we assembled in the North African sunset, he said, 'Now I want you to remember that no sonuvabitch ever won a war by dying for his country. He won it by making the other poor dumb sonuvabitch die for his country.'" James M. Gavin, *On to Berlin: Battles of an American Commander, 1943–46* (New York: Viking Press, 1978), 9.

5. After purchasing two mules from the local natives, a team from the 505's Second Battalion (under orders from Division Headquarters and against Gavin's wishes) managed to get them up in a plane and hooked to large parachutes. Pushed out the door, both mules broke their legs upon landing and had to be destroyed. Once on Sicily, however, the paratroopers soon realized that there were plenty of mules on the island for their use.

6. While serving with the 505 at Fort Benning, Barney Oldfield drew on his civilian expertise as a publicist to showcase the regiment's daring paratroopers in

the press—making their dog famous, too. However, on the day that *Movietone News* came to Benning to shoot a sequence on the "paracanine," Max was hit by a truck. He recovered, though never jumped again. Recruiters for the paratroopers were nevertheless able to use Max as an example, saying that the dog proved "it was more dangerous to walk across the road than jump from a plane." Barney Oldfield, *Never a Shot in Anger* (Santa Barbara, Calif.: Capra Press, 1989), 301.

7. Gavin was often frustrated in dealing with the Division staff because "Gen. R[idgway] wants certain things, Gen. Keerans comes around and wants something else. Gen. Taylor [artillery commander] calls and wants something else. Each thinks his requirements the most pressing." Gavin Diary, entry of May 25, 1943. The James M. Gavin Papers, Box 8, "Personal Diaries, December 1939–September 1945, June 1958–May 1960," United States Army Military History Institute, Carlisle Barracks, Pennsylvania.

8. In Detroit, though the workforce of the war plants was integrated, the affordable housing areas available due to the influx of workers were segregated. Needing somewhere to live, African American workers moved into those areas that were not allotted to them, and race riots were often the unfortunate result. Elsewhere, John Lewis called out the members of the United Mine Workers, whose work was crucial to the war effort, to strike for higher wages.

9. Gavin Diary, entry of June 1, 1943.

10. H. L. Covington, *A Fighting Heart: An Unofficial Story of the 82nd Airborne Division* (Fayetteville, N.C.: privately published by Ted Davis, 1949), 31.

CHAPTER 3: OPERATION HUSKY—SICILY

1. Excerpts from "SOLDIERS OF THE 505TH PARACHUTE COMBAT TEAM," enclosure in letter to Barbara, dated July 8, 1943.

2. Jack Foisie, "Paratroopers Were Ready When Zero Hour Came," *Stars and Stripes Algiers Daily*, July 12, 1943.

3. Gavin insisted that the 505's officers lead by example and put the needs of the enlisted men before their own by emphatically telling all officers reporting to him that they were to be "first out of the door of the airplane and last in the chow line." Clay Blair, *Ridgway's Paratroopers* (Garden City, N.Y.: Doubleday, 1958), 50.

4. Jack Thompson filed several news dispatches from Sicily, including the account of Gavin's victory at Biazza Ridge: "Despite the smallness of his force, the colonel went into position on the lower hill in the orchard and then began working through the tall grass, gnarled little trees and vineyards. The armored grenadiers—for that is what the opposition proved to be—fought back with their fast firing machine guns, mausers, artillery, and mortars. Our first rush

shoved the enemy back up and over the hill altogether. He outnumbered us then about three to one. The troopers had him on the run, but he came back strong with more artillery fire, and then tanks. . . . The next hour was our worst. Everyone expected an attack by the tanks in force and it looked as if there were a good chance that we would be overrun. . . . Then the colonel called on his last hope and ordered three available howitzers wheeled up for direct fire. . . . They opened fire at 800 yards, knocking out two tanks. . . . At 8:10, our tanks opened fire and we charged in two waves while the Germans replied with intense mortar fire and sweeping machine gun fire. Overhead their Messerschmitts prowled to observe or strafe. Half an hour later it was quiet. And in the gloom of the gathering night our men came back to their lines. . . . We counted many dead and wounded, but it was a victory beyond question." John Thompson, "Heroism of Airborne Force Opened Way to Vittoria Area," *Washington Evening Star*, July 16, 1943.

5. General Ridgway was unable to make contact with Gavin and his scattered combat team; on July 11, at General Patton's direction, he ordered the Division's follow-on contingent, the 504th Parachute Infantry Regimental Combat Team, to drop on Sicily that night. As the planes flew over the drop zones, tragedy struck—antiaircraft guns from the naval convoy offshore and from Patton's forces on the beaches opened fire, mistaking the planes as German. Twenty-three of the one hundred forty-four planes were shot down, and approximately sixty were damaged. In all, eight-one troopers were killed, one hundred and thirty-two were wounded, and sixteen were listed as missing. Brigadier General Keerans survived the crash of his plane just offshore and was seen heading inland from the beach, but he was never heard from again, nor was his body ever found.

6. As an airborne adviser to Fifth Army and observer of Operation HUSKY, Lieutenant Colonel William Ryder jumped from Gavin's plane and also fought with him at Biazza Ridge. A pioneer in the field of "vertical envelopment," Ryder (then a lieutenant) commanded the original parachute test platoon in 1940; in 1941, he encouraged his longtime friend—Jim Gavin—to apply to the Parachute School.

7. The citation read in part: "For extraordinary heroism in action lasting throughout daylight on the 11th day of July 1943 . . . Colonel Gavin . . . together with a small portion of his regiment, held and drove back a superior force of German Infantry and tanks in the face of heavy gunfire and counterattack, led by tank, which reached to within fifty yards of his Command Post. This successful action enabled the . . . 45th Division, which had been held up all day, to continue its advance. Colonel Gavin displayed cool, courageous leadership of the highest order throughout the day's fighting, and inspiring his men by his heroic example,

achieved decisive success in the face of greatly superior odds." Distinguished Service Cross citation, included in "Official Biography of Lieutenant General James Maurice Gavin," Department of Defense, Office of Public Information, News Branch, archived at the Airborne & Special Operations Museum, Fayetteville, North Carolina. The Distinguished Service Cross is the U.S. Army's second highest combat award, with the Congressional Medal of Honor the highest.

8. Gavin equated jumping out of an airplane with riding a reluctant horse over a difficult jump—both had in common "a high degree of mixed apprehension and elation." James M. Gavin, *War and Peace in the Space Age* (New York: Harper & Brothers, 1958), 36.

9. For officers going into combat behind enemy lines, maps printed on silk were easy to conceal, durable, water-resistant and, most important, silent when folded and unfolded.

10. James M. Gavin, *Airborne Warfare* (Washington, D.C.: Infantry Journal Press, 1947), 17.

CHAPTER 4: OPERATION AVALANCHE—ITALY

1. "I feel that many of the fine boys now buried on Biazza Ridge are much more entitled to decorations than I am." Gavin Diary, entry of August 10, 1943. The James M. Gavin Papers, Box 8, "Personal Diaries, December 1939–September 1945, June 1958–May 1960," United States Army Military History Institute, Carlisle Barracks, Pennsylvania.

2. Gavin Diary, entry of September 11, 1943.

3. Mark W. Clark, *Calculated Risk* (New York: Harper & Brothers, 1950), 199 and 203.

4. A few days later, Gavin recorded his feelings about wearing the stars of a general officer: "I do not believe that I wear them particularly well, I may in time." Gavin Diary, entry of October 19, 1943.

5. To encourage volunteers for the extremely hazardous parachute branch of the U.S. Army, incentive pay was offered—an additional monthly stipend of $50.00 for enlisted men and $100.00 for officers.

6. Clay Blair, *Ridgway's Paratroopers* (Garden City, N.Y.: Doubleday, 1958), 170.

CHAPTER 5: OPERATION OVERLORD/NEPTUNE— UNITED KINGDOM

1. James M. Gavin, *On to Berlin: Battles of an American Commander, 1943–46* (New York: Viking Press, 1978), 87.

2. To conserve fuel during World War II, the British set their clocks one hour ahead of their standard time (Greenwich Mean Time). From spring to fall, clocks were set ahead two hours—"British Double Summer Time."

3. Paul Gallico's *The Snow Goose* (New York: Alfred A. Knopf, 1941) is the story of a reclusive crippled hunchback living in an abandoned lighthouse on the English coast who turns the grounds into a wildfowl sanctuary. He is befriended by a young girl who seeks his help with a migrating injured Canadian snow goose, amazingly blown to the English coast by a freak storm. A deep and trusting friendship, and the promise of love as the girl becomes a young woman, develops but tragically ends when the hunchback, bolstered by her faith in him, adds his small boat to the flotilla rescuing British soldiers from the French beach at Dunkirk in 1940, dying heroically in the process.

4. SPAM, canned processed ham and pork shoulder produced by Hormel Foods, was a staple in GI rations.

5. "Short-snorter bills" were dollar bills on which soldiers collected signatures of friends or famous people. If asked to exchange signatures and caught without your "short-snorter," you had to pay for drinks ("snorters") at the closest bar.

6. *The White Cliffs* (New York: Coward-McCann, 1940) by American author Alice Duer Miller, was very popular in both England and America and was also made into a film, *The White Cliffs of Dover* (1944). Its speaker is an American girl raised to disdain all that is British because her ancestors fought them in the Revolutionary War; she nevertheless marries an English aristocrat and settles in England, only to become a widow with an infant son when her husband dies in World War I. In 1939, she faces an awful truth—her son may face the same fate as her husband: "My child, my child, why should you die for England, too? . . . Is she worth dying for?" But then she remembers: "And were they not English, our forefathers, never more English than when they shook the dust of her sod from their feet forever, angrily seeking a shore where in his own way a man might worship his God. Never more English than when they dared to be Rebels against her. . . . The tree of Liberty grew and changed and spread, but the seed was English. . . . [I]n a world where England is finished and dead, I do not wish to live."

7. Gavin recalled how veterans would gather on May 30 "and then walk in a long column to the cemeteries. . . . Each would carry a small American flag . . . and place it upon the grave of a departed comrade. We boys would run and walk alongside the column . . . convinced that the finest thing that could happen to us would be . . . to serve our country . . . if ever a war should come. . . . We learned at an early age that those liberties that Americans enjoy were not easily won."

James M. Gavin, *War and Peace in the Space Age* (New York: Harper & Brothers, 1958), 26.

8. Excerpts from letter dated October 19, 1945, signed "A Lieutenant of the 82nd Airborne Division," enclosure in letter to Barbara, dated October 26, 1945.

CHAPTER 6: OPERATION NEPTUNE — NORMANDY

1. William Walton, "Parachute Landing in Normandy," *TIME*, June 19, 1944.

2. Matthew B. Ridgway and Harold H. Martin, *Soldier: The Memoirs of Matthew B. Ridgway* (New York: Harper & Brothers, 1956), 14.

3. The citation read in part: "For extraordinary heroism in action against the enemy on 9 June 1944, in France. In a battalion attack . . . extremely heavy and intense enemy artillery fire inflicted heavy casualties among the officers and men, causing disorganization in the battalion. General Gavin, observing the results of this action, went immediately to the front lines. There he took charge and personally effected a reorganization of the battalion and directed it to a renewed attack. . . . General Gavin, in order to better control the assault, moved to an exposed position. . . . Although enemy fire was particularly intense at this point, General Gavin remained in this position until the battalion had completed a successful assault." Oak Leaf Cluster to Distinguished Service Cross citation, included in "Official Biography of Lieutenant General James Maurice Gavin," Department of Defense, Office of Public Information, News Branch, archived at the Airborne & Special Operations Museum, Fayetteville, North Carolina.

4. Given the choice to either be sent to a slave-labor camp or fight for the *Wehrmacht*, many young men of Nazi-occupied countries opted to fight — hoping for the opportunity to surrender to American or British forces.

CHAPTER 7: COMMAND OF THE 82ND AIRBORNE DIVISION

1. With the 504th Parachute Infantry Regiment having been a part of the 82nd since the beginning, it was only natural that it would return to the Division once refitted, meaning that either the 507 or the 508 would have to be transferred out — Ridgway and Gavin chose the 507. After the 507's commanding officer, Zip Millett, was captured, command of the regiment was given to Colonel Edson D. Raff. Unlike Roy Lindquist, commanding officer of the 508, Raff was already a seasoned veteran going into Normandy, and with the newly arrived 17th Airborne Division arriving in the European Theater, it made sense to assign the 17th a parachute infantry regiment that would best serve the untried division. It was also no secret that Raff had very little respect for Ridgway — whether or not that affected the decision would be conjecture.

2. Gavin Diary, entry of July 23, 1944. The James M. Gavin Papers, Box 8, "Personal Diaries, December 1939–September 1945, June 1958–May 1960," United States Army Military History Institute, Carlisle Barracks, Pennsylvania.

CHAPTER 8: OPERATION MARKET-GARDEN — HOLLAND

1. Gavin Diary, entry of September 14, 1944. The James M. Gavin Papers, Box 8, "Personal Diaries, December 1939–September 1945, June 1958–May 1960," United States Army Military History Institute, Carlisle Barracks, Pennsylvania.

2. Allen Langdon, *Ready: The History of the 505th Parachute Infantry Regiment, 82nd Airborne Division, World War II* (Indianapolis: Western Newspaper Publishing Company, Inc., 1986), 87.

3. The citation read in part: "For gallantry in action . . . [w]hen two simultaneous attacks by enemy forces against the thinly held sector in the vicinity of Beek and Mook were made by the enemy, Major General (then Brigadier General) Gavin moved the division reserve to a position of vantage and went personally to Mook, the most critical sector. Upon arrival at the railroad overpass immediately west of the village, he came under intense artillery and mortar fire. Pressing on to obtain a more accurate picture of the situation, he came upon elements of a defending infantry unit which had lost many of their leaders. . . . [He] directed and carried out the reorganization and disposed the unit to effect a counterattack. The ensuing attack broke the desperate bid of the enemy to break through. [His] presence with the assault echelon encouraged and inspired our troops, and his personal leadership at a critical moment resulted in the shattering of the enemy attempts to break through our lines." Silver Star citation, included in "Official Biography of Lieutenant General James Maurice Gavin," Department of Defense, Office of Public Information, News Branch, archived at the Airborne & Special Operations Museum, Fayetteville, North Carolina.

4. In *A Bridge Too Far*, Cornelius Ryan wrote that after General Bernard Montgomery outlined his plan to General Frederick "Boy" Browning, First Allied Airborne Army's deputy commander, Browning pointed to FAAA's most northern objective on the map—the bridge at Arnhem—and asked how long it would take the armor to reach them. After hearing Montgomery's reply of "two days," Browning then said, "We can hold it for four, but, Sir, I think we might be going a bridge too far." Cornelius Ryan, *A Bridge Too Far* (New York: Simon and Schuster, 1974), 89.

5. One of the small towns that appeared to be within Holland (astride the Dutch-German border) on Division maps was, in fact, within Germany.

6. Gavin Diary, entry of October 8, 1944.

7. Gellhorn's article, "Rough and Tumble," appeared in *Colliers*, and an excerpt was also included in the Division's official history, published in 1946. "The troops of the 82nd Airborne Division look like tough boys, and they are. They are good at their trade, too, and they know it, and they walk as if they knew it. This trade is war: most of them are too young to have learned any other profession. . . . The mission of the 82nd Airborne Division in Holland . . . was completed in three fierce and sleepless days. It was entirely and successfully completed with a total of five bridges and a piece of essential ground taken. Then it became necessary to hold, and they are holding still—sweating it out in the long rain that means another ugly winter of war. . . . The 82nd is a very proud outfit, having earned the right to this pride. They do not boast when they say that where they fight, they fight without relief or replacements and that they have never relinquished a foot of ground. . . . From the general on down, they are all extraordinary characters and each one's story is worth telling, for men who jump out of airplanes onto hostile territory do not have dull lives. . . . You wonder what happens to a magnificent division of brave men after the war. And you wonder who is going to thank them, and how, and will it be enough?" Martha Gellhorn, "Rough and Tumble," in William F. Dawson, *Saga of the All American* (Fort Lauderdale, Fla.: Hoffman Publishing Company, n.d.), n.p.

8. The American commander of FAAA later agreed that because of British control over the war correspondents and their dispatches "everyone will remember Arnhem, but no one will remember that two American divisions fought their hearts out in the Dutch canal country and whipped hell out of the Germans." Lewis H. Brereton, *The Brereton Diaries: The War in the Air in the Pacific, Middle East and Europe, 3 October 1941–8 May 1945* (New York: William Morrow and Company, 1946), 371.

9. After Gavin, command of the 505 passed to its executive officer, Herbert Batcheller. Batcheller was relieved of regimental command in early March 1944 and replaced by William E. Ekman (executive officer of the 508), who led the 505 in Normandy and throughout the remainder of the war. Batcheller, given command of the First Battalion, 508th Parachute Infantry Regiment, was killed in action in Normandy. Harry Lewis, commander of the 325th Glider Infantry Regiment, fell seriously ill in Normandy and was returned to the States; he was replaced by Charles Billingslea (executive officer of the 504).

10. The use of an absentee ballot and its restrictions resulted in a very small percentage of overseas military personnel voting in 1944. While collecting the ballots, Gavin was also surprised to discover that in one company only two men were of the then legal voting age of twenty-one.

CHAPTER 9: THE BATTLE OF THE BULGE — BELGIUM

1. The stamps were sent, and the Division received a thank-you note from President Roosevelt that would eventually appear in the May 1945 issue of the Division's newspaper, *The "All American" Paraglide.*

2. Anticipating a lull in the fighting, General Ridgway felt it safe to dispatch Major General Maxwell Taylor, commander of the 101st Airborne Division, to Washington for conferences at the War Department.

3. Wanting to gauge the readiness of his Corps' third division — the untried 17th Airborne Division not yet on the Continent — Ridgway had gone to England.

4. Letter from Major General James M. Gavin, reproduced in Wayne Pierce, *Let's Go!* (Chapel Hill, N.C.: Professional Press, 1997), 261.

5. Major J. C. H. Lee Jr. was the son of Lieutenant General John Clifford Hodges Lee, responsible for services and supply (SOS) in the European Theater of Operations.

6. The citation read in part: "For gallantry in action . . . 21 December–25 December 1944. Moving his division into a fluid situation caused by the German counter-offensive of 16 December . . . Major General Gavin, by his personal and outstanding leadership, contributed materially to the success of his division. Constantly with the forward elements of his command . . . [he] imparted to his troops the positive, aggressive spirit which stopped the German in his offensive effort and inflict[ed] punishing losses upon him. Throughout the period the heroic and fearless leadership . . . was a source of inspiration to the troops he commanded." Oak Leaf Cluster to the Silver Star citation, included in "Official Biography of Lieutenant General James Maurice Gavin," Department of Defense, Office of Public Information, News Branch, archived at the Airborne & Special Operations Museum, Fayetteville, North Carolina.

7. Another soldier near Gavin and Olson had a leg severed above the knee during the same artillery barrage; Gavin applied a tourniquet and had him evacuated to an aid station.

8. Benjamin Vandervoort's serious wound (his left eye was surgically removed) ended his Army career, but didn't stop him from serving with the CIA for twenty years.

9. Throughout his postwar career, a copy of this photo hung in Gavin's office.

10. Fighting the Japanese, many soldiers in the Pacific Theater worried that they wouldn't see America for several years, hence "Golden Gate in '48." "End the war in '44," didn't happen in Europe, so a new European Theater catchphrase became "Home alive in '45."

CHAPTER 10: CRACKING THE SIEGFRIED LINE — GERMANY

1. Gavin Diary, entry of February 15, 1945. The James M. Gavin Papers, Box 8, "Personal Diaries, December 1939–September 1945, June 1958–May 1960," United States Army Military History Institute, Carlisle Barracks, Pennsylvania.

2. Gavin's "boys" often referred to their commander as the "Two-Star Platoon Leader."

3. Gavin's letters of condolence were compassionate and kind. He wrote to one family after the loss of a young officer in Holland that their son had been "destined to be one of our outstanding higher commanders," and that his "fairness in dealing with others and unusually high courage in combat brought him the admiration and respect of all his subordinates." Gavin had also visited the officer's field grave and assured the family that it was "properly marked and well cared for." Excerpts from letter of Major General James M. Gavin to A. S. Raymond, Lincoln, Nebraska, dated December 13, 1944, on the death of Raymond's nephew, Lieutenant Jack Gavin (no relation). Copy of letter provided to Starlyn Jorgensen by Mike MacLean, nephew of Jack Gavin.

CHAPTER 11: A BRIEF RESPITE — FRANCE

1. The champagne cooler, perfectly sized for a prop-blast mug, came from the Hotel Groot in Berg en Dal that was very close to the German border but still within Holland. The hotel's owner presented it to General Gavin, and it is now part of the 82nd Airborne Division's War Museum collection at Fort Bragg, North Carolina.

2. Munro Leaf's children books, *Ferdinand the Bull* and *Manners Can Be Fun* (which included the "Watchbird" stick character that kept an eye on the behavior of children) were, and still are, very popular with children. However, when *Ferdinand the Bull* was published in 1936 it also came to the attention of adults — political activists saw the character of the peaceable bull as a satirical attack on fascist aggression, and in Germany, Hitler ordered the book burned. During World War II, Leaf helped create animated films for the U.S. military, using bumbling cartoon soldiers to teach by negative example. It's assumed that Leaf found no soldiers within the 82nd upon whom he could base the characters.

CHAPTER 12: BACK ON THE LINE — THE FINAL FIGHT

1. During World War II, Radio Berlin employed a female American expatriot, Mildred Gillars, to broadcast propaganda aimed at American troops. Though she was referred to as "Axis Sally" or "The Berlin Bitch," Gavin was obviously exercising parental censorship with his use of "Berlin Bess."

2. Wendell Wilkie's *One World*, published in 1943, called for an international peacekeeping force after the war.

CHAPTER 13: VICTORY, RUSSIAN CAMARADERIE, AND A VISIT HOME

1. Gavin Diary, entry of May 6, 1945. The James M. Gavin Papers, Box 8, "Personal Diaries, December 1939–September 1945, June 1958–May 1960," United States Army Military History Institute, Carlisle Barracks, Pennsylvania.

2. James M. Gavin, *War and Peace in the Space Age* (New York: Harper & Brothers, 1958), 35.

3. Excerpts from burial service read by Major George B. Wood, Division Chaplain, enclosure in letter to Barbara, dated May 7, 1945. The "Burial of Atrocity Victims" is also reproduced in full in Robert P. Anzuoni's *"I'm the 82nd Airborne Division!" A History of the All American Division in World War II After Action Reports* (Atglen, Pennsylvania: Schiffer Military History, 2005), 261.

4. Prior to becoming Gavin's aide, John Thompson was a platoon leader in the Second Battalion of the 504th Parachute Infantry Regiment. Largely due to his platoon's efforts during the first hours of Operation MARKET-GARDEN, the key bridge over the Maas River at Grave was quickly seized and held. In 2004, for the sixtieth commemoration of the operation, the Dutch government renamed the bridge in his honor.

CHAPTER 14: OCCUPATION DUTY — BERLIN

1. Gavin Diary, entry of August 10, 1945. The James M. Gavin Papers, Box 8, "Personal Diaries, December 1939–September 1945, June 1958–May 1960," United States Army Military History Institute, Carlisle Barracks, Pennsylvania.

2. James M. Gavin, *On to Berlin: Battles of an American Commander, 1943–46* (New York: Viking Press, 1978), 294.

CHAPTER 15: THE CALL HOME

1. Barney Oldfield, *Never a Shot in Anger* (Santa Barbara, Calif.: Capra Press, 1989), 301.

EPILOGUE

1. Meyer Berger, "82d Airborne Set for Parade Today," *New York Times,* January 12, 1946.

2. Martin Kivel and Art Smith, "4 Million Cheer Fighting 82d," *Sunday News.* Jan. 13, 1946: A3. The article continues: "And march he did behind a rank of color-bearers who carried the American, British, French and Russian standards. You knew by his carriage and by his step that here was a man any soldier would follow."

★ SELECTED BIBLIOGRAPHY ★

PRIMARY SOURCES

Gavin, James M. *Airborne Warfare*. Washington, D.C: Infantry Journal Press, 1947.

———. *On to Berlin: Battles of an American Commander, 1943–46*. New York: Viking Press, 1978.

———. *War and Peace in the Space Age*. New York: Harper and Brothers, 1958.

The James M. Gavin Papers, box 8, "Personal Diaries, December 1939–September 1945, June 1958–May 1960," United States Army Military History Institute, Carlisle Barracks, Penn.

SECONDARY SOURCES

BOOKS AND ARCHIVED MATERIAL

Biographies of General Gavin

Biggs, Bradley. *Gavin: A Biography of General James M. Gavin*. Hamden, Conn.: Archon Books, 1980.

Booth, T. Michael, and Duncan Spencer. *Paratrooper: The Life of Gen. James M. Gavin*. New York: Simon and Schuster, 1994.

Official Biography of Lieutenant General James Maurice Gavin. Department of Defense, Office of Public Information, News Branch. Archived at the Airborne and Special Operations Museum, Fayetteville, N.C.

World War II Airborne Operations

Breuer, William B. *Geronimo! American Paratroopers in World War II*. New York: St. Martin's Press, 1989.

Devlin, Gerard M. *Paratrooper! The Saga of U.S. Army and Marine Parachute and Glider Combat Troops During World War II*. New York: St. Martin's Press, 1979.

———. *Silent Wings: The Saga of the U.S. Army and Marine Combat Glider Pilots During World War II*. New York: St. Martin's Press, 1985.

Warren, John C. *Airborne Missions in the Mediterranean, 1942–1945*. U.S. Air Force Historical Study, no. 74, U.S. Air Force Historical Division, Research Studies Institute, Maxwell Air Force Base, Alabama, 1955; reprint, MA/AH Publishing–Sunflower University, Manhattan, Kansas, n.d.

———. *Airborne Operations in World War II, European Theater*. U.S. Air Force Historical Study, no. 97, U.S. Air Force Historical Division, Research Studies Institute, Maxwell Air Force Base, Alabama, 1956; reprint, MA/AH Publishing–Sunflower University, Manhattan, Kansas, n.d.

82nd Airborne Division Histories

Anzuoni, Robert P. *"I'm the 82nd Airborne Division!" A History of the All American Division in World War II after Action Reports*. Atglen, Penn.: Schiffer Military History, 2005.

Covington, H. L. *A Fighting Heart: An Unofficial Story of the 82nd Airborne Division*. Privately published by Ted Davis, Fayetteville, N.C., 1949.

Dawson, William F. (Buck). *Saga of the All American*. Fort Lauderdale, Fla.: Hoffman, n.d.

Nordyke, Phil. *All American All The Way*. St. Paul, Minn.: Zenith Press, 2005.

———. *The All Americans in World War II: A Photographic History of the 82nd Airborne Division at War*. St. Paul, Minn.: Zenith Press, 2006.

Campaign Histories

Atkinson, Rick. *An Army at Dawn: The War in North Africa, 1942–1943*. New York: Holt, 2002.

Balkoski, Joseph. *Utah Beach*. Mechanicsburg, Penn.: Stackpole Books, 2005.

Breuer, William B. *Drop Zone Sicily: Allied Airborne Strike, July 1943*. Novato, Calif.: Presidio Press, 1983.

———. *They Jumped at Midnight*. New York: Jove Books, 1990.

Hastings, Max. *Armageddon: The Battle for Germany, 1944–1945*. New York: Knopf, 2004.

Kershaw, Robert J. *"It Never Snows in September": The German View of Market-Garden and the Battle of Arnhem, September 1944*. Hersham, England: Ian Allan Publishing, 1994.

MacDonald, Charles B. *The Siegfried Line Campaign*. Washington, D.C.: Center of Military History, 1963.

———. *A Time for Trumpets: The Untold Story of the Battle of the Bulge*. New York: Morrow, 1985.

Margry, Karel, ed. *Operation Market-Garden: Then and Now*. Vols. 1 and 2. London: Battle of Britain International, 2002.

Murphy, Robert M. *No Better Place to Die: Dropped Behind Enemy Lines to Protect Utah Beach on D-Day!* Croton Falls, N.Y.: Critical Hit, 1999.

Ruggero, Ed. *Combat Jump: The Young Men Who Led the Assault into Fortress Europe, July 1943.* New York: HarperCollins, 2003.

———. *The First Men In: U.S. Paratroopers and the Fight to Save D-Day.* New York: HarperCollins, 2006.

Ryan, Cornelius. *A Bridge Too Far.* New York: Simon and Schuster, 1974.

———. *The Longest Day, June 6, 1944.* New York: Simon and Schuster, 1959.

Regimental Histories

Francois, Dominique. *The 507th Parachute Infantry Regiment.* Bayeux, France: Heimdal, 2000.

Langdon, Allen. *Ready: The History of the 505th Parachute Infantry Regiment, 82nd Airborne Division, World War II.* Indianapolis: Western Newspaper Publishing Company, 1986.

Lord, William G., II. *History of the 508th Parachute Infantry.* Nashville: Battery Press, 1977.

Mandle, William D., and David H. Whittier. *Combat Record of the 504th Parachute Infantry Regiment: April 1943–July 1945.* Paris: Draeger Frères, n.d.; reprint, Nashville: Battery Book Shop, 1976.

Morgan, Martin K. A. *Down to Earth: The 507th Parachute Infantry Regiment in Normandy.* Atglen, Penn.: Schiffer Military History, 2004.

Nordyke, Phil. *Four Stars of Valor: The Combat History of the 505th Parachute Infantry Regiment in World War II.* St. Paul, Minn.: Zenith Press, 2007.

Pierce, Wayne. *Let's Go! The Story of the Men Who Served in the 325th Glider Infantry Regiment.* Chapel Hill, N.C.: Professional Press, 1997.

Personal Memoirs

Burns, Dwayne. *Jump into the Valley of the Shadow: The War Memories of Dwayne Burns, Communications Sergeant, 508th Parachute Infantry Regiment.* Drexel Hill, Penn.: Casemate, 2006.

Burriss, T. Moffatt. *Strike and Hold: A Memoir of the 82d Airborne in World War II.* Washington, D.C.: Brassey's, 2000.

Carter, Ross S. *Those Devils in Baggy Pants.* New York: Appleton-Century-Crofts, 1951.

Lebenson, Leonard. *Surrounded by Heroes: Six Campaigns with Divisional Headquarters, 82d Airborne, 1942–1945.* Drexel Hill, Penn.: Casemate, 2007.

McKenzie, John D. *On Time, On Target: The World War II Memoir of a Paratrooper in the 82d Airborne.* Novato, Calif.: Presidio Press, 2000.

Megellas, James. *All the Way to Berlin: A Paratrooper at War in Europe*. New York: Ballantine Books, 2003.

Oldfield, Barney. *Never a Shot in Anger*. Santa Barbara, Calif.: Capra Press, 1989.

Renaud, Alexandre. *Sainte-Mère-Église: First American Bridgehead in France*. Translated by Deena Stryker. Sainte-Mère-Église, France: Famille Renaud, 2004.

Tucker, William H. *Parachute Soldier*. Harwichport, Mass.: International Airborne Books, 1994.

Wurst, Spencer F., and Gayle Wurst. *Descending From the Clouds: A Memoir of Combat in the 505 Parachute Infantry Regiment, 82d Airborne Division*. Havertown, Penn.: Casemate, 2004.

Other

Bierbaum, Margaret, ed. *As Ever, John: The Letters of Col. John V. McNally to His Sister, Margaret McNally Bierbaum, 1941–1946*. Fairfield, Conn.: Roberts Press, 1985.

Blair, Clay. *Ridgway's Paratroopers*. Garden City, N.Y.: Doubleday, 1958.

Boroughs, Zig. *The Devil's Tale: Stories of the Red Devils of the 508 Parachute Infantry Regiment, 82nd Airborne Division in World War Two*. College Park, Ga.: Static Line Books, 1992.

Brereton, Lewis H. *The Brereton Diaries: The War in the Air in the Pacific, Middle East, and Europe, 3 October 1941–8 May 1945*. New York: Morrow, 1946.

Clark, Mark W. *Calculated Risk*. New York: Harper and Brothers, 1950.

Hastings, Max. *Warriors: Portraits from the Battlefield*. New York: Knopf, 2005.

O'Donnell, Patrick K. *Beyond Valor: World War II's Ranger and Airborne Veterans Reveal the Heart of Combat*. New York: Free Press, 2001.

Pfannes, Charles E., and Victor A. Salamone. *The Germans*. Vol. 1 of *The Great Commanders of World War II*. New York: Zebra Books, 1980.

Ridgway, Matthew B., and Harold H. Martin, *Soldier: The Memoirs of Matthew B. Ridgway*. New York: Harper and Brothers, 1956.

Wills, Deryk, ed. *Put on Your Boots and Parachutes*. Leicester, England: AB Publishers, 1992.

ARTICLES

Berger, Meyer. "82d Airborne Set for Parade Today," *New York Times*, January 12, 1946.

Foisie, Jack. "Paratroopers Were Ready When Zero Hour Came," *Stars and Stripes Algiers Daily*, July 12, 1943.

Kivel, Martin, and Art Smith. "4 Million Cheer Fighting 82d," *Sunday News*,
    January 13, 1946.
Thompson, John. "Heroism of Airborne Forces Opened Way to Vittoria Area,"
    Washington Evening Star, 16 July 1943.
Walton, William. "Parachute Landing in Normandy," *Time*, June 19, 1944.

WORLD WAR II:
THE GLOBAL, HUMAN, AND ETHICAL DIMENSION
G. Kurt Piehler, series editor

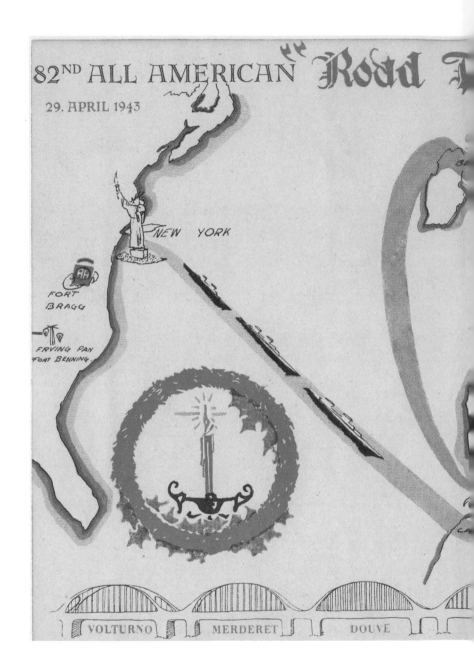